Erik Bloodaxe
His Life and Times

Erik Bloodaxe
His Life and Times

A Royal Viking in his Historical and Geographical Settings

William Pearson

authorHOUSE®

AuthorHouse™
1663 Liberty Drive
Bloomington, IN 47403
www.authorhouse.com
Phone: 1-800-839-8640

Published by AuthorHouse   07/19/2012

ISBN: 978-1-4685-8330-4 (sc)
ISBN: 978-1-4685-8329-8 (e)

Contents

To June

Preface

This work involves some critical assessment of received opinion about the period covered. To facilitate appreciation of this, comment on the text is integrated with it, the two modes being distinguished by two sizes of font. The larger deals with the narrative passages: any discursive material here is minimal, uncontroversial and serves to promote continuity.

The smaller considers elements of comment, discussion and argument that arise from omissions and misrepresentations in the sources that can give rise to doubts and misconceptions in the minds of modern students of history. The two font sizes allow readers to be aware of the nature of the particular passage under perusal and spare them the inconvenience of referring continually to notes segregated on later pages or as footnotes.

Chapters 2 to 11 include in narrative form Erik's career in Norway, England and elsewhere, but the account is not intended to take the form of a historical novel. The events portrayed are as contained in the various sources, with a minimum of embellishment; this does not however imply that the sources themselves are completely reliable.

While historical accuracy has been aimed at by the use of original sources, in order to appeal more to the general reader the use of notational devices has been kept to a minimum. Some archaic spellings have been used, but these are usually subsequently dispensed with by the use of an acceptable modern version. Diacritical marks have been used sparingly, except the one used here to cover various mutations (*umlaut*), e.g. *ö*, etc.

Old Norse inflexional endings are normally not shown, except that the genitive is always maintained when enclosed in personal names and other compounds. Of the archaic letters "thorn" and "eth", the former (þ, and as in "bath") is not used at all and always shown "th"), while the latter (ð and as in "bathe") only appears in italics, but otherwise as "dh", both for example as in "Thordh". Hence Erik represents *Eirikr,* Egil represents *Egill,* and Thori Hersi represents *Thorir Hersir,* while forms like Thoruson contain weak genitives implying "Thora's son".

Chapter 1

Introducing Erik and his
10th Century Setting

Many people will have heard of Erik Bloodaxe without understanding exactly when he lived or who he was. Most will understand that he was a Viking, but perhaps even this fame rests mainly on the form of his by-name "Bloodaxe", which invokes everything a Viking was supposed to have been. He has certainly come more to the fore with the creation of the body known as the "York Archaeological Trust" in that ancient city of northern England, with its on-going excavation programme, together with the creation of the "Jorvik Viking Centre" and the possibilities being exploited of sales of "Erik Bloodaxe" souvenirs in the form of mugs, tee-shirts, etc. The knowledge that Erik met his death "on Stainmore" also kindled additional interest in the archaeological effort that occurred in 1990 in advance of the conversion of the Bowes Moor section of the A66 road over the Stainmore Pass to dual carriage-way, even though in the event no direct association was found. The small stone monument known as Rey Cross has been traditionally associated with Erik and his death, but its removal brought no evidence to light.

The major source for Erik in England is Egil's Saga. There are obvious chronological difficulties in this, which have been held to be so irreconcilable by historians that doubt has been cast on the saga as a historical document of any worth at all. The chronology is reassessed below so that the apparent errors can be reconciled, if not completely overcome.

Important figures in Erik's life were his father King Harald, his wife Gunnhild, his brother Hakon, his henchman Arinbjörn and, according to Egil's Saga, Thorolf and Egil Skallagrimsson; but these last two hardly feature at all in other sources. Despite his fearsome reputation Erik's prowess has nowhere inspired description in detail when taking part in a specific military encounter; unlike Harald, Hakon, Thorolf and Egil, there is no account of him personally killing anybody.

As is usual for the time, the sources appear to be a record of continuous warfare and brutality: these were the events which impressed themselves on folk at the time, and especially poets, chroniclers and those collecting material later to appear in written sagas. Men of eminence and honour were expected to take up arms to right the wrong when events were otherwise going against them and those dependent on them, although this often followed failed attempts at reaching a peaceful solution. Violence itself was not condemned; it was a way of life and greatest dishonour ensued when the sword was not taken up when it was called for.

The other vehicle for settling disputes was the law, at the time unwritten in Scandinavia and prone to diverse interpretation. It was a sense of the rule of law being flouted that drove Egil Skallagrimsson to extraordinary lengths in his quest for justice, which he could back up in the event by his prowess as a warrior. Try as he might to obtain what he considered to be his right, he was continually frustrated by Erik and Gunnhild, with dire results. Much of the trouble was created by Norway being one of the last outposts of heathen barbarian Europe and the governing system that went with it. It was being overtaken by Christianity and an incipient feudal system whereby everything was owned by way of rewards from an all-powerful monarch, who demanded loyalty and whose rule was ultimately backed by God.

Well, what sort of historical figure was Erik Bloodaxe? Was he really such a hard man as he is traditionally thought of? Did he really deserve his nickname? Or was he a bit of a softie underneath a tough exterior? Is it possible for a Viking king to be hen-pecked, or influenced by sorcery? Was his queen Gunnhild devoted to him, or driven by her own personal ambition (which she considered he lacked to the same degree) in the manner of Lady Macbeth? Why do Egil's Saga and the Kings' Sagas disparage her as being a sorceress and a harridan? What drove Egil Skallagrimsson to keep leaving Iceland to face up to the Norwegian royal house, particularly in the shapes of Erik and Gunnhild, at great risk to his safety and largely over the inheritance of a specific piece of land? How did it come about that, despite his enmity of Erik and Gunnhild, Arinbjörn—Erik's right-hand man—was Egil's best friend? By what right was Erik able to come to England and claim the throne of Northumbria, when he ostensibly had no historical connections with the area, nor with the dynasty of Irish-Norse kings who were trying to hang onto power there? It is the answers to questions such as these that it is felt can be illuminated by parting the misty curtains of time by means of the presentation and discussions on the pages that follow.

Chapter 2

Erik's Background

King Harald Hairfair (or, as some render it, Finehair) was a descendant of the ancient Yngling dynasty that had its roots in Sweden. His more recent forebears had moved into southern Norway and created a kingdom for themselves there. Relevant burial mounds have been found in various locations, with some of the kin having been laid to rest in fine ships, sunk into the ground and over which earth had been heaped. One such was Queen Asa, who gave the name *Asuberg* to the barrow in which she lay, and which has probably been rightly identified in modern times as the excavated Oseberg ship burial.

The rest of Norway (in the south-west, west and north) consisted of a string of petty kingdoms, whose rulers had rather limited powers over their subjects; strictly speaking their status resembled that of a headman rather than a king. The history of the Ynglings was one of rivalry, ambition and warfare, and Harald himself was certainly cast in this same mould. He surveyed those petty kingdoms of the interior and strung out along Norway's west coast (the "north way") and decided that they were all going to be united, with himself as over-king. On making this decision he swore an oath to the effect that he would not have his hair cut until his ambition was fulfilled. Because of this he became known as Harald Lufa (i.e. Shaggy).

Harald's father was Halfdan the Black, King of Vestfold in south eastern Norway. From this ancestral base alongside the huge sea inlet called *Viken* (the Vik or Wyke, now Oslo Fjord), Harald's campaign carried him through the dales of the interior to reach the coast at Trondheim, with its own great fjord. From here he set out to subdue those small maritime states to the north and south. Those to the north were a push-over. Conquest of the rest was accomplished by means of two major naval victories. The first was at Solskjel and gave him control of Sunn (i.e. South) Möre. King Arnvidh had persuaded

Audhbjörn, king of Fjordane, i.e. The Firths (in the Old Norse of the time *Firðir*) to his south, to create a joint defence force. It was all in vain, for both kings were slain in the defeat. After this Harald had among his henchmen Rögnvald (now created Earl of South Möre) and Kari of *Berðla*. The latter had sons called Ölvir Hnufa and Eyvind Lambi, and a daughter Salbjörg, who will feature again later.

Earl Rögnvald became King Harald's favourite. After Solskjel, Vemund became King at the Firths. Harald intended to deal with him once winter was over, but in the meantime Rögnvald took care of the matter for him. He learned that Vemund was sojourning at Naustdal. Despite the time of the year, Rögnvald crossed the isthmus with a force and burnt Vemund in, along with his men. Kari of Berdhla sailed in to support Rögnvald with a longship and both sailed away well satisfied, Rögnvald taking Vemund's ships, as well as other booty. Kari carried on north to Trondheim and became firmly established as Harald's man. After these events the districts of Gaular and Sogn also came under Harald's control.

There are two possible candidates for the Naustdal in question, but the circumstances of the attack on Vemund make the one in Nordfjord more likely, despite it being a more constricted site than the Sunnfjord one, There has been an opportunity to visit places that had been provisionally identified as being mentioned in the relevant sagas. While the possibilities of pinpointing tofts exactly was originally considered unlikely, in the event one was able to locate them with some confidence, a surprising circumstances. Excluding thingsteads and temple sites, and concerning oneself provisionally only with the great family homesteads (which for want of a better term can be dubbed "halls" or "seats"), two conditions can be seen as likely to be satisfied in their locations: 1) each will be in a position to give a clear view of approach by water, either across a lake or from the seaward end of a fjord; 2) as much as possible of the surrounding farmland will be in view from the hall. The settlements may be near the mouths of rivers, but these are generally too swift to serve as havens; harbouring was provided by nearby small wykes where ships or boats could be either moored out on the sheltered water or pulled up onto a sloping pebbly beach. The inner reaches of such wykes have often been filled in during recent years to enable a quay to be constructed in deeper water and to make a gain of flat land.

In the case of Naustdal/Nordfjord there is no *vang* of alluvial land and no infilling of the wyke has occurred. Aptly enough this is still lined by several 'nausts', i.e., boathouses. The hamlet consists of a scatter of farmsteads near the shore, but none of these are in a position to view the farmland in anything like its entirety. However, above them is a small field in the form of a level platform and filling a promontory out of the surrounding less even landscape. This is clearly an earlier dwelling platform of unknown date, but from it one has an excellent view down the Nordfjord and virtually all the farmland can be viewed. Some antiquity for this site is suggested by a tall grey monolith standing near the edge of the platform; this was not examined closely, (Ref, photos, 1-4, App, 6)

While Harald was preoccupied with problems elsewhere in Scandinavia, the remaining kings of western Norway formed themselves into a coalition, including such districts as Hordaland, Rogaland, Agder and Telemark. After a hard battle on Hafrsfjord (near Stavanger), several of the opposing leaders were dead, leaving Harald as victor and master of all Norway. Even so, his troubles were far from being over. He instituted a policy which cancelled the old allodial system of land occupation ("odhal") and replaced it with one in which men held land as a right granted by the king, indeed virtually feudalism. This was too much for many landed men, and emigration to lands over-sea to the west became increasingly prevalent, especially from western Norway. In this way pockets of disgruntled expatriates appeared in places like Man, Scotland, the Hebrides, the Orkneys, Shetland, the Faroes and Iceland, all with a desire to hit back at Harald's Norway and its trade. To the king however such attacks were nothing but piracy, and in the end he is said to have mounted a punitive expedition that took in Scotland and the western isles, and penetrated even as far as Man. The recalcitrant Norse settlers were slaughtered if caught, although those on Man are said to have gained foreknowledge of his arrival and fled with whatever they could carry, although their homes were destroyed. To secure the situation Harald gave the Orkneys and Shetland to Rögnvald, and made him earl over them. In this way the name Ronald—in Anglicised form Reynold—was firmly introduced to Britain; it can be seen to feature anciently in Ronaldsay (Orkneys) and Ronaldsway (Man). But Rögnvald soon gave up his earldom in favour of his brother Sigurdh and returned to Norway to rejoin Harald the Shaggy. The king at this time concluded that he had fulfilled the terms of his oath in that Norway was now unified under him and pacified. His hair had grown unkempt and uncut for ten years; it was Rögnvald himself who was allotted the task of shearing it off. After this everybody seems to have agreed that Harald's hair was "fair", i.e. beautiful.

The creation of the earldom of the Orkneys by the Norwegian king rendered the Scottish islands unsafe for those opposed to him; this made Iceland a more favourable choice of destination for those wishing to shake off his influence. Among the earlier arrivals there was the kin of Ketill Flatnose. He himself had sailed to Scotland c890. His daughter Unn had a son Thorstein who made successful war on the Scots until they managed to kill him. Unn left Caithness and sailed off to the Orkneys. Among her following was Koll Hersi. There she married off Gro, the daughter of her son Thorstein. Her daughter Greilad became the wife of Earl Thorfinn, son of Turf-Einar and grandson of Earl Rögnvald of Möre. In this way did the Earls of the Orkneys come to be descended from Ketill and his daughter Unn. By way of the Faroe islands she eventually arrived in Iceland with her remaining offspring, including Olaf "Feilan". There she joined her brothers and their brother-in-law Helgi.

Among others who had sailed directly to Iceland was Kveldulf and his kin. They abandoned their home, which must have been on the Norwegian mainland somewhere near the mouth of the Sognefjord.

Before the Battle of Solskjel, King Audhbjörn had approached Kveldulf for help; but the latter refused, saying that he was only committed to defending his own district, not The Firths and Möre.

> It is clear from the context that Kveldulf's seat lay south of The Firths and Möre. The reluctance to name the site will be returned to later. (Pálsson 1976 p24)

Eventually Kveldulf was summoned to court by the victorious Harald, but demurred, claiming to be too old to make the journey. His younger son Skallagrim also resisted the summons, refusing to acknowledge any other superior while his father yet lived. They were indeed clinging to the spirit of the old independence of men sitting on their odhal under the ancient Germanic system. The elder son,

Thorolf, was away at the time. The replies were hardly designed to please Harald and he despatched another messenger who conveyed his insistence. Kveldulf dodged the issue again by promising that Thorolf would be glad to become the king's man when he returned from his expedition.

Upon Thorolf's homecoming, Kveldulf, far from persuading him to the king's cause, argued against it, sensing the inevitability of disaster from that quarter. But Thorolf disappointed him by showing enthusiasm for the king, having heard how generous he was to those who joined him, while those in opposition were brought to their downfall, one way or another.

From his base at Trondheim, Harald also summoned the landed men of Helgeland, the district to the north, to come to him. This brought Brynjolf Björgolfsson with his son Bardh from their seat at *Torgar* (now Torget). This appears to have been a very desirable place, with the name meaning "market places", apparently because of the lucrative exchanges with the Lapps that went with it. At this court Bardh met Thorolf Kveldulfsson, and they were to become firm friends. Bardh was betrothed to Sigridh, the daughter of Sigurdh of Sandnes, and Thorolf accompanied him north on the occasion of his wedding.

The two friends were subsequently together with Harald at his victory on the Hafrsfjord, when Norway was secured as a single realm. Both suffered wounds, which in Bardh's case proved to be fatal, but before he died he bequeathed everything he had, including his wife and his inheritance prospects, to his friend. It seems evident that Thorolf needed the marriage to Sigridh to secure the bequest, even though he had the king's backing in the arrangement. Agreement was also required by both the widow and her father; in the event the proposal was accepted, while shortly afterwards Sigurdh died so that Thorolf inherited the estate of Sandnes too, thus making him a quite powerful as well as wealthy man.

There were however those who envied Thorolf his good fortune. Foremost among these were two brothers called Harek and Hrærek, who took their grievances to King Harald. They were the sons of Hildiridh, daughter of Högni of Leka, a landowner but not high born. They were about the same age as the late Bardh, but their father was his grandfather Björgolf, whose marriage to their mother Hildiridh was considered by some as of dubious legality. When Björgolf died his son Brynjolf had thrown Hildiridh and her sons out, and they returned to Leka where they remained with festering thoughts about their lost inheritance at Torgar. While they had to put up with Bardh, the brothers were frustrated and furious when the estate went to Thorolf Kveldulfsson, who was not even kin. He rejected their claims, even as had Bardh before him, on the grounds that they had been born out of wedlock, an allegation they were at pains to refute. (For genealogies see App. 2)

For some reason King Harald seems to have harboured suspicions about Thorolf's position at Torgar; he came to visit his man, who laid on a huge feast. Yet the king remained in a bad mood until his host led him down to the shore and presented his ruler with a fine ship he had just had built. Until then the king had been showing every sign of being uncertain about Thorolf's attitude towards him and had been waiting for a proper sign of gratitude and allegiance for having allowed Bardh to bequeath as he did. Was Thorolf indeed getting too big for his boots?

But the sons of Hildiridh later again went to the king and slyly discredited Thorolf, even to the extent of suggesting that he had planned the king's death on his visit. They proposed that there were better and more reliable men in the north to look after the king's interests and that if Thorolf must have lands at all they should be further south where he belonged. A further suggestion was that the king should enlist Thorolf into his bodyguard so that an eye could be kept on him.

> It would seem that Harald was not entirely deaf to all this, perhaps because Thorolf was after all a son of Kveldulf, but one might also infer that, owning both Torgar and Sandnes, he had quite independently grown too wealthy and powerful for the king's liking.

The affair dragged on, with Thorolf in the end being ordered to go to the king in person. This culminated in Harald offering him charge of the royal bodyguard, but this implied that Kveldulfsson must then sever from his own men, his private army. He declined and left for the north. The king responded by ordering him to relinquish his stewardship and hand over Torgar, his inheritance from Bardh, to the sons of Hildiridh. However, having complied, Thorolf still retained Sandnes, his inheritance from Sigurdh, and remained a man of standing.

> The way in which Thorolf Kveldulfsson inherited property through marrying a widow was to be reflected in Egil's later marriage to Asgerdh, with similar dire results. (Pálsson 1976 pp36, 133)

The brethren Harek and Hrærek had promised King Harald better returns than those received from Thorolf; however, they fared far worse and blamed Thorolf for this, perhaps with some justification. It turned out that Thorolf had established such good relations with the Lapps that they preferred to deal with him than with the king's new stewards. Thorolf's illegal foraging and exchange completely undermined the business of the official operators.

But Thorolf Kveldulfsson could not now dispose of his vast surplus of materials in Norway, so he loaded them onto a ship under the command of his man Thorgils Gjallandi, who then sailed to England on a trading mission. Harek and Hrærek, however, knew well enough what was going on and reported it to the king. Harald had by him another pair of brothers, his kinsmen Sigtryg Snarfari and Hallvardh Hardhfari, who he employed sometimes to do his dirty work. They were from eastern Norway, the Oslofjord area. This pair observed the return from England of Thorgils Gjallandi, when he made landfall off Hordaland, and they set off northwards in pursuit. His heavily laden trading ship was encountered as it lay moored and unguarded, thus enabling them to seize it without trouble and bring it back as a prize to Harald, who one can readily assume regarded the cargo of wheat, honey, wine and clothing as his by right.

Thorgils and the rest of Thorolf's men obtained transport and arrived at the home of Kveldulf, which must have been fairly close by.

> Although there is mention of Torgar and Sandnes, as well as places like Eyrr, the name of Kveldulf's home is again for some reason not mentioned.

The old man soon drew to Thorgil's attention that the disaster had now begun that he had foretold would occur at the time his eldest son Thorolf first wanted to become the king's man. His counsel was that Thorgils should tell Thorolf that the only course now left open to him was to seek service abroad with some other king, either of England or Denmark or Sweden.

Thorolf did not take his father's advice; instead he became a Viking, with the goods and property of Harald his main target, and with the brethren Sigtryg and Hallvardh high upon his black list.

It would appear that Harald's apparently illogical fear and distrust of Thorolf had been self-fulfilling; open suspicion and provocation had inevitably brought about the very misdemeanours that were hitherto hypothetical. The disastrous course of events had somehow been obvious to Kveldulf (and one might suspect to Harald too); only Thorolf appears to have believed in his ability to escape from a cruel destiny.

In order to avoid detection, Thorolf sailed southwards down the coast outside of the Skerries to make his way eventually to the Baltic, where he raided without great success. He returned to Danish waters and waylaid Norwegian ships heading northwards out of Eyrr (now Skanör, at the south west tip of Sweden). It was Autumn and he caught up with one of Harald's fat merchantmen at Mostrarsund on the east side of the Kattegat and seized it in the evening as it lay in the shelter of a haven, leaving the crew stranded on land, just as his ship had been taken by Harald's men. With both ships he sailed northward along the coast.

In those days Norway and Denmark shared this coast, presently all Swedish. The boundary was at the river now called Göta-Älv, beside which, on the island called Hising, stood a dwelling belonging to the brothers Sigtryg and Hallvardh, on whom Thorolf duly took his revenge. He and his men rowed up the river and surrounded the house. A third member of the unloved brethren, Thorgeir by name, tried to make a run for it, but while clambering over the surrounding fence had his hand cut off by Thorgils Gjallandi. The fourth brother, called Thordh, was one of more than a score cut down there. The house was then ransacked and burnt. Thorolf sailed out of the river with his booty and steered north for The Vik, where they took another merchant ship without resistance.

With his three ships he sailed round Lindesnes, the southern tip of Norway, pillaging on the way until Sogn was reached, where Thorolf called in to see his father.

That Thorolf came home to Kveldulf in Sogn confirms that the seat was immediately south of The Firths. (Pálsson 1976 p55)

Kveldulf's response was in the "I told you so!" vein, while also observing that no good was to come of recent events, either for Thorolf or for his kin, just as he Kveldulf had already prophesied. It seems obvious that time was now running out for Thorolf in Norway, but he carried on northwards notwithstanding, homeward bound for Sandnes. While there was ample provision laid in for winter, the sanctuary of exile seemed the inevitable course for the following year.

King Harald spent that winter at Trondheim with a goodly army. With him were Sigtryg and Hallvardh, and they had received reports of the havoc wreaked by Thorolf. The brethren were keen on vengeance, for custom would expect them to take it if they were to live on with any honour. They asked the king for leave to descend on Sandnes with their own men. Harald discouraged them, while expressing the opinion that he did not think them up to it against the likes of Thorolf; but they pressed their need for revenge, involving the necessity that Thorolf must die. So the king granted them such leave, entreating them to return with Thorolf's head and much booty. They sailed down and out of the fjord to turn northwards up the coast, where they were met by strong head winds.

The king immediately showed his disbelief in their competence, together with his own need to take vengeance personally on Thorolf because of his latest exploits. He however chose to sail up the fjord to the isthmus called Elden, which he crossed on foot to commandeer boats on the far side. By rowing hard, day and night, he came quickly and unannounced to Sandnes with a force of 300 men. Thorolf's ship lay there, all ready for the departure that now seemed unlikely to take place, due to the fate creeping up on him out of the gathering dusk.

The house was surrounded and the war-cry sounded; those inside, though caught unawares, reached quickly for their weapons. All who were not warriors, i.e. the women, the young, the old, the thralls and the servants, the king allowed out. Sigridh appealed for her husband and Harald promised his life, though his men must pay for their crimes. Thorolf's uncle and friend, Ölvir Hnufa, conveyed the message to Thorolf; but he rejected all offers and demanded to be let out to fight. The king ordered the hall to be burned down around them, but they escaped their hellish fate by breaking down a wall with a beam. A battle ensued, but the burning building at their backs made it go ill for Thorolf's party. He made a desperate charge towards Harald, and though he lost his man Thorgils in the foray, reached the shield wall and felled the royal banner bearer. But edges had found him and he fell at the king's feet. Harald himself had the satisfaction of finishing him off. It was over. Or was it?

Thorolf's uncles Ölvir Hnufa and Eyvind Lambi stayed behind to perform the necessary services following such a bloody encounter. This incident, as well as others preceding it, had placed them in a dilemma that was a common experience of noble warriors in the last centuries of barbarian Europe; namely whether to be loyal to their kin or to their lord. They had followed the growing trend by staying loyal to Harald, although the death of Thorolf must have been very painful for them, above all because it was impossible for them to avenge it.

All the later troubles between Egil Skallagrimsson and Erik Bloodaxe were derived from this incident, at least as a precedent and justification for the kin of Kveldulf to use violence to settle disputes. Features highlighted by the affair at Sandnes were the need to avenge a kinsman's death, but this being inhibited by the growing predominance of loyalty owed to one's lord over that due to one's kin. (Very similar themes are explored in the Old English poem "Beowulf".) The growth of kingship, with traditional loyalties being abandoned to the detriment of the bonds of kin, can be seen in Harald's attitude in the future, even towards his own sons. This devolved to lesser families, as evident with regard to the strife that accompanied the succession of the Earls of the Orkneys in the Orkneyinga Saga. (Anderson 1873 *passim*)

An odd aspect of this Sandnes affair was that King Harald was able to return to Trondheim without meeting those would-be avengers. Those brothers had found the going along the coast so hard that they had taken frequent shelter, little realising that the king had got ahead of them and taken care of the business. When news of events did reach them, they must return shamefacedly to Trondheim. It would seem that Thorolf had been expecting attack from this quarter, keeping a watch on the coastal approaches. Harald had by-passed such outposts, however, by dint of his overland manoeuvre and twilight approach.

The above accounts tell one how threatening clouds had been gathering around Thorolf before the storm finally broke over him. Despite this, many had been flocking to his cause; one such was Ketill Hæng, a distant member of Thorolf's kin and also related by marriage to his deceased friend Bardh. Ketil saw his own downfall now tied to the fate of Thorolf, but before he left Norway struck a blow at what was obviously considered to be the very root of the trouble. He fell upon Torgar and killed the sons of Hildiridh. Then, gathering together everything he could lay his hands on, sailed off with wife, family and all his men out onto the open sea, away from his homeland to become one of the earliest settlers of Iceland.

The death of Thorolf Kveldulfsson put his kin in a difficult position. As usual the go-between was their relative Ölvir Hnufa, a staunch king's man, but Kveldulf's brother-in-law by way of Ölvir's sister Salbjörg. He came to their home and urged them to seek atonement from the king, although Harald in fact had not promised this. However his visit really made things worse, for Thorolf's father and brother thus heard how it had been the king himself who gave the *coup de grace*. Kveldulf declined to make the journey on the grounds of old age, but his son Skallagrim agreed reluctantly to go, yet asserted that he would waste no words in seeking atonement.

The king was sojourning at Voss, an inland settlement of western Norway situated at the east end of a lake. Skallagrim commandeered a boat to cross this, having marched from their coastal landfall with his men.

The route taken to sail from the mouth of the Sognefjord to Voss can be determined with a high degree of certainty. (Ref. Map 3, App. 3) The settlement of Vossevangen lies at the eastern end of Lake Vangsvatn, where there is a large vang—"plain". The original settlement will have been near the area where the church, thing-house and St. Olaf's Cross lie in a line. They are on a low ridge, presumably of Ice Age origin, with the stone cross being on a small mound at the southern end of this. The ridge has apparently caused the river to diverge to the south, with the consequent building up of a spit. It is suggested that the "hall" where Skallagrim met King Harald was on the landward end of the ridge, with good views both over the *vang* behind and along the lake, and with easy access to the latter down a former sloping beach, largely now filled in behind a low quay. It would be down such a beach that Harald's men would pour in pursuit of Skallagrim's party who were escaping in the last serviceable boat. Alternatively one might consider that the ridge and growing spit constituted a cult site, and this is why the church and St. Olaf's Cross stand on it. Could there originally have been a temple or runestone here, or both, with these later replaced by the Christian structures? This possibility is echoed and promoted by the circumstances at Hestad. (See Chap. 3 below) If the comparison with Hestad is just, then the "hall" site at Voss would be harder to pinpoint, but could well have been at the foot of the fell side north of the church, near the railway, and more directly below the famous preserved site of Molstertun on its high ledge. (Ref. photos 5-8, App. 5)

The twelve companions of Skallagrim at Voss were all big men and Ölvir introduced the party to the king. However, he would only offer atonement if Skallagrim would become his man, as had once been his brother. In view of what had befallen the latter at the hands of Harald, it is hardly surprising that Skallagrim turned this down flat; the ruler turned red with anger. Ölvir tactfully led Skallagrim's party out and back to the boats, urging them to flee the king's wrath. To aid the escape, he stove in all the other boats there, thus preventing pursuit; a necessary precaution, for soon after a horde of armed men rushed down to the shore, bent on spilling Skallagrim's blood. Harald had motivated these pursuers by pointing out that anyone who had had a hand in the slaying of Thorolf was now liable to be the butt of Skallagrim's revenge. But they were thwarted in their aims by Kveldulfsson's temporary monopoly of local water-borne transport.

Later, while at Trondheim, Harald heard of the bereavement of certain youthful kinsfolk in The Vik, so he commissioned Hallvardh to fetch them to him, and for this purpose provided the longship that had formerly been Thorolf's. On the way back to Trondheim they were spotted by the keen-eyed Skallagrim, who recognised the ship as his brother's. He reported what he had spied to his father. After the incident at Voss they had decided not to remain in Norway. Ships had been prepared for emigration to Iceland, but they first sailed to the much indented Solund islands at the mouth of the Sognefjord, an ideal place for Vikings to lie in wait. In their two ships father and son sailed forth and pounced on the other as it lay hove to. Then a strange change came over Kveldulf, who was supposed to be suffering from the weakness of old age. He was overtaken by a condition that ran in his family and exhibited itself especially after sunsets. His strength miraculously increased, and he went battle-mad in the manner of a berserk. It was on account of this trait that he got his full name; he was originally simply Ulf, but because of his prowess in the evening became Kveldulf, "Evening Wolf".

There was much butchery aboard that ship. Kveldulf, coming upon Hallvardh, clove him through helmet and head with a battle-axe, heaved him up in the air with it and slung him overboard. Skallagrim in the meantime had slain Hallvardh's brother Sigtryg, and thus did they pay in full for their hostility towards Thorolf. Many men escaped, including Harald's youthful relatives: so knowledge of the event was not going to be withheld from the king for long. For Kveldulf and Skallagrim the point in time had definitely arrived when departure for Iceland was expedient, if they were to avoid the same fate as Thorolf. They transferred their gear from their own ship to the one formerly owned by Thorolf, then scuttled the other. But the efforts of Kveldulf had taken it out of him; he was soon to breathe his last. Like Moses he was destined not to set foot on the promised land. His dying wish was to be thrown overboard in a wooden chest, with the instruction that wherever this came ashore Skallagrim was to settle. And so it came about that Borg was founded in Iceland on the fjord later named after it, while Kveldulf was buried in his chest on the nearby headland and stones heaped over him.

This seems a very dubious means of choosing a place suitable for settlement. Another reason for the founding of Borg where it still is will be advanced later. As for King Harald, he had a very long reign. While his hair may have been regarded as "fair", the same can hardly be said of his nature: he was quite ruthless and pragmatic. But one might argue that these were the qualities that made a king successful in those times: they allowed one to seize the throne and hang on to it. Weakness could manifest itself in a number of ways, anyone of which could bring a leader down.

Harald demanded that his kin be regarded as the only royal family in all Norway, that land was only to be held by licence from the king, and that all folk holding land should support the king, while those in his immediate entourage and receiving gifts should in their turn give unswerving loyalty. These were his ideals, but he must fight hard to sustain them. Yet by his own lights he has to be adjudged successful, for those who opposed him either died violently or were constrained to leave the country. He was succeeded by his favourite son Erik, but with him the results of attempts at power wielding were quite different.

Chapter 3

Erik in Norway

King Harald's prowess also ran in another direction: he had many children by a number of women, both high- and low-born, within and without wedlock.

It is almost as though he were trying to repopulate Norway out of his own gene-bank. With this sort of attitude one can understand that he was perhaps not too bothered whether the sons of Hildiridh were illegitimate or not.

Initially his favourite son turned out to be Erik (*Eirikr*), who he intended to be his heir. In general Harald let his children be fostered at the place where the mother came from; in Erik's case it was different. His mother was Ragnhild, daughter of a certain King Eirik in Jutland. When Harald took up with her he set aside all his other women. She only lived for three years after coming to Norway and when she died Harald arranged for Erik to be fostered with Thori Hersi (*Thorir Hersir*, son of Earl Hroald in The Firths. (For genealogies see App. 2) But when he was only 12 years old his father Harald equipped him with five longships so that he could go a-Viking. It is clear that Harald saw in him a "chip off the old block". He first sailed up into the Baltic and then southwards back as far as Denmark, Frisia and Saxony. He was away for three years. After returning from this he turned westwards to harry the coasts of Scotland, Wales, Ireland and northern France, this keeping him away for another four years. Such journeys must have enhanced his reputation and self-esteem. Then he made a foray to Lappland, and even beyond. Retracing his route as far as Lappland he had a strange encounter that would seem to have affected the rest of his life. In a hut his men discovered a woman of unsurpassable. beauty, who said her name was Gunnhild and was a daughter of Ossur Toti who lived in Helgeland. She said she was there to learn sorcery from the Lapps. She warned that her two instructors were out, but because of their powers it was advisable that the shipmen kill them instantly upon their return. She went to great lengths, first to allay the Lapps suspicions and then to render them helpless. At a sign from her the Norwegians leapt out and slew them. They then took Gunnhild with them to their ship and introduced her to Erik. Sailing south they called in at Helgeland and Ossur agreed that Erik should have Gunnhild to wife. She then accompanied him back to the south.

> The saga account of young Erik's exploits indicates that his father thought more of him than of his other sons. Yet the Kings' Sagas and Egil's Saga seem to go to some length to disparage him. One has no reason to doubt that he was a doughty warrior and competent leader of men, but the sagas will insist that he was under the influence of witchcraft. Yet Harald used Erik to destroy the band of sorcerers led by one of his brothers, and he appears to have shown some zeal in this task. (Holtsmark 1959 p74) It is possible that the explorers did encounter a Norwegian woman among the Lapps, but it seems extremely unlikely that a royal personage like Erik would have married the daughter of someone like Ossur Toti. The way she conspired against her so-called teachers suggests that she was somehow being held against her will by them and that Erik rescued her, (Holtsmark 1959 pp71, 72) But the saga was meant to show that Gunnhild was treacherous and bloodthirsty, as well as being a witch. Whether or not Erik did have a liaison with this "Gunnhild" is of course beside the point. Witchcraft was associated with the Lapps. Harald's dislike of it was due to him too being seduced by a Lappish woman called Snefridh. When she died, he was spellbound with grief for three years, while her body remained uncorrupted. However, the spell was broken when he was advised that her clothes needed changing. As soon as an attempt to move the body was made it burst open and all the evil hidden by that beautiful skin escaped. (Holtsmark 1959 pp66, 67) He had four sons by this wife, but it is clear that he valued them hardly at all because of their mother, in contrast to Erik, whose mother Ragnhild was the daughter of a Danish king, (Holtsmark 1959 p63)

By the time King Harald reached the age of 50 many of his sons were grown up; some were even dead. On the whole they were an unruly bunch, riddled with personal ambition and envy. They were constantly complaining about being short of land to govern and, apart from squabbling among themselves, sometimes took to driving the king's earls from their properties. Just after the king was 40, two of them called Halfdan and Gudhrödh had had the nerve to descend on Earl Rögnvald of Möre and burnt him in, together with 60 men. Halfdan then went overseas, while Gudhrödh settled down at Rögnvald's seat. King Harald would not tolerate this and dislodged him, handing the earldom back to Rögnvald's son called Thori.

Earl Hroald's son Thori is not to be confused with Thori, son of Earl Rögnvald of Möre. Thori Hroaldsson inherited The Firths from his father, which district lies immediately south of Möre. Thori Rögnvaldsson had a brother called Hrolf, who became a Viking and because of his activities was made an outlaw by Harald. (He eventually became the first Duke of Normandy, the ancestor of William the Conqueror.) Earl Rögnvald of Möre was surrounded and burnt in at his seat by two of Harald's sons by Snefridh, namely Halfdan and Gudhrödh. The latter tried to hang onto the ill-gotten lands, but Harald removed him to Agder and replaced him with Thori Rögnvaldsson, while the former made for the Orkneys.

Rögnvald's brother Sigurdh had died on the Orkneys. The Earl of Möre had eventually allowed a certain Einar to replace him. But Harald's son Halfdan descended on him; so he fled, only to return to take his replacement by surprise, to capture him and to subject him to the brutal death known as the blood eagle. Halfdan's kin were naturally outraged at this and screaming for revenge. In response the king gathered a force and sailed to the Orkneys, whereupon Einar fled to Caithness. A meeting was convened at which Einar's right to the earldom was confirmed, provided the king was recompensed. This was Einar's responsibility, but to support him all the odhal in the Orkneys was transferred to him. From then on the farmers there only held their land by consent of the earl.

When one of his four sons by the Lappish Snefridh, Halfdan Hålegg, was thus killed on the Orkneys by being given the dreaded "blood eagle" treatment by Turf-Einar there, Harald sailed over seeking redress, but instead of taking revenge in blood, as one would have expected of him, he allowed Einar to remain Earl of the Orkneys on the payment of wergild. Harald was clearly not too fond of his sons born of a sorceress.

On the other hand, it seems unlikely that Harald would have continued to show such favour towards Erik if he really had made a lifelong marriage to a woman steeped in the sorcery of the Lapps. Someone was trying to use the saga to bring him down to the same level as the others. The foundation and continuance of the earldom of the Orkneys can be noted as the reason that, throughout the ages, these islands remained the main seat of the representative of the Norwegian crown in the west, when other territories tended to change hands intermittently, especially with the Scots.

One of Erik's companions on that same expedition to the Lappish far north was, rather surprisingly, a son of Skallagrim, Thorolf by name.

On the expedition to the arctic, with Thorolf Skallagrimsson taking part, a battle was fought beside a river Vina and near a forest called Vinuskogr. Virtually identical names were used in the description of the Battle of Vinheidh in Egil's Saga, where Thorolf was to meet his death. This has been used to cast doubt on the presence of Thorolf at Vinheidh at all. Evidence to refute this notion has been presented by this author below.

The circumstances that brought Erik and Thorolf Skallagrimsson together had arisen long before. (For genealogy See App 2) A certain Björn Brynjolfsson, who came from Aurland on one of the headwaters of the Sognefjord, had set his heart on marrying Thora Hladh-hand, sister of Thori Hersi. However, he was rejected by her brother even though Björn's father, being also a "hersi", was apparently of equal rank. Undeterred, while Thori was away, the single minded Björn came along and made off with Thora. Unfortunately this breach of etiquette was also frowned upon by his own father Brynjolf, because the act had brought shame to Thori, to whom Brynjolf had long been a friend.

The rift was so serious that Thori Hersi would not even accept atonement from Brynjolf, but demanded Thora back, to which Björn refused to comply. To relieve the situation Björn decided to become a Viking, but was frustrated in that his father would not provide him with a ship for that purpose; instead he offered a merchantman, with instructions to sail her to Dublin and Björn must settle for this. Before he left he called at the farm where his mother was living with Thora and took the latter with him, along with her goods. This displeased his mother greatly and it was done quite without the knowledge of his father.

The weather was bad, but they made landfall on Shetland at the island of Mousa, and Björn made his winter quarters at *Moseyarborg;* this can hardly be other than the still well preserved Iron Age fortification known as Mousa Broch. But that Autumn a longship sailed to the western isles to inform Earl Sigurdh that King Harald had made Björn an outlaw, against whom any man's hand might turn. This message was passed all the way to Dublin. Björn was clearly in need of a refuge beyond Harald's reach. He had married Thora soon after his arrival on Shetland and next Spring he headed for Iceland, where he came ashore at Borg and was welcomed there by Skallagrim.

While Brynjolf expressed his disapproval of the abduction of Thora and offered compensation to Thori (which he refused), he was unable to persuade or force Björn to return her. One can best explain this by Thora being a willing partner in the escapade, which would also explain how Björn was able to take her from his parents' custody without any trouble, to marry her on Shetland and to take her to Iceland without her giving the game away to Skallagrim. Thori's rejection of Björn was probably because he had her earmarked for marriage into a kin of higher standing, and this was most likely in the form of his foster son Erik, a prospect that Thora presumably was not too keen on. Erik's intentions are unknown, but one might suspect that his father Harald at least was in favour of the arrangement: hence Harald's annoyance.

That autumn seafarers arrived in Iceland from Norway and revealed the truth about Björn and Thora; Skallagrim was not at all pleased, especially since he had had friendly relations with Thori Hersi in the past. Things thus became difficult for Björn in his refuge, but he was saved by the intercession of Skallagrim's son Thorolf, who had taken to Björn and spoke up for him. Next summer Thora gave birth to a daughter called Asgerdh.

The birth of this daughter to Björn and Thora at Borg was an event of great importance to the Skallagrimssons, since it was through her that they were later to lay claim to estates in Norway.

After the birth and through the good offices of his son, Skallagrim was persuaded to send men to Norway to plead Björn's case, which they did with success. So, after three winters at Borg, Björn was able to return to Norway and Thorolf went with him; but Asgerdh was left fostered with Skallagrim. The friends came to the dwelling of Brynjolf in Aurland, Sogn, and the rift between Björn Brynjolfsson and Thori Hersi was soon settled amicably.

Although Harald had his roots in the *Viken* area of eastern Norway, he spent a great deal of his time in the fjord country of the west, where he had a number of seats, His favourite son Erik, as already mentioned, was living as a fosterling with Thori Hersi. It was here that the paths of Erik and Thorolf were about to cross. Björn and Thorolf made a Viking expedition into the Baltic and returned laden with loot. They first went back to Björn's home at Aurland, but later paid a visit to Thori, using a ship they had acquired on their foray, with places for 12 or 13 rowers on each side. In this way did a son of Harald find himself in confrontation with a member of the kin of Kveldulf, which was outlawed, and indeed subject to the laws of vengeance because of wrongs done and lives taken earlier. It would appear that the fine ship they had with them was meant as a gift of atonement to Erik from both Björn and Thorolf.

The fact that the ship was a gift from Björn as well as Thorolf was presumably connected with the loss of prospects of Erik with Thora. It would be this, rather than the insult to Thori, that had persuaded Harald to make Björn an outlaw in the first place. If Erik were placated, then Thori would have to be, even if reluctantly.

The two friends went down to the shore and found Erik looking at the vessel. Without too much difficulty they persuaded him to accept it as a gift in exchange for promising to intercede with the king on behalf of Thorolf, which eventually Erik did with an element of success, although Harald demanded that Thorolf stay out of his sight. Thus did Thorolf Skallagrimsson establish friendly relations with Erik. The gift of a ship was ominously reminiscent of how his namesake uncle Thorolf Kveldulfsson placated for a while Erik's father Harald. Still, for the time being Erik and Thorolf (the younger) took to each other and became quite firm friends. Upon reaching maturity Erik became head man in The Firths and Hordaland, and it was under these circumstances that he made a foray beyond the North Cape with his constant companion Thorolf and is supposed to have met his wife Gunnhild, as told above.

Björn's wife Thora died and he remarried, the bride being Ålof, daughter of Erling the Wealthy, who lived on Osteröy off the coast of Hordaland. One summer Thorolf returned to Iceland on a trading visit and went to see his father. Before he set sail from Norway, Erik had given him a magnificent axe as a gift for Skallagrim: it was apparently a peace offering. Upon receiving it Skallagrim did a strange thing: he caused two oxen to be held with their necks one above the other over a stone, brought the axe down mightily onto them, thus severing both heads at a stroke and ruining the axe edge on the stone below. Without a word, Skallagrim hid the spoilt axe in the house, where it stayed untouched all winter. The test seems to have been devised so that whatever happened the axe would be shown to be imperfect: the placing of the stone underneath might indeed be thought of as unfair. The axe having been shown to be worthless, the implication was clearly transferred to the giver of such a gift, namely Erik.

The gift of the magnificent axe from Erik was apparently meant as a gesture of reconciliation to Skallagrim: so what then is the explanation for his behaviour upon receiving it? He clearly did not want to "bury the hatchet" in the sense of a truce, for he could neither forget nor forgive how he and his father had been driven off their land and out of Norway, The slaying of the two oxen has all the signs of being a sacrifice, in a manner similar to that even recently carried out by the Gurkhas, which ceremony culminates in an adult bovine being beheaded with a very large kukri, with it having to be accomplished with one stroke to be effective, The axe can hardly be said to have failed if it severed the heads of two oxen at once, although contact with the stone below could have blunted it. Was it thus unfairly adjudged useless? Perhaps Skallagrim was disappointed and annoyed that the axe proved to be so effective and put it somewhere in the house where it would indeed be spoilt. Otherwise it might simply be that use for animal butchery was an insult to Erik in itself, and one must not overlook the fact that Skallagrim was a skilled smith and he may have inferred that the axe was meant to imply that it was better than any he could make.

This seems to be the only incident in which Erik "Bloodaxe" is actually associated with an axe, and one must hence suspect that his byname results from this incident. One can immediately see signs of a pun in which *bloð-öks* was confused with *blot-öks* - "sacrifice axe". This punning can be furthered by replacing *öks* by *okse* 'ox'. However the real insult was probably served with the further pun using the Norse word *blautr* - 'soft'. Erik was presumably called *blaut-öks* - "soft axe" - behind his back. The punning would be understood throughout the Scandinavian world, and perhaps is visually more obvious in Modern Danish *blød-okse*—"soft axe"—while one might see it still in "blunt-axe", even though any early etymology of "blunt" is obscure, However this sort of word play was more characteristic of the ancient Celtic world and the attitude behind it will have been picked up by visitors to the British Isles, as were indeed Irish personal names introduced to Iceland, e.g. Kormak and Njal. Even a Gaelic component of the pun can be seen in the word *bloighdeach* - "(cut) in pieces" - as were the oxen.

The next autumn Thorolf set out again for Norway, taking Asgerdh with him to see her father Björn. With them was his petulant younger brother Egil, who had insisted on being taken along, despite his father's and brother's opposition. Before his departure Thorolf announced that when next he returned to Iceland it would be to settle down. As he was about to set sail Skallagrim came from the house carrying that axe, the blade now rusty and the whole blackened with smoke. He suggested that Thorolf give it back to the sender, an insult that was bound to provoke the prince; tactfully he threw the weapon overboard at the first opportunity. However, the real instrument of a rift with Erik was still on board, namely Egil!

Although Egil was still quite young at the time, he went to immense lengths to force his father and brother to let him accompany the latter to Norway. This provokes two questions; why was he so keen to go and why were they so reluctant that he should? One must bear in mind that Thorolf sought to marry Asgerdh and she was an heiress. So did Thorolf intend eventually to claim the inheritance on her behalf? It would seem not, for he announced that this was going to be his last trip abroad and Iceland was to be his future home.

It is clear that Egil did not agree with his brother, but wanted a claim on this inheritance to be staked out in full. He clearly saw Thorolf's friendship with Erik as the bugbear in this matter. He was envious enough of his brother's situation and prospects, but this was a matter of importance for the kin and he in particular still wanted them to be developed to the full. His father and brother would be well aware of his nature and attitude and resisted his demand to go to Norway in the knowledge that it would lead to trouble. Skallagrim does not seem to have been interested in the inheritance, otherwise he would not have insulted Erik by sending his axe back. His concern was that Egil would place both brothers in peril because the lad harboured thoughts of the unavenged death of his uncle Thorolf at the hands of Erik's father Harald.

By the time Thorolf and Egil arrived in Norway, Erik had come of age and had been made a king in The Westland, his favourite seat apparently being Aarstad (*Alreksstaðir*), near Bergen in Hordaland. To placate his sons, Harald had decreed that the men of his kin should receive the various kingdoms, while earldoms would descend only to those in the kin through their mother's line. The land was divided thus. Originally Sogn and Hordaland fell to Rörek and Gudhrödh, but Erik stayed close to his father, for he was held in highest esteem and received Helgeland, North Möre and Romsdal. Yet those brothers were still dissatisfied and envy was rife. Internal strife alternated with forays abroad. Thorgils and Frodhi received warships from the king and raided Scotland, Wales and Ireland. They were the first Northmen in Dublin, where Frodhi is said to have died of poison. Thorgils ruled on there until finally killed by the Irish, who knew him as Turgeis.

Erik wanted to establish himself as over-king of all his brothers and Harald backed him up in this ambition. Although Harald was a heathen, he had no time for some of the superstitious elements within the pagan practices. This is perhaps because he thought he had once been bewitched by the Lappish mother of four of his sons. One of these had Hadeland, but was practising sorcery. Harald sent Erik to admonish him: he found this Rögnvald at it along with eighty other sorcerers. He burnt them all in. He also fell out with his brother Björn over taxes due to Harald. His lands were in the east and, when it eventually came to war, Björn was killed in battle. Erik was winning renown, but losing friends in many areas.

When Harald was approaching seventy he had a son by one of his serving women. He was named *Hákon* after the Earl of Lade and it is said that he was eventually fostered with King Athelstan in England, which would take him beyond the reach of a potentially hostile Erik. Upon reaching the age of ninety, Harald could no longer manage the affairs of state and gave the high seat over to Erik, which definitely confirmed him as over-king. Yet some of his brothers would not accept this and declared themselves independent kings in their own realms. This was the situation developing when Thorolf came back to Norway, accompanied by Egil, and one might suspect that Erik was easily persuaded "to bury the hatchet" because he needed all the friends he could get.

Three years after making Erik sole king Harald died in Rogaland. He was buried in a large and complex howe beside the Karm Sound, and this feature has given its name to the town of Haugesund—"Howe Sound".

Erik eventually came into strife with his two main remaining brotherly rivals in Norway, and they died in the warfare, leaving him as sole ruler. He is said to have been big and handsome, strong and brave, but of unruly temperament. His wife Gunnhild, though beautiful and clever, had the reputation of being devious and cruel. While she suffered the friendship between Erik and Thorolf, she did not approve. She was supposed to be gifted in sorcery.

> Her witchcraft was no doubt a notoriety spread by detractors and justified by her being identified with the would-be sorceress met by Erik in Lappland. Perhaps there were two women who both happened to be called Gunnhild, and Erik was enthralled by the first, just as his father had been overwhelmed by the attractions of a Lappish woman. However, unlike his father, Erik did not earn the reputation of being a shaggy womaniser, and he remained with his formidable queen; this Gunnhild is far more likely to have been the daughter of a Danish king from Jutland, than of some farmer up in Helgeland.

The sagas seem to be making the point that once Harald was rid of Snefridh, he was free of sorcery, while Erik failed to do this because of the continuing presence of Gunnhild.

After delivering Asgerdh to her father Björn, and reporting to Erik with a diplomatic replacement present for the. axe, Thorolf Skallagrimsson found quarters with Thori Hersi, who had a son called Arinbjörn. The latter took particularly to Egil and they became friends for life.

Arinbjörn was a little older than Egil. The friendship forged between them was to prove one of great constancy. One presumes it was because they had natures with a lot in common.

One might perceive with hindsight that the real purpose for this visit had to do with Asgerdh. Thorolf broached the matter of permission to marry to her cousin Arinbjörn. Once armed with his blessing, Skallagrimsson fared into Sogn to ask Björn for his daughter's hand and she was promised to him, whereupon he returned to Thori's place. At last the day of the wedding drew nigh, so Thorolf, Thori and Arinbjörn set out for the home of Björn. Egil, however, claimed to be unwell and stayed behind at Thori's house.

Now Erik owned a house on the island called Atley, off the mouth of the Dalsfjord. (See Map 3, App. 3) On this dwelt a man named Atley-Bardh, a close friend of Erik, but especially of his queen Gunnhild. The king and queen arrived at the hall to find that Bardh was bedding down guests. Erik required that they should be brought before him; but who should they include but Egil Skallagrimsson and a companion called Ölvir.

Once Thorolf's wedding party had left, Egil's recovery appears to have been swift enough. Accompanied by Ölvir, who was accustomed to travelling about collecting rents for Thori, they had set out in a twelve seater, but were driven by the weather to the isle of Atley. Wet and weather-worn, they asked for shelter. At table earlier that night Atley-Bardh had kept deploring the fact that he did not have a decent drink to offer them, such as ale. After what appears to have been a rather frugal meal, the guests were being bedded down in another building where straw at least was not in short supply!

The reason for Egil not attending his brother's, wedding is questionable: the "illness" seems very dubious, considering what he got up to instead. There seem grounds to maintain that he did not want to go there because it was at Björn's house, in other words the former odhal of Egil's kin and that Egil was not content with an outsider occupying it, even a friendly one about to be linked by marriage. To reach Björn's home - say involving a journey from Naustdal to Sogn - the wedding party would need to sail southwards past Atley. It would seem that Egil was following in their wake when he was diverted to Atley, either deliberately or by accident. It may be that Erik and Gunnhild came out of Dalsfjord to Atley with the purpose of making their presence felt to the returning wedding party, an occasion to which they had not been invited, or had declined to attend.

With the arrival of Erik and Gunnhild, the means to have real festivities were miraculously provided, and one might be tempted to describe the subsequent proceedings as heathen debauchery. Ale now appeared in plenty, which Egil found infuriating. He then proceeded to demonstrate how he could out-drink all of them. Bardh went to Gunnhild and told her that there was one present bent on shaming them. Gunnhild's solution to this problem was quite simple: she and Bardh added poison to Egil's drink, for he was by now in a wild mood. For some reason Egil became suspicious and spilled the drink on the floor with some ceremony. The festivities meanwhile had caught up with Ölvir and he fell ill, so Egil, sword in hand, led him to the door. Bardh followed and demanded that Ölvir drink one more health, but it was Egil who snatched and downed it. It was dark in the doorway where Egil threw down that empty horn and then thrust his sword right through Bardh. As he slumped dead, the sick Ölvir collapsed. Egil made off. The two bodies, one lifeless, the other senseless, were found in the doorway. Erik sent men to seize ships all round the island, so that in the morning it could be searched for the fugitive.

Egil soon made the discovery that no boat or ship was available to him for escape: resourceful as ever, he swam across to a nearby islet called Saudhey. Erik's men searched Atley all day without success, and it was not till eventide that a twelve seater came to the islet. While three men guarded the boat, the rest searched ashore. Egil broke cover to attack the boat watch. One man was killed outright, the second had his foot cut off as he clambered up a bank, while the third leapt aboard and attempted to push off, but in vain: he too met his end. Egil took the boat and rowed it single handed back to the dwelling of Thori Hersi.

No blame for the outrage was attached to Ölvir and his men: they were allowed home, which they reached before Egil. Thorolf and Thori had by then come back from the wedding. Considering what had been reported to them, they were rather surprised when Egil turned up, having supposed his fate to be sealed. Once they had heard Egil's side of the story, Arinbjörn and Thori became sympathetic and the latter made his way to the king to offer him atonement on behalf of the rugged Icelander. It is now that one can perceive a sign of weakness in Erik which was absent from his father. One must feel that Harald would only have been satisfied with proper vengeance for Bardh and the others; but it was not so with Erik. He blustered a lot, but eventually showed himself vulnerable to alternative offers, here a goodly sum of wergild.

> Of course, one might feel inclined to award him some excuse in that his heart was not really in the campaign of hatred being waged by his wife Gunnhild.

The isle of Atley *(Atla-ey)* appears to have been named after Earl Atli. Earlier, Harald Hairfair's father, Halfdan Svarti, while trying to hold sway over The Westland, had put a friend called Atli of Gaular in charge of Sogn. After the Battle of Solskjel and the subsequent death of King Vemund, Harald made a certain Hakon Earl over The Firths. With Harald absent in the east, Hakon sent word to Atli that he should surrender Sogn and go back to Gaular, where he had been before. He refused, and it came to a battle in Fjaler. Hakon was killed and the wounded Atli was taken to Atley, where he died of his injuries. After this Sogn went to Brynjolf and The Firths to Thori; Atley-Bardh may not have been a subsidiary of Thori, but rather was in charge of the lands of Fjaler around the Dalsfjord and at Gaular which were then under Erik's direct control.

> Atley-Bardh's special friendship with Gunnhild will not have gone down well with Egil, since he was probably only too aware of her aspirations for Erik. In view of Egil's behaviour one must suspect that she had plans

for Atley-Bardh which boded ill for the two earls (especially Brynjolf), as well as anyone called Skallagrimsson. The attempt by Gunnhild to poison Egil may simply be a fabrication to justify further Egil's actions, which culminated in the slaying of Atley-Bardh. At the very least he had become a threat to any inheritance of the Skallagrimssons through the marriage to Asgerdh. Thori and Arinbjörn may have been aware of the threat that Atley-Bardh posed, and it was therefore that they were eager to support Egil against Erik and Gunnhild. Atley is indeed quite a mountainous island, separated from Askvoll by the Granesund, but the name Sauesund occurs at the south end of this. The main settlement and church are now at Vilnes, near the southernmost point, but near Vilnes is Bardnes; this could refer directly to Atley-Bardh or namesake descendants. (See also Chap, 3 below and ref, Photo, 30, App. 5)

While Thorolf and Egil were thus allowed to stay on with Thori, Erik was not at all happy with Egil within his realm. The next spring the brothers prepared a longship and sailed into the Baltic as Vikings. In Courland (Latvia?) they were captured by natives, who prepared to put them to death. Egil's huge strength helped them to escape and to loot and burn down the hall of their captors. At the same time they released a Dane called Aki and his two sons, thus making good friends. On the way back they topped up their booty by raiding Lund, then Danish, but now a university city in the south of Sweden.

Although Aki was a Dane, he appears to have had no compunction against looting the Danish settlement of Lund, together with his new friends Thorolf and Egil. This was not anywhere near his home territory, as is clear from the fact that he was later able to contact them on a future occasion when they were cut off along the west coast of Jutland.

They eventually parted from Aki, who returned to Jutland, and in the autumn Thorolf set a course which brought them back to the long coast of Norway, to reach once more the home of Thori Hersi. Arinbjörn wanted Egil to overwinter there, but his father was worried about the attitude of King Erik. Then Arinbjörn proclaimed with some force that if Egil went, so would he, and that seems to have settled the matter in Egil's favour, at least for the time being.

That autumn Thori went to visit Erik to explain who would be staying with him. The king accepted the situation, but only because of the involvement of Thori; had it been someone else it would have been different! Once more Erik can be seen as acting with a certain indecisiveness towards Egil, through not wanting to cross Thori. This was not lost on Gunnhild who told Erik straight that if he continued to give in thus to the sons of Skallagrim he would one day be faced with the necessity of avenging someone of near kin. Even the slaying of Bardh had been passed over too lightly in her view. Erik spoke words in defence of Thorolf, which even she seemed inclined to accept provisionally. Even so, Egil had now come to Norway and spoilt him. Thori reported these discussions to Thorolf and Egil.

There was thus an explosive situation in The Westland that was just waiting for someone to light the fuse.

The next spring there was a great sacrificial festival at Gaular in The Firths, where there was an important temple. Folk gathered there from all over The Firths, Fjaler and Sogn. King Erik attended with Gunnhild, who made the suggestion to her brothers Eyvind Skreya and Alf Askmann that they should attempt to slay one or other of the sons of Skallagrim, but preferably both.

Thori foresaw that there were dangers at Gaular for his Icelandic guests and put it to his son that he should keep Egil away from the festival altogether, while he himself would attend with Thorolf. Once there, Thori never left Thorolf's side. Since both Egil and Thorolf proved to be inaccessible, Gunnhild instructed her brothers to switch target to some close companion of the pair. Thorvald Ofsi and Thorfinn Strangi were kinsmen of Björn Brynjolfsson, son-in-law to Thori, and they had become henchmen of the sons of Skallagrim, Thorvald close to Thorolf and Thorfinn close to Egil. Those brothers of murderous intent, Eyvind and Alf, took to drinking with the pair and, as can easier be arranged under such circumstances, a quarrel arose whereby Eyvind stabbed Thorvald to death.

One might suppose that Egil and Gunnhild had an instinctive distrust of each other and the events on Atley had converted this to an implacable hatred. Each realised that the other stood in the way of the realisation of ambition. Gunnhild must play down any bad feelings she actually harboured against Thorolf, because he had given no grounds for complaint, except for being Egil's brother. It seems quite plausible that she would try to do away with the brothers at Gaular, but, because of the precautions, had to settle for secondary targets. It should come as no surprise that these were not only henchmen of the Skallagrimssons, but also kinsmen of Björn, for he sat and lorded it over Sogn, which benefit should have come to the heir of Earl Atli—Atley-Bardh perhaps. Her brothers are said to be the sons of Ossur Toti. If so they were probably not her brothers at all. However, it would seem more probable that this erroneously complied with the belief that she was his daughter. The meeting at *Gaular* here, since it concerned the provinces of The Firths, Sogn and Fjaler, ought to have occurred somewhere convenient to all three districts. This would be at the River Gaula that runs into the Dalsfjord, near the border of The Firths and Sogn (rather than the River Gaula far to the north near Trondheim), and indeed at the head of Dalsfjord, near whose mouth lies the isle of Atlöy.

The exact location of the cult site at Gaular would seem difficult to locate without direct evidence. However, a visit to Hestad provided circumstantial evidence to make this the likely situation. On the course of the Gaula are two lakes here, the Hestadfjord to the east and the Viksdalsvatn to the west, which are really one lake almost cut in two by a spit of glacial origin attached to the north shore. (App 3 Map 3; App 10 Photos 9 to 12) This spit is now a nature conservation area. The *gardstun* hamlet is at its root, at the foot of the slopes, but at its southern end is a knoll upon which sits the church in isolation. Information on site states that this timber structure replaced a former stave church. The peculiar physical circumstances here suggest that this was indeed the important heathen cult site in Gaular, and this is enhanced by the consideration of the place-name Hestad on a later page.

The deed earned banishment for Eyvind, for one was not supposed even to be carrying a weapon at the temple. King Erik may not have known anything about the complot, but offered compensation to Thorolf and Thori for the slain man. They replied that they had never accepted such atonement and would not start now; they left Gaular forthwith. These remarks must have struck home, for as has been remarked, in the past Erik had shown himself to be only too willing to accept treasure by way of atonement. As far as Eyvind was concerned, his fate supports the Danish origins of Gunnhild, for he was sent back to Denmark by his sister and Erik to be appointed warden against the Vikings infesting its waters.

The refusal of Thorolf and Thori to accept wergild should however not disguise from one that Erik was indeed intent on doing the best he could to atone for this deed. That Eyvind was sent to Denmark may have been for his own safety, rather than punishment; but Erik has the appearance of trying to be reasonable towards the two seeking redress. However, wergild refused meant that a blood feud was still open. Guilt clearly lay with Gunnhild and she is not reported to have made protestations in this case: a diplomatic silence? Since Thorolf and Thori would not accept compensation for Thorvald's murder meant that they were honour bound to spill blood to avenge it. And so was especially Thorfinn Strangi. Eyvind may have escaped, but this would put others at risk as substitute targets. Now Thorolf had joined his brother as an enemy of the royal kin. It is clear that the brothers had to leave and so they sailed off the next year as Vikings. It is in the aftermath of the gathering at Gaular that the discrepancies in chronology and personalities between Norse and English sources start to build up; one must suspect that it was all done to cover up any failings that Egil had and increase his status as a warrior and hero. There is indeed a gap of several years between them leaving Norway and eventually turning up in the army of "Athelstan" ready to fight at Vinheidh, during which hiatus their activities are obscure.

After the affair at Gaular, Thorolf and Egil set off on another Viking foray. This time, rather than sailing eastwards into the Baltic, they passed down the west coast of Jutland towards Friesland. At the border between Denmark and Friesland they were hove to for the night when a message came to Egil from his old friend Aki warning that Eyvind was aware of their presence and lying in wait for them on their return from the south. His force was vastly superior to that of Thorolf and Egil. The latter's reaction was typical. He immediately set sail and caught Eyvind's ship unawares. The "warden" and a deal of his men escaped by swimming ashore, but ships were taken, along with clothes and weapons. When he rejoined Thorolf, his brother expressed the fear that now they dare not attempt to return to Norway that autumn. Egil's response was that they should therefore seek another land in which they could gain winter quarters. It was under these circumstances that the brothers were indeed fortunate in that, while cruising by Saxony and Flanders, they heard that Athelstan, King of England, was in need of men skilled in the ways and weapons of war. The Skallagrimssons joined the forces of the English king, but Thorolf was eventually killed at the Battle of Vinheidh.

That Thorolf and Egil as armed Vikings were operating off the west coast of Jutland can hardly be a matter of chance; they and their brother-bereft man Thorfinn Strangi were surely seeking any means they could to bring harm to Eyvind, to either his reputation, his property, or his life. One must assume that they had specifically sought out their friend Aki, who owed them one, and he could keep them informed. Eyvind would think that he was the hunter, but became the hunted and in the end was fortunate to escape with his life. The action made their position off Denmark untenable and a return to Norway was out of the question. This would particularly apply since Arinbjörn had also felt under pressure to leave.

So they eventually turned up in the service of King Athelstan. However, there is the mentioned gap of several years in which neither the Skallagrimssons nor Arinbjörn Hersi are mentioned. Where were they and what were they doing? It is evident that the brothers at least did not return to Iceland and could not find safe quarters in either Norway or Denmark. This problem is deferred and will be addressed in the next chapter.

By the time Egil got back to The Firths, Thori was dead and Arinbjörn had succeeded to his estates. Together with eleven men, Egil stayed the winter with him, but kept showing signs of discontent. Eventually it was disclosed that this was on account of his feelings for his brother's widow Asgerdh. His suit was accepted and they were wed, which cheered him up no end. Next spring he got ready a merchantman and, accompanied by Asgerdh, sailed back to Iceland, for Arinbjörn had warned him against staying in Norway while Gunnhild was still in a position to wield power, especially after the affair with her brother Eyvind off Jutland.

Despite what is said in Egla, Egil may well have returned to Norway together with Arinbjörn. The saga could not mention this without disclosing something it was shy of, namely that this man had also been in England with Athelstan.

Egil is said to have stayed many winters at Borg. But at last news reached Iceland that Björn Brynjolfsson had died and that Bergönund, who had married Björn's daughter Gunnhild by his second wife Alof, had assumed the inheritance, even going to the extent of transferring goods to his own place at Ask in Hordaland. Bergönund was the son of Thorgeir Thornfoot, and had two brothers called Hadd and Atli. It occurred to Egil that Bergönund might not have claimed the estate entirely on his own initiative, but through the influence of more powerful people, for Thorgeir's son was a great friend of King Erik, though an even greater one of Queen Gunnhild.

Egil was stung into action. The next spring he sailed away from Iceland, taking Asgerdh with him, but leaving behind Thordis, her daughter by Thorolf. They arrived at Arinbjörn's seat, who welcomed them and took them in. Egil enquired of his friend about the possibility of claiming what he took to be his inheritance, but was advised that there was little chance, for Bergönund was difficult to deal with and had the backing of the king and queen, while Gunnhild held Egil especially in enmity. But Egil would not be put off; yet he must have been feeling his age a bit, for he decided to take the matter to the law.

So by 943 King Harald had died and his preferred son Erik was over-king in Norway; but his days there were numbered. Erik was kept busy brutally suppressing the claims of other members of his kin, but in the meantime had been trying to win support (Holtsmark pp. 79-83; Pálsson p. 32). He confirmed the ownership of some land to a certain Bergönund, which Egil had a pressing claim on. So, sometime after 939 Egil in Iceland had heard that his legacy in Norway had been "illegally" seized in this way by others, thus compelling him to go back once more to retrieve it. The upshot was that the matter was taken to the Gulathing court.

The details of the confrontation with Bergönund and the proceedings at Guli, and of Egil's subsequent taking of retribution are as follows. Taking a ship with twenty men he sailed to Ask and demanded his share of Björn's estate, adding that in his opinion

Asgerdh was higher born than Bergönund's wife, her half sister. The other showed amazement at Egil's aspirations, especially as he had been declared an outlaw by King Erik. Bergönund added that he had overcome the likes of Egil before with less cause and, as for Asgerdh, she was the daughter of a thrall on her mother's side. This was a reference to Björn's first wife Thora, who had been taken against the will of Björn's father Brynjolf and her brother Thori Hersi.

Egil demanded that the matter be taken to the regional assembly (or "thing") at Guli and the other agreed, but not without making threats against Egil's person. Then Egil reported back to Arinbjörn Hersi in The Firths, who became furious at the denigratory remarks Bergönund had made about his aunt Thora. He went to Erik and proposed a meeting of the thing. This was granted, but the ruler reproved him for taking Egil's part in such matters, especially against those who were the friends of the King of Norway.

When the appointed time for the Gulathing was nigh, Arinbjörn made his way there accompanied by Egil and with a large body of men. King Erik too had a goodly band, with Bergönund among them, and his two brothers. The thing took place on a level area marked out with hazel wands set in a ring and strung with ropes. Inside this sat the judges, twelve each from The Firths, Sogn and Hordaland. One would expect The Firths to go with Arinbjörn and Egil, while Hordaland would clearly vote with Erik and Bergönund, leaving Sogn as the deciding factor. Björn's brother had inherited Aurland and was one of the representatives of Sogn. With him being related by marriage to both Arinbjörn and Egil there was clearly a chance that he would swing Sogn against King Erik in this matter. The situation was very tense and with the forces assembled there a conflict of some magnitude was possible.

Egil stepped forward to make his claim to the inheritance of Björn Brynjolfsson, which was based on the rights of his wife Asgerdh in this matter: through her he laid claim to half of the estate. He thus appears to have conceded the right of Bergönund to the rest by way of his wife Gunnhild.

Arinbjörn Hersi took up the word and recalled how reconciliation had been achieved between Thori and Björn. At this the king was beginning to show signs of indecision; Queen Gunnhild chided him about this and added that she was not going to allow judgment to take place when it concerned someone like Egil. She called on her brother Alf, who with his men cut down the poles and ropes, then scattered the judges. Egil by this time had had enough of the law being dispensed at this thing; he challenged Bergönund to personal combat, that kind of duel known as "holmgang". But the king intervened, saying that if it was a fight Egil wanted, then they were ready enough to give it to him. Egil then indicated how unfairly the odds were in the king's favour, but if he cared to fight it out with equal numbers he was willing enough to oblige. The developing situation obviously created a problem for Arinbjörn; to avoid such strife he intervened and urged that they all leave, seeing as there was clearly nothing to be gained by staying. Before departing in a hurry to escape Erik's wrath, Egil banned the estate of Björn to Bergönund or anyone else. Reaching their ships, and on the advice of Arinbjörn, Egil's folk went their own ways to avoid any further confrontation.

Rather than risk Erik winning his case, Gunnhild had had her brother Alf organise a total disruption of the Gulathing proceedings. Egil then took a series of actions to satisfy his honour, before eventually returning to Iceland and resuming life at Borg, which he was soon to inherit upon the death of his father. (Pálsson pp. 34-50)

The Gulathing, like the festival at Gaular, was held somewhere near the mouth of the Sognefjord, but in this case on the south side. Here is the Gulefjord and the district still called Gulen, The institution of the Gulathing lasted for several centuries, mainly in the time of the later Christian kings. It was held at Eivindvik. "Things" were open air meetings and essentially had a flat space or spaces (*thingvöllr* or *thingvellir*) and a high point, either natural or artificial, from which law speeches could be delivered. Such places can be recognised in Britain in place-names like Tynwald (Isle of Man) with its artificial square stepped hill, Tinwald (Dumfriesshire), Dingwall (Ross and Cromarty), Tingwall (Orkneys and Shetland), and Thingwall (Cheshire, Lancashire and a lost one in Yorkshire), which all can be compared with *Thingvellir* in Iceland, The use of prehistoric burial mounds as "thing-howes" is suggested by names like Thingoe (Suffolk) and Fingay Hill (Yorkshire). At Eivindvik the speakers' level is up on the ridge of rock on which stands the church. On the north side is a stone cross which may have replaced a standing stone at the "pulpit". This point overlooks the only flat area available for the assembly and now largely occupied by the cemetery. (Ref. Photos 13-16, App. 5).

Like Gaular, Gulen was a central spot, in this case for the representatives of The Firths, Sogn and Hordaland to meet, twelve men from each. The parties came in some strength and well armed, although they were not allowed to take weapons onto the thing-stead. [The way this was marked out with hazel wands and rope reflects how an area at the battlefield of Vinheidh is described as similarly treated. (Pálsson 1976 pIl9)] The argument revolved around the legitimacy of Björn's first marriage to Thora. Although Björn had been reconciled with Erik, Bergönund totally rejected that marriage, while Arinbjörn made a speech outlining the legal niceties in Egil's favour and thingmen came forward to support him. The king and the judges were then invited to take oaths on this, but Erik demurred. It is quite clear that Gunnhild had her brother Alf Askmann at hand just in case the king should weaken, and they overran the thing.

It is to be noted that Egil was not out to take all of Bergönund's inheritance through his wife Gunnhild and her and Asgerdh's father Björn, but only those estates descending to him from Björn through Asgerdh. He was really trying to settle this in law and saw his case as unanswerable. But the risks were huge. So why did he persist so strongly to get possession of this particular parcel, when he was going to inherit Borg in Iceland in any case? Borg was safe, so he showed little special interest in it. This matter of Björn's legacy had driven him from an early age and he was determined not to be cheated out of it. Bergönund's argument that Asgerdh's claim to the land was invalid because of the suspect marriage of her mother to Björn is not mentioned as being compared directly with the way that Thorolf Kveldulfsson lost half of his inheritance to the sons of Hildiridh, yet whose marriage to Björgolf was questionable. (See Chap. 2 above) Perhaps it was to be inferred without prompting. Since King Harald had come down in favour of the Hildiridharsons, then King Erik should really have done the same for Egil. Another perceived weak point in Egil's case is that Björn, after reconciliation, had not taken service with the king, and was therefore known as Björn Hold. Even some in the king's service had been demoted; Thori Hroaldsson should have succeeded his father as an earl, but was called a hersi, as was eventually also his son Arinbjörn. Björn's brother Thordh succeeded their father Brynjolf as hersi in Aurland. But

Björn had his own estate. The nagging question remains: why was Egil so keen to get his hands on it? Where indeed was it?

The first question has already been aired to some extent, but there may be an extra element that is not brought out in Egil's Saga, The name of Björn's estate is never mentioned. Perhaps it was not known; but rather it was a deliberate omission. An earlier deliberate omission was the name of the estate in Sogn which Kveldulf and Skallagrim were forced to abandon. Thori Hersi had been Kveldulf's foster son and thus became a great friend of Skallagrim, which was some cause for the bond that quickly developed between Arinbjörn and Egil. When Kveldulf left, it is said that nobody dare buy the estate because of fear of the king's power. The farm must have been unoccupied and the land unused. Yet when Björn came back and, along with Thorolf Skallagrimsson, was reconciled with the king, he obtained a "fine, impressive farm". How was such a property available? The easiest answer is that because of the renewed good relations with Erik he was able to reoccupy the abandoned farm of Kveldulf and taking this on board allows us to perceive with greater clarity a very strong reason why Egil wanted to get his hands on it. Apart from his legal rights through Asgerdh, it was also ancient odhal that his kin had been driven off. This of course does not explain the secrecy over the name. It must have been known; so why not disclose it in the Saga?

It could well be that when Kveldulf and Skallagrim left Norway their old home became a no-name place, because the name went with them. This suggests that their former home was called Borg. Be that as it may, it would seem that the descendants of Egil were determined not to name it because the kin never managed to regain it for all practical purposes. Another consideration is that the name was originally omitted for effect, with the audience obtaining dramatic pleasure by working the situation out for themselves. With the passage of time the underlying facts would be forgotten by everyone in Iceland and resolution would no longer be possible. From pointers in Egil's Saga, as well as argument above, it is clear that it lay near the mouth of the Sognefjord on the north side. A lesser inlet here is called Böfjord, taking its name from a settlement called Bö. Böfjord and the branch of Borgarfjördhr in Iceland on which Borg lies are remarkably similar both in shape and orientation, while Bö and Borg occupy the same relative position on the north-west shore respectively, (See Map 3, App 3)

The element *bö* occurs in Norwegian place-names, often specifically with the sense "abandoned place". (Olsen 1939 p15) This would be particularly appropriate should one consider Bö to have been abandoned by Kveldulf, then by Bergönund after he ransacked it, and finally by Egil who was unable to stay in Norway. Egil clearly sealed the fate of the settlement when, at the break-up of the thing, he angrily declared to everybody that the estate descending from Björn was not to be occupied by anyone, no matter what his status. (Pálsson 1976 pp 138-9)

At the time that Björn Brynjolfsson first came to Borg the place is said to be named after a rocky hill that overlooked it and resembled a castle. (Pálsson 1976 p83) Be that as it may, it can be claimed that the word *borg* in place-names refers to "rock", whether a fort is present or not. In Scotland two places called Borgue suggest Nordic origin of this kind. They do have ancient coastal forts nearby, the one a broch and the other a cliff-top promontory fort. In Cumberland the upper valley of the River Derwent is known as Borrowdale. The river was called *Borgará* in Old Norse and the dale *Borgarárdalr*. The *borg* here is a precipitous rocky eminence rising from the floor of the dale and known as Castle Crag. The small area on top has been partially quarried away, but has been made even more inaccessible, assuredly in prehistoric times, by the provision of a low rampart around the periphery. Not far from the nearby town of Keswick is a lower hill with rocks outcropping on its summit. Although no actual fort is in evidence, this is known as Castle Head, with a later translation from *borg* being inferable. Elsewhere in Cumberland, overlooking the Vale of St. John, a huge rock is known as the Castle Rock of Triermain. The last represents Welsh *tre'r maen (tref yr maen)*—"settlement of the rock". The original Cumbrian farm will have been under this crag, without any fort being present, It would be the Northmen who introduced the sense "fort" as *borg,* which we can infer as having been translated to "castle" after the appearance of the Normans.

One can observe that Bö similarly nestles right under a large sheer cliff. This is reminiscent of Borg and Triermain, with an overhanging crag itself being enough to secure comparison with a fort. Bö sits on a ledge that may be partially artificial and of much earlier origin. From here can be observed all the associated farmland, the small natural harbour and the approach up the Böfjord, (Ref, photos, 19-24, App. 6) The association of *borg* with natural rocks can be observed with Borgund, Lærdal, not so very far from Aurland, Inner Sogn. The *gardstun* lies just to the east of the famous stave church, with the latter confirming the place's antiquity. The place does not lie under a crag, but appears to be named because it sits on a raised platform of rock, much of it outcropping, Such a rocky platform does give an aspect reminiscent of a prehistoric fort. (Ref. photos, 25-21, App 6) This argument leads one towards discussion of the ancient Burgundians and the island of Bornholm, which must however be deferred here. Sufficient to say that Bö is overlooked by a crag and stands on a platform, either of which features could have suggested a *borg,*

Björn's brother Thordh inherited the estate of Aurland. The Aurlandsfjord is one of the inner reaches at the head of the Sognefjord. (Ref. Photos. 28 & 29, App. 5) He would also inherit the title *hersi* from his father, with the whole vast province of Sogn as his domain, while Arinbjörn was *hersi* in The Firths, It would be under these circumstances that Björn was able to reoccupy a place like Bö. Aurland is a huge distance from Bö, while the latter would be rather closer to the seat of Arinbjörn; but the exact location of the latter is another problem and as yet not fully addressed.

Erik was made furious by Egil's parting words, but was inhibited from attacking him there and then because attendance at a thing required one to be unarmed, a precaution justified by the events described. However, he swore to have Egil's life and those of any who would defend him. Crunch time had arrived for Arinbjörn. He was overhauled by Erik at Saudesund as they sailed north; but, wisely, he had parted from Egil. Upon demand, Arinbjörn informed the king that Egil, in a twenty-seater, had sailed towards Steinsund, which was indeed the truth. Egil had by then reached his merchantman there, which was ready to sail; but in the early light he saw ships approaching. There was no time to get the trader under way, however, so Egil ordered his men to get back swiftly aboard the twenty-seater; yet, despite the urgency, he did not neglect to take with him the two chests obtained from "Athelstan". In the poor light he managed to hug the shore and slip past the approaching fleet. The nearest ship, which he brushed past, was Erik's. Egil let fly a spear, which struck the steersman; it was perhaps a case of mistaken identity, for he was a near kinsman of Erik and resembled him. Egil's merchantman was taken and some ten men perished who had not made their escape. The ship was looted and burnt.

In his haste to get away from Gulen, Egil had forged ahead of Arinbjörn's fleet. The latter, heading north across the mouth of the Sognefjord to get to The Firths, probably sailed along the sound to the east of the island of Hisaröy and was overhauled by Erik's ships. As a ruse they may have split, with Egil keeping to the south of this island before turning north. (*See* Map 3, App. 3: Ref. Photos 17 & 18, App, 5)

Erik actually caught up with Arinbjörn in Saudesund. This lies between Atlöy and Askvoll, just north of the Dalsfjord, and is a clear indication that the seat of Arinbjörn, and Thori before him, was at least as far north as Sunnfjord (the Fördefjord). Here one might recall that when Egil was escaping from Erik on Atley he swam to a small island called Saudhey; a suitable island exists in the short strait still known as Sauesund. It can be argued that Arinbjörn's seat was actually at Naustdal, and since Egil managed to row there after his strenuous adventures on Atley, it would seem that some destination on the Fördefjord would be far enough for him to manage, rather than anywhere even further north.(Ref, Photos 30-33, App. 5)

Arinbjörn had to choose between defying his lord or betraying his friend. To have lied would have been disloyal, as well as putting his relationship with Erik in the greatest jeopardy, together with his status and very life in Norway. He told the truth, but did not take part in the pursuit. Egil's ship was at Steinsund, on one of the outer isles of Solund, which are separated by long and narrow channels. The settlement of this name lies at the head of a small wyke off one of these sounds, a place where one could easily get trapped. Hence Egil was only able to escape in his light ship, with some of his men. The rest were scattered from his merchantman by the king's men, after which the craft was looted and burnt, with ten killed. Yet Egil had rescued those two chests. He had been back to Iceland and ought to have handed them over to his father, but he clearly considered them his own private property that he took with him wherever he went. Just before Skallagrim died he challenged Egil about them, but was told that he had silver enough of his own. Skallagrim's response was secretly to bury his own treasure in a bog to put it out of reach, and died immediately after. One might suppose that Egil intended to use his own treasure to buy the land he so desired in Norway, if all else failed. In the event he was never parted from them, for, in a similar way to his father, as an old man about to die in Iceland, he took them and hid them in a place where he intended them to remain undiscovered, although this was after he had been dissuaded from scattering the contents of the chests indiscriminately at the thing for folk to scramble after, with prospects of chaotic and unpredictable results ensuing. In any case he was making the point that this treasure was his alone to dispose of as he liked; it represented after all the tangible sum total of all his efforts abroad.

Egil too might have been caught at Steinsund, but escaped by rowing over shallows where the longships could not follow. He made his way back to Arinbjörn again, who provided him with another ship so that he could return to Iceland. This he did not do immediately, but secretly took refuge among fisherfolk on some outer isles called *Vitar*; merely to return to his home with his journey and endeavours having been almost a complete failure was not in his nature.

It would appear that about the time of these incidents King Harald finally died. Now in pursuit of his greater ambitions Erik drove eastwards to Viken to do battle with his brothers, as described on a previous page. Arinbjörn Hersi went with him. This afforded Egil an opportunity which he seized.

Bergönund was nervous when the king left and kept plenty of men by him, including his brother Hadd. A kinsman of Erik, called Frodhi, who the king had left behind to guard Bergönund, was in residence at the royal seat of Aarstad, and with whom was staying a boy, a son of Erik called Rögnvald. Before he drove eastward, Erik had made Egil an outlaw throughout Norway, for any man to slay at will. That man thus banned skulked on his islands, but arranged for his fishermen hosts to bear to the mainland false reports of his departure. Reassured, Bergönund let his men go and rowed to Aarstad to see Frodhi, inviting him to his own house where there was plenty of ale. The pair hence went back together and duly celebrated.

Rögnvald had a six-seater and, after Frodhi left, with twelve men in all he rowed out to Herdhla. Egil in the meantime had sailed out to sea at night, but found himself becalmed at dawn, whereupon the ship was allowed to drift for some time. In the end a sea-breeze sprang up and Egil decided to head back to land while the wind was reasonable, for any freshening could have forced them to some hostile shore. As it was, Egil happened to reach Herdhla and sent men ashore to spy out the land, thus learning that Rögnvald was there and much was being drunk. Leaving his ship by Herdhla, with eighteen shipmates Egil rowed a boat to the island of *Fenhring* (now Asköy) and once there pulled into a small inlet. Fully armed, he went up onto land and came across some boys with several large hounds, learning from them that a bear had been abroad in that place. When the boys asked why he was going around so heavily armed, Egil took to lying, claiming that he too was in fear of the bear and had in fact seen it beside the wood. Saying that he must now be off home, he suggested that the boys inform the revellers in the house as to where the bear was lurking. This resulted in Bergönund, Frodhi and Hadd arming themselves and coming out to hunt down the animal, which soon betrayed its presence to them by moving about among the bushes.

Bergönund ran toward the thicket where Egil lay in wait to come at the other with thrusting spear, to which reply was given in kind. Unfortunately for Bergönund Egil's spear held fast in his shield, making it completely unwieldy. The landowner then attempted to draw his sword, but Egil already had his to hand because it was attached to his wrist by a thong. He thrust his opponent through and then nearly severed his head with a second blow. Then he recovered his spear.

Hadd and Frodhi came to the attack. Once more Egil struck home, his spear transfixing the latter after passing through his shield, then, after a short swordplay, Hadd too was killed. Egil's men came to seek him, and became aware of his deeds. Then all together they stormed the farmhouse, killing all the men within. The loot they could not carry away they spoilt, then escaped to the sea.

As they rowed back towards Herdhla, it so happened that Rögnvald was sailing in the opposite direction. He had found out that Egil was in the area, and intended to warn Bergönund. Egil recognised the ship at once and rammed it without hesitation, so that it shipped water. He was still in a bloodthirsty mood and with his men clambered aboard and slew all thirteen defenceless crew, including Rögnvald. Thus did Egil avenge himself on Bergönund and also on Erik and Gunnhild through their lad.

It seems that Erik had other problems and finally lost patience with the irritating Egil. Before the king set out on a campaign against his two brothers, who were eventually slain, he formally made Egil an outlaw to be killed by any man's hand. This threat probably assisted with the success of Egil's feigned departure overseas, whereby Erik's kin and friends in Hordaland were put at their ease. The *Vitar* were west of the island of *Alden,* and the place on them where Egil took refuge was a fishing station. The largest of these outer isles even now has a place called *Værøy,* which as it stands means "fishing station island". Of the other three places involved in these episodes Aarstad is at Bergen, Ask is on the island of that name *(Askøy),* and Herdhla is a small island at the northern tip of Askøy. The most rash act was that of young Rögnvald in sailing to Herdhla, and one can imagine his panic when he got wind that Egil's ship was moored there. These encounters resulted in a number of deaths among Egil's enemies, including Gunnhild's favourites the brethren Bergönund and Hadd, Erik's kinsman Frodhi, and Erik's (and presumably Gunnhild's) son Rögnvald. With this on top of everything else one might have cause to suppose that Erik could hardly have any compunction against putting Egil to death at the first opportunity.

As they approached Herdhla again, Egil and his party were observed by those remaining at the farmhouse, who fled: this too was then looted. Before he left, Egil set up a horse's head on a hazel post upon a rocky outcrop. The head pointed towards the mainland and was an emblem of scorn directed at Erik and Gunnhild. He is said to have inscribed certain runes upon the post!

One might again note the use of hazel in a ritualistic manner. The association of horses with rocky headlands is more a feature of the Celtic west, (a point which this author hopes to expound elsewhere), but how the horse's head in itself could be an instrument for insult is not so clear. The claim that Egil added his insulting words to the pole in runes can hardly be accepted; at best it is more likely that they were rudimentary and not understood by his companions, especially in view of the lack of runic inscriptions in Iceland.

There would seem to be signs of a horse cult in the Gaular/Fjaler area and with King Erik, Thori Hersi and the Skallagrimssons being among its devotees. It is suggested that the sacrifices at Hestad involved the slaughter of horses. The use of hazel posts or stakes for ritual purposes may also have been connected with this owing something to the alliterative connection between the two words, i.e., *hest*—"horse"—and *hesli*— "hazels". While one is not in a position to refer directly to British horse cults yet, attention can at least be drawn to one link with headlands in that Old Norse *hross*—"horse"—is a homophone of Gaelic *ros*—"headland". Perhaps the association between headlands and horses was imported from Britain. At any rate, apart from the affair at Gaular, one can indicate Egil's horse's head on a hazel post on a headland immediately after the Gulathing, the latter having been marked out with hazels, and that shortly after he got home to Borg his father died and then buried together with his horse on the tip of a headland.

Hestad perhaps can be thought of as "hest-stad", but such a settlement is more likely originally to have involved the plural *stadhir*—"steads". However, the church knoll appears to have been called Kyrkjeli, which would represent Old Norse *Kirkju-hlið*. This may have replaced an earlier name such as either *HesIa-hlið*—"hazel slope"—or *Hest(s)-hlið*—"horse('s) slope". Any representation of a horse would perhaps be known as a *hlið-hest*. An exact linguistic route cannot of course be determined, but one way or another it would be normal to arrive at a form like "Hes-stad" for the settlement by suppression of the "li", (earlier "hlidh"). With the present church having replaced a stave church it is tempting to consider that this was either a converted temple building or a replacement built in the temple style. Stave churches can be divided into two categories: 1) those which visually resemble churches elsewhere, despite the stave construction, as at Kaupanger: 2) those of apparently outlandish design, with multiple roofs and a more symmetrical fabric, as at Borgund. Any temple at Hestad may not have been converted directly to become the former stave church there, but this structure, as well as such as Borgund, and the eventually destroyed Fantoft one near Bergen, may owe their design to that of temples. The stronghold for the stave churches is around the Sognefjord and the Fantoft one was transferred from there.

Were they the descendants of the temples of the horse cult, and could the characteristic grotesque carvings forming roof finials be stylised horses' heads? (App 5 Photos 9 & 27)

Bö church is one of the three parish churches of the Hyllestad commune. This and the fjord-name suggest a former importance for Bö which seems misplaced today, being overshadowed in size as it is by its neighbour Leirvik, at the head of the fjord. It may be noted that nearby Hyllestad is overlooked by a spectacularly precipitous mountain called Lihest—"slope-horse". From the east its outline can be thought to resemble the head and back of a horse. Did it in some way symbolise the horse cult? The present position of the church at Hyllestad may not be significant. An earlier heathen shrine may have been on a nearby pronounced peninsula jutting into the Åfjord. On this is the place-name Lien, which is reminiscent of the Kyrkjeli at Hestad and may represent earlier *hlíðin*—"the slope"—with reference to the hill there. The Lihest *(hlíð-hest?)*, and the neighbouring Lifjell, with Lifjord between them, may incorporate the same element. That a heathen shrine of some importance did exist hereabouts is suggested by the name Hyllestad, but it is proposed that the original "hylle" stood on the mentioned headland. A. Houken deals with an element *hillæ, hyllæ* in Danish place-names, and links it with modern *hylde*—"shelf" . . . . *I stednavne bruges det om tømmer bygning, gudehus af træ, specielt om et forhøjning, hvorpå gudebilledet er opstillet, og hvor gudsdyrkelsen øves*—"In place-names it would be used for a timber structure, a temple of wood, especially with regard to an eminence where a representation of the god was erected, or where the god was worshipped". . . . . Among place-names involving *hyllæ* one can mention Onsild and Vonsild (2), all from original *Oðins-hyllæ*. (Perhaps a *hylle* could in some places take the form of a scaffold which traditionally was supported by eight posts and on the top of which the heads of sacrificed horses could be displayed. In this case one might note that Odin rode an eight-legged horse called Sleipnir which may have been derived from a "Li-hest" on a "hylle".)

Also pertinent are the two names Harild, from *harg-hyllæ*. *Harg* itself bore the sense "place of sacrifice, temple", but an earlier meaning may have been "heap of stones". The Old Norse form was *hörgr*. The word is of great antiquity, with an Old English form being present in a few names in England, like Harrow-on-the-Hill. In Cumberland an Old Norse version seems to occur in Harras, from a theoretical *hargar-hreysi*, where it was deemed necessary to reinforce the sense of "stone heap" by the addition of *hreysi*. In Denmark Trelde is from *træ-hyllæ*, where the wooden nature of the structure has been emphasised. (This is comparable with Stokeld, Yorkshire (*stok-hylle?*). Further apparently relevant names are Horsens (3) *(hors-næs)* and Hesnæs *(hest-næs)*. Not all of these Danish names can be readily associated with headlands, although Trelde (near Fredericia) clearly refers to the pronounced peninsula called Trelde Næs. Apart from Hesnæs (Falster) and one Horsens (Vend Syssel), all of these names are concentrated in east Jutland between the Limfjord and Kolding Fjord. Hesnæs can be seen to refer to the pointed east end of Falster now called Hestehoved - "horse head". (Houken, 1955, pp97, 100, 255, 256) Not only does this give an insight into the situations at Hyllestad and Hestad, but also into Egil's setting up of a horse's head on a hazel pole upon a rocky point, (Ref, photos, 9-12 & 24, App. 5)

With a favourable and freshening wind they made good time back to Iceland, where Egil took over the running of the estate at Borg, for Skallagrim was now very old and indeed soon to die and be given a heathen burial under a howe on Borgarnes (Digranes), together with his horse and smith's tools.

The howe-laying of Skallagrim is interesting in that it describes a pagan burial involving a horse(!) and with grave goods, yet with the latter comprising mundane tools, rather than ornaments or weapons. However, they must have been considered as being among Skallagrim's most valued possessions (since he had hidden his treasure), with him having been a proud and skilful craftsman. At this point Egil would seem perforce to have abandoned his overseas ambitions and grown resigned to being a landed man on Iceland.

News of King Harald's death reached England. It was of course of great interest to his son Hakon, supposedly fostered with King Athelstan there. His foster father provided him with men and ships and he set out for Norway. Learning of the dire fates of his other brothers and that Erik was still in The Vik, he sailed north to Trondheim, where he was well received. He apparently bore a strong resemblance to his father Harald and this seems to have stood in his favour. In any case, promises he made to return allodial rights to their lands to those lately deprived of them must have swayed more than a few to support him. At the time he was still only fifteen.

> Harald's son Hakon may well have still been in England but could not have been at the court of King Athelstan; by the time he left (944) this English king had been dead for some years and his half brother Eadmund was reigning. It may be surmised that this was not a normal act of fostering, but that Hakon had been sent abroad for his own safety, in view of Harald's enfeeblement and Erik's attitude towards his brothers. It could well be that the English royal house saw something in this situation that could be turned to their advantage.

Hakon journeyed around, seemingly giving away much of what Harald had obtained and clung to, but nevertheless gaining thereby massive backing wherever he went. When the time for showdown eventually arrived, Erik paid the price for unpopularity and could only muster support in The Westland; and meagre at that. He had no other choice but to flee the country and it seems clear that most were glad to see him go.

> No sooner had Erik secured Norway, than his youngest half-brother Hakon, who had been "fostered with Athelstan" in England, arrived in the land in 944 the year after Egil had left for Iceland. He was able to exploit the immense unpopularity of Erik, so the latter had no choice but to leave the country in the same year and sailed to the Orkneys. (Pálsson p, 151: Holtsmark pp. 81-3)

Upon reaching the Orkneys, Erik made vassals of the sons of Earl Einar who were ruling there. Yet this was hardly a satisfactory position for a man who had of late been the king of all Norway and its dependencies; but he consoled himself for the time being by using the islands as a base for harrying in Scotland and northern England.

> Harald Hairfair had been able to hold his kingdom of Norway together by his ruthlessness, his reputation and, indeed, his ability; Erik was not able to maintain his position in face of unpopularity, presumably lacking some of his father's qualities, but perhaps suffering also from the reputation

of his wife Gunnhild. Hakon shrewdly bought popularity once back in Norway by the return of allodial rights. Erik sought refuge in the only part of his kingdom beyond Hakon's immediate reach - the earldom of the Orkneys - but as a king this was hardly a satisfactory outcome, and especially for his queen Gunnhild with her "Lady Macbeth" qualities. However, opportunity was beckoning further south, namely in England.

Through his prestige and prowess as a war-leader and Viking, Erik was soon able to dominate the seaboards of northern Britain. There are saga accounts of how he came to an agreement with the English king Athelstan, who had been victorious but badly mauled at Brunanburh. Erik was to hold "Northumberland" as a sub-king of Athelstan and protect it against "Danes and other Vikings", alternatively "Scots and Irish" (Holtsmark p. 83; Pálsson p. 151). The bulk of this kingdom was modern Yorkshire (the Deira of yore) and potential intruders were mainly the Irish-Norse (who were infesting the Irish Sea) and the Scots.

However, since Athelstan died in 939, Erik could not have left Norway in time to meet him, The king who appointed him must have been Eadmund (since we know that he was excluded by Eadred early in the latter's reign). Erik's career in the British Isles hence could have started by 944, but hardly before.

Meanwhile in Iceland, Skallagrim died sometime around 944 and Egil inherited Borg. But Egil spent two miserable winters there after the death of his father. He decided that in the next summer he would visit England, but because of delays it was autumn before he could set sail. (Pálsson p. 152)

Chapter 4

England before Erik

The Viking flood over Britain sprang from two main sources; while the folk involved were closely related in race and language, and to a lesser extent culture, their homelands were vastly different. The provenance of the earliest raiders, such as those who sacked Lindisfarne in 793, may be arguable, but the Vikings most active in England during the following 9th century were predominantly from Denmark. While one might presume that their enterprises attracted to their ranks Swedish and Norwegian adventurers, they were basically "Danes": for convenience these particular groupings will henceforth be referred to collectively as such.

However, Northmen (Norwegians) from the west side of the Scandinavian peninsula mainly reached western Britain by the "westerway" route, via Shetland, the Orkneys, the Hebrides, Man and Ireland. In the latter land they came to clash during the 9th century with Danes who had extended their activities to the west beyond England. Despite the fact that the Irish appear to have regarded the latter as the lesser of two evils, the Northmen gained the upper hand and it seems to have been in an attempt to cope with the situation that Halfdan, the "Danish" king of Northumbria, lost his life at Strangford Lough in 877. Apart from Ireland and Man, the Irish-Norse active around the Irish Sea eventually made their presence felt on the coasts of south-west Scotland and north-west England.

After many years of raiding, it was not until 865 that the first serious attempts at conquest were made by Danes in England. After over-wintering in East Anglia, an army attacked a politically disrupted Northumbria, seized York and harried further north. With Northumbria beaten, York was used as a base for expeditions against Mercia, which kingdom obtained temporary relief by buying off its tormentors. By 870 large parts of eastern England had been conquered, but the marauders did suffer a major setback when defeated at Ashdown by the forces of Wessex in 871. Yet the so-called "great heathen army" remained active and forced payment of "Danegeld". In 875 this force was weakened by division, with a large component heading north under Halfdan, who became acknowledged as king of Northumbria, while the remaining contingent under Guthrum made forays around Wessex until defeated by Alfred. The area later known as the "Danelaw" was then established in 886, with Watling Street as a major part of its southern border. Even so, further attempts were made to subdue Wessex, but without success, so the Viking elements among the Danes eventually turned their main attention towards the Franks, which resulted in 911 in the acquisition and ensuing settlement of Normandy.

Subsequent to the Danish defeats in England the Anglo-Saxon Chronicle for 896 commented that: "the Danish host broke up, some to East Anglia, some to Northumbria, and those who were without fee got themselves ships there and went south across the sea to the Seine". "Northumbria" here basically means the earlier Deira, i.e. the southern of the twin realms into which it was traditionally divided. This was confusingly (yet with geographical accuracy) referred to as "Northumberland" in sagas.

With the death of King Guthred in 894 the situation again became obscure. King Alfred himself died in 899, to be succeeded by his son Edward. Since the death of Guthred, Alfred had claimed the whole of England as his domain, but Edward was in no position to do the same. The Danes south of the Humber started to assert their independence again and indeed seem to have resurrected hopes of completing the conquest of England. But Edward was a resolute and resourceful ruler in Wessex, who was ably and loyally assisted by his sister Ethelfled and her husband Ethelred, the earl of English Mercia. By dint of successful military campaigns, followed up by the strategic building of forts, the resistance of the Danes was gradually worn down and the territory under their sole control reduced. Ethelred died in 912, but by the time Ethelfled followed him in 919, the Mercians and West Saxons were again in a position to threaten Northumbria at the Mersey, its south-west border. However, it was not just Anglo-Saxons who were by now giving the Danes a hard time. From the north and north-west they were coming under increasing pressure from Norwegian Vikings who had established strongholds all around the

Irish Sea, especially in Ireland and Man, and were poised to seize either southern Northumbria or northern Mercia, or both.

Because of a common dislike of the Anglo-Saxon dominance, these Northmen could find willing allies among the Celtic peoples of Britain, if not those of Ireland. For a while the other two parties put the Danes of eastern England in a squeeze, but when it came to a choice their preference appears ultimately to have been for the Anglo-Saxon kingdom, rather than the greater chaos spreading from the west.

North of the Tyne the residual country of Bernicia was becoming untenable as a kingdom, being threatened by the Scots to the north and the Norwegians to the west, as well as lately by the Scandinavians immediately to the south. For survival it was natural for them to look to the Anglo-Saxon king in the far south. Things were different for the Danes in their part of Northumbria, namely in Deira and based in York. While their compatriots failed to maintain their independence south of the Humber, because of Saxon and Norwegian pressure, between Humber and Tees they appear to have managed to blend with both Angles and Norwegians in the wake of Guthred in order to form a kingdom independent of the West Saxon dominated south. However, the retention of ethnic factions can be seen as a latent problem.

Norse control of Deira was initiated by the appearance on the scene of a certain Rögnvald. Leading his men from their lairs in western places like Ireland and on the Isle of Man, he burst into English history by doing battle against the Northumbrians at Corbridge, near the Tyne, and thus gaining control of the lands of St. Cuthbert. It was the temporary weakness in the south brought about by the death of Lady Ethelfled of the Mercians in 919 that then allowed him to seize York and establish himself as king there. He awarded lands annexed from St. Cuthbert, and generally lying southward from the river Wear, to two of his men. Onlafbal in particular was an oppressive heathen and was eliminated by the will of the saint in the doorway of the church at Chester-le-Street because of his depredations at the shrine there. The followers of Cuthbert thereby recovered the more northerly part of his seized holy lands.

The probable basis for Rögnvald's claim on York was that he was one of the kin of Ragnar and hence of the Halfdan who had been killed in Ireland in 877. The drive from there back into Yorkshire appears to have commenced in 902, when the Irish took Dublin and it is reported that Ingimund left Ireland to settle on the Wirral peninsula in Cheshire. However, the Northmen were not to be denied for long in Ireland, being back in force in 914. Ascendance was aimed at on both sides of the Irish Sea. Another of the kin, Sigtryg Gali, seized power by killing Niall. Moving to England he stormed Davenport (Cheshire) in 920.

Rögnvald did not last long in York, dying in 924. King Edward the Elder had meanwhile marched to the north-west to build a fort on the south bank of the Mersey at Thelwall and to restore the one at Manchester. From this renewed position of strength he called a meeting with all the Northumbrians, the Scots and the Strathclyde Britons. As a result of the treaty they would all recognise him as their master, but at the same time their rights to rule were confirmed. Thus did Rögnvald secure for himself the kingship in York. Upon his death the problems of the English succession enabled his brother Sigtryg Gali to succeed him without great difficulty. He had already seized Dublin before crossing the sea to sack Davenport, as mentioned above.

The Anglo-Saxon Chronicles attribute the taking of York by Rögnvald and the rebuilding of Manchester fort to the year 923. While Rögnvald had been more successful, his brother Sigtryg also wanted a realm and had set his eyes on Mercia. Both brothers had been bent on making inroads from the north-west coasts of England, the one from the Dee and Mersey estuaries (the Wirral) and the other probably from the Eden estuary (Solway Firth, from where the Tyne valley was best accessible). Edward had apparently forestalled the threat to Cheshire and the wider Mercia by building forts at Nottingham and Bakewell (Derbyshire) and then established the forts on the Mersey so that this could live up to its name as "border river" between Mercia and Northumbria. Direct links between the Norse settled around Chester and on the Wirral with York were thereby severed. The situation was eventually resolved after the deaths of Edward and Rögnvald in 924. The latter was quickly succeeded by Sigtryg. It seems unlikely that either of these Norse brothers was welcomed by everyone in Northumbria, but as long as Sigtryg would abide by the agreement on overlordship with Edward any succeeding English king might feel obliged to give him his grudging support.

The west coast of Northumbria had been nominally under Rögnvald's control. However the coast-lands of the future Lancashire show all the signs of being infested by Irish-Norse Vikings and one might suspect that Sigtryg, his southern ambitions frustrated and before his brother died, became prominent among these. Initially the important access points for him were the Ribble estuary and Morecambe Bay. There are indications that Athelstan closed these areas to Irish-Norse intruders by seizing Amounderness and Sigtryg's sons were forced into maintaining their coastal activities in areas further north.

When King Edward the Elder died in 924, he was eventually succeeded by his son Athelstan in 925, who promptly gave his sister in marriage to Sigtryg Gali. However, the benefits of this arrangement did not last long because the latter died in the next year. His son Gudhfridh attempted to succeed him, but Athelstan drove him out of York. His brother Olaf was also expelled and sailed to Ireland. Their uncle, another Gudhfridh, found sanctuary with King Constantine of the Scots. The English king was clearly laying his claim to Northumbria by exploiting the additional significance of his sister's predictably childless marriage to Sigtryg. At this point in time Athelstan decided to renew the arrangement established by his father Edward, so called together the rulers of the various other parts of Britain. The place chosen for the meeting was by the River Eamont (namely at Dacre). A notable absentee was any king (or earl) from York. He will have called for the assembly on the banks of the Eamont, a tributary of the Eden in Cumbria, because this was then claimed to be the limit of his own direct rule.

The passage in William of Malmesbury that covers this relationship after the expulsion of a Gudhfridh by Athelstan in 926 is somewhat ambiguous: "Analaf the son of Sihtric then fled to Ireland, and his brother Godefrid to Scotland"; the "his" must relate to "Analaf". In reality both brothers will have fled to Ireland, causing historical confusion in that it was Olaf's uncle Gudhfridh who took refuge in Scotland at some time. However, Simeon states that Sigtryg had a son called Gudhfridh, who was driven out by Athelstan in 926. While uncle Gudhfridh went north, the brothers found refuge in the west. The Rögnvald Gudhfridhsson driven out with Olaf Sigtrygsson in 944 by Eadmund would be Olaf Gudhfridhsson's brother and named after another uncle, {"Egla" (51-3) pp,117-24; William of Malmesbury p117; Simeon pp,88-9}

The situation was made more difficult by the multiplicity of Olafs, Guthfriths and Reynolds abroad in the British Isles in the 920s, 930s and 940s. In the analysis below screening techniques are used to separate the desirable from the dross in both the English and Nordic sources, with the intention of clearing up the identities of the York kings and illustrating that the sagas are rather more reliable than allowed for by much academic opinion. The events in question are covered by the reigns of three members of the dominant West Saxon ruling house in England, namely Athelstan and his two half-brothers, Eadmund and Eadred, covering the years 924-55.

Once Athelstan had settled his sister in marriage to Sigtryg Gali he probably always had the intention of using this eventually as a reason to annexe Northumbria to the southern realm. But Gudhfridh, the brother of Rögnvald and Sigtryg, also had a poignant name, redolent of the Godfred of Danevirke fame and "good" King Guthred of Northumbria. But the Gudhfridh mentioned together with Olaf Sigtrygsson, and who attempted to succeed Sigtryg, was Olaf's ill-fated brother. Sigtryg was related to Rögnvald and Ragnar, yet may appear to have a name with no relevant English precedent. Yet the mentioned East Anglian king Rægenhere had a brother called Sigbert. Names with this first element later came into use in the East Saxon royal house, namely Sigbert, Sighere, Sighard and Sigbald. But the most appropriate use of "Sig-"in the English royal strains is in the legendary past of the Deirans, with Sigegar and Sigegeat, and this must have had significance with regard to a kingdom based on York. The first element of Olaf is more accurately rendered by the English form Anlaf. Apart from the vowel alliteration particularly preferred by the Anglian royal houses (to go with their supposed origins in Angel), this specifically fits certain precedents, such as Eni and Anna of the East Angles and Eanfridh of Deira. Olaf itself is hardly an original Scandinavian form, but can be argued as having developed in Ireland, apparently from a Norse original. The Irish form Am(h)laibh has given rise to surnames like Macauley and McAuliffe. Gudhfridh has given rise to Irish surnames like MacCaffery, as well as English Godfrey (and presumably Welsh Gruffudd).

The English records are reticent about any kings or earls that Athelstan had installed in Northumbria after he drove out Gudhfridh and Rögnvald. However, he must eventually have found it necessary to delegate governance and defence of the two halves of this realm to leaders whose status would be at the level of an earl.

Eventually Constantine broke the allegiance he had rendered to Athelstan. This resulted in the English king marching north in 934 and harrying Scotland by land and sea. He thereby forced the King of the Scots to hand over his own son as a hostage.

Olaf Sigtrygsson (or Cuaran) would appear to have become less prominent at the time of these events and his name ostensibly does not feature later in the various actions around the great battle at Brunanburh (otherwise Vinheidh), which were dominated by Olaf Gudhfridhsson, son in law to Constantine, King of Scots. Yet it might appear that Athelstan had found it expedient to reinstate him and his brother Gudhfridh when he decided on that invasion of Scotland in 934.

At some time Athelstan is said to have received the gift of a magnificent ship from King Harald of Norway. In similar vein he was also visited by a boatload of men from Norway. Under their leader Hauk Håbrok they entered the court in close file with concealed swords, as though expecting trouble. With them was a young lad who Hauk proceeded to place on the king's knee, explaining as he did so that his master, King Harald of Norway, wanted to know if he would take a serving wench's child as a fosterling for him. Athelstan was furious and drew his sword as if to kill the boy; but Hauk pointed out that he had already taken him on his knee and, even if he did kill him, he could not eradicate all of Harald's sons by the act. With that Hauk and his men withdrew. The affair is said to have been in retaliation for an earlier incident when Athelstan sent an ambassador to Harald, who was tricked by him into accepting as a gift a sword presented in such a way that it indicated Athelstan's superior standing. A king accepting a child in foster would be very unusual, for it was the custom to foster children out to families of inferior status. Be that as it may, the English king is believed to have accepted the lad, who became known in Norse tradition as "Athelstan's Fosterling". Eventually, when he was about 15, Hakon learned of his father Harald's death. He returned to Norway to drive out Erik and claim the crown.

Athelstan's supposed refusal to accept Harald as an equal appears to have led to a deterioration in the relations between the two men. Harald himself had been fostered with Earl Hroald, while his son Erik was fostered with Hroald's son Thori, who himself had been fostered by Kveldulf. The above paragraph reeks of unlikelihood and alternative implications of the gifts and the fostering are discussed below.

Harald Hairfair had been taunted by a princess called Gydha in that she would not accept him until he had a realm of the same size as those of King Eirik in Sweden and king Gorm in Denmark. It was by her that he eventually begat the sons Sigtryg, Frodhi and Thorgils. During his struggles to fulfil his ambitions he spent a long time in Trondheim. Once while there he learned that King Eirik of Sweden had laid claim to some of his lands in the south. The latter had let it be known that he would not spare himself until he had just as big a realm round "The Vik" as had earlier been held by Sigurdh Hring and his son Ragnar Lodhbrok.

The last named is either confused with or is identical to the leader who harried in France and England, eventually to meet his death in a snake pit in York by order of Ella. His vengeful sons, Ivar, Ubbi and Halfdan, defeated and captured Ella. They dispatched him by means of the brutal blood-eagle treatment and the last of them eventually became king of Northumbria. Whether this Ragnar is identifiable as the Ragnar (Lodhbrok) cannot be completely discarded satisfactorily, but the name is identical to Old English *Rægenhere,* seventh century king of the East Angles and once thought to be commemorated by the ship burial at Sutton Hoo (although later opinion has veered towards it being his father, King Rædwald, who is buried therein). The same reasoning would help in the pursuance of the claims of anyone with a version of "Ragn" beginning his name, as with Rögnvald, in Old English rendered *Rægenwald* (later Reynold). This name also reflects the second element of that of the great Northumbrian king Oswald (as well as the great East Anglian Rædwald). It is to be noted that the earlier Anglo-Saxon kings used names that were unique, at least to Britain, but Scandinavians often repeated names in their royal houses, as long as at least one generation or other relationship intervened. After the Scandinavian intervention it became prevalent among the English to repeat names from the past and distinguish them by means of by-names in the Scandinavian manner, e.g. Ethelred "the Unready" and Alfred "the Great". Alliteration was also commonly used among the English royal kins, while originally they had kept the custom of having favourite elements from which to construct different or even unique names within the royal strain. On the other hand it would seem that the kin of Ragnar were using elements in their names that had earlier been favoured by the royal houses of the Angles.

The problems arising from references to Egil, Erik and the English succession in the period 937-54 result from certain key points needing to be resolved. When exactly did Athelstan die? How reliable is the relevant Nordic material and why does it claim that Erik was killed during Eadmund's reign? How do the tales in contemporary Iceland and Scandinavia fit into the English chronology? Who were the various Reynolds, Olafs (Anlafs) and Gudhfridhs who were involved with York? How many times did Erik reign in Northumbria? What drove the characters to behave as they did?

Looking to the English side of these matters, both English and Nordic sources claim that Athelstan reigned for fourteen and a bit years, although in "Simeon" he died in the sixteenth year, This source agrees with the "D" and "E" Chronicles that his death was in 940. (Garmonsway pp. 110-1; Holtsmark p, 84; Stephenson p. 89). This particular discrepancy may be due to confusion between when his father Edward died (924) and when he was crowned (925) after a struggle for the succession. (Wood p. 130-31). Chronicles "A" and "D" add the information that the death was almost exactly 40 years after that of King Alfred, recorded inaccurately earlier as October 901. Most Chronicles and Simeon agree that Eadred died in 955, with the "A" adding that it was in November after a reign of 9½ years. (See Appendix 2, Table 9)

As briefly mentioned above the apparent deterioration in the relationship between the kings Athelstan and Harald is indicated by three events. At the start of Athelstan's reign and while at York (926) he received from representatives of Harald the gift of a magnificent ship. The gift was delivered by Helgrim and Osfrid. (Stephenson p.118) If true, this was clearly a loaded gesture of friendship by the Norwegian king; he must have expected something in return. One can provisionally perceive that Harald was indicating that he considered himself to be a ruler to be reckoned with, since he could afford to present a gift of such splendour. There was also a suggestion of an intended carve-up into two spheres of influence. In particular the Vikings active around the Irish Sea were irritants to both sovereigns, but Harald did not want Athelstan to use this as an excuse to expand westwards; they were after all basically ethnic Norwegians. However, since these Northmen were continually trying to gain control of the realm based on York, action against them by the English king was inevitable, at least on the British mainland. Since this is an English source (William of Malmesbury) it may be less distorted, but suspicions are aroused. The ship as described is hardly a warship, but rather a royal galley, with its "golden beak and a purple sail, furnished within all round with a close-set row of gilded shields". Why were the shields already in position, in the Viking manner?

The other question is to how Harald knew that Athelstan would be in York. This would be after the English king had driven Gudhfridh and Olaf Sigtrygsson out of the city and, according to Malmesbury, slighted the defences. (Stephenson p. 117) Presumably Harald had learned of Athelstan's efforts to get control of York and expected that he would be there. This would then be the start of any direct link between York and the Norwegian royal kin. However, the suspicion arises that the recipient of this ship was someone else. This other person may also be inferable when Snorre recalls that Athelstan tried to humiliate Harald when he sent an ambassador to him who presented a fine sword, but in such a way that it indicated Harald's inferiority. (Holtsmark p77)

However magnificent with its gold and silver decoration and inlaid jewels, this sword was not on the same scale as a ship. Athelstan's message to Harald appears to have been that, though a king, he was not of the same class as himself. As such he would be advised to stay out of areas of influence that were considered to be those of the English royal house, especially the Irish Sea where the Irish Norse were active. The fact is that Harald was indeed soon to be virtually squeezed out of the British Isles, except for the Earldom of Orkney. This would be c932, by which time Athelstan was very powerful and had been in control of Northumbria for some years. Yet, he was about to find it necessary to act against the Scots.

The sword may have been used as a sign of the cross, the implication being that one could not be a proper king without being a Christian. On the other hand one might suspect that the sword was not a gift handed personally to Harald at all, but rather presented to someone else who must acknowledge Athelstan as his lord and agree to be converted if he wished to enter the king's service.

The third incident took place a year after the gift of the sword and was the fostering of Hakon Haraldsson on Athelstan. As described by Snorre the lad was dumped on Athelstan in London by Harald's men, led by Hauk Habrok, who made off immediately. (Holtsmark pp. 77-9)

If the King of Norway were indeed involved, the message could have been that if he accepted, this king was to consider himself insulted, for Hakon had been born of a low-bred woman and he who fostered another's son would in any case normally be considered of lesser status. Why then did Athelstan accept him, rather than sending him away? Perhaps it is true that as claimed by some, he too had been begotten out of wedlock by his father Edward and this, rather than being a demeaning circumstance, perhaps provided a parallel that induced a certain empathy. In the event he seems not only to have brought him up as a Christian foster son and anglophile, but also as a warrior, for the saga informs us that he gave him a sword called Kvernbit, said to be the best sword ever taken to Norway. It would seem that Athelstan got his revenge by the grooming of Hakon by himself and Eadmund to succeed to the Norwegian throne and forcibly convert all those heathens over there. This is indeed what happened, whether or not one believes in the direct involvement of Athelstan rather than some intermediary. Hakon drove Erik out of Norway but took no interest in the latter's subsequent activities in the British Isles. Erik had to seek his fortune in Britain, because there was no way he could return to Norway while Hakon remained popular there.

However, in view of the confusion of names in the sagas it is suggested that Hakon was not fostered directly on Athelstan in 933, but on Arinbjörn, who Harald knew had left Norway to take up service in York on behalf of Athelstan. The location for the presentation of the sword as "London" has to be suspect. Before Hakon left England and sometime before 938

Thori died. This was after the Battle of Vinheidh and Arinbjörn must then return to Norway to inherit The Firths.

Hakon's return to Norway can be dated to 944 when he was fifteen years old. This would put his birth to 929. His delivering to "Athelstan" (i.e. Arinbjörn) must have occurred while he was quite young, for he was lifted onto the recipient's knee. Assuming him to be a four-year-old would place this incident in 933.

The Chronicles report that Athelstan attacked Scotland by land and sea in 934 (or 933), the naval expedition reaching as far as Caithness.

That the action did not extend as far as the Orkneys may indicate that Athelstan was acknowledging that the earldom based on them was subject to the King of Norway. Caithness was that part of the earldom on the adjacent mainland of Britain and this action was clearly meant to be a warning to that Norse entity. It would seem to have been a pointless exercise with regard to the Scots, at whom the hostilities were mainly aimed. Gudhfridh had taken refuge among them, but died in 934. It would seem clear that to forestall the stirring up of the Scots by him and his son Olaf was the prime reason for Athelstan's move.

Yet something else sparked Athelstan into making a naval expedition unusually far north. The Orkneys were too far north for him to subdue permanently, but he wanted to ensure that they would not be used on Harald's behalf as a base to attack England. In reality the aging Harald's authority on the distant isles was becoming increasingly difficult to wield, and Harald's position was one of weakness when confronted by a king who was intent on demonstrating that he was far from being his inferior when it came to affairs around Britain.

Yet a showdown was coming. Gudhfridh's son Olaf was married to the daughter of Constantine and between them they planned a concerted attack on Athelstan's realm, starting with Yorkshire. Constantine was to lead his Scots, while Olaf would recruit a following in Ireland: as an ally they had King Owen of the Strathclyde Britons. The resulting battle in 937 was called Brunanburh in an English poem and the result was a significant victory for Athelstan and his young half-brother Eadmund. Among his troops there was a contingent of Northmen in which the Icelandic brothers Thorolf and Egil Skallagrimsson played leading roles. It was on this field that Thorolf met his bane and the conflict was recorded in Icelandic tradition as Vinheidh. Egil received particular compensation from "Athelstan", in the form of chests of treasure, which he was supposed to pass on to their father Skallagrim. Afterwards Egil prepared a longship and sailed from England, parting in great friendship from Athelstan; but many of his men chose to stay behind in the service of the English ruler.

> Much of the above paragraph must be held as suspect; it can be regarded as part of the myth that was created about Athelstan's high opinion of Egil and his appointment as a royal commander, as well as the influence and prominence he had at the English court after the battle. It is at this point and for this reason that the Icelandic accounts of Egil's career started to conflict with the English chronicles. Apart from the intention of elevating Egil's heroic status, a confusion of personal names caused chaos, both with regard to the identification of persons and the chronology.

With the death Athelstan in 939 and Harald c943 the situation changed. Any notion of a Norwegian empire stretching round the north and west of Scotland and including lands bordering the Irish Sea was soon to evaporate. While Erik Bloodaxe might still think of himself as the rightful king of Norway, as a result of Hakon's ascendancy there he had to content himself with hopes of the creation of a kingdom in Britain. Its initial power base would be the Earldom of the Orkneys, with the eventual prize being York. However, there were other Norse contenders.

> One hindrance to the formation of such a Norse empire was that it was never going to include Ireland on a lasting basis. The problem was that the Scandinavian presence there was one of trading stations and unruly Viking bases, rather than widespread settlement. The idea of a realm based mainly on the power of the ship was as yet before its time. While Cnut the Great later managed to create a Danish North Sea empire, it barely outlasted his lifetime. Even the Normans could not retain for ever their Continental lands once England became the seat of their power.

The stage had not yet been reached for the kinds of ship-linked empires that were eventually created by western states and survived until modern times.

What had been the aims of the coalition against Athelstan in 937? One can again perceive the prospects of a carve-up. The Scots were to get the Bamburgh earldom of the Anglian north-east. The Strathclyde Welsh were to regain control over lands in the north-west, at least as far as Cumberland. Olaf Gudhfridhison would get the realm based on York and with possibilities for extending this southwards. The results of failure were that the Bamburgh earldom survived and Strathclyde soon collapsed and thereby became vulnerable to takeover by the Scots, although they would find themselves in dispute with certain Vikings over the more southerly parts. As for Olaf Gudhfridhsson, he was now a spent figure reduced to making petty Viking forays from his refuge among the Scots.

With his ambitions in Norway being thwarted, it seems inevitable that Erik would eventually take advantage of the political chaos that was taking place around that commercially rich prize that was York and the substantial northern English realm that naturally went with it. While he at least temporarily succeeded in attempts to rule in York, the threat from Norway had receded. Right from the time of the death of Sigtryg Gali and Athelstan's ejection of Gudhfridh and Olaf in 926, the threat had been apparent to the English king: any successful back door seizure of the realm centred on York by Norwegians might lead to action by the Norwegian king, who could continue to claim that he was their overlord.

The main ruling family of the Irish-Norse soon split. After one faction threw in its lot with the Scots, the other sought a future as allies of the English monarchy, although the best they could then achieve was as sub-kings to this. Athelstan's death in 939 led to the arrival in England of an Olaf from Ireland. He is conventionally identified as Olaf Gudhfridhsson, the prominent defeated opponent of Athelstan at Brunanburh and who wished to renew his ambitions in England. Another Olaf, son of former king of York called Sigtryg, has come to be regarded as a weaker character. While both of them were available for this opportunity that arose, one should consider the likelihood that Gudhfridhsson was a much weakened man after the battle.

The question arises as to any grounds for Olaf Gudhfridhsson to have a claim on the Northumbrian kingdom. He appears in history as a Viking sea lord who had sufficient influence in Ireland to be able to raise an army there in order to provide a major component of the force that faced Athelstan. The first apparent record of this Olaf's activity in Ireland is in 919. (Beaven p.6 n.19} This would probably relate to him exploiting a power vacuum in Ireland due to Rögnvald and Sigtryg being distracted by involvement in Northumbrian affairs at that time. That Olaf Gudhfridhsson was not in Ireland c940 is shown in that his brother, Blackare arrived in Dublin as the temporary Norse leader about this time. The latter died there in 948, apparently having returned to rule there in that year after Olaf Sigtrygsson again left to return to Britain.

However, is it even possible that the Olaf who seized power in Northumbria on the death of Athelstan could be Gudhfridhsson? Well, after Brunanburh (Vinheidh) it would seem that he gave up his serious southern aspirations and settled permanently among those other losers, his former allies the Scots. Constantine, King of Scots, was said to be his father in law and they were comrades in adversity at the time. (Simeon p.89). From there he sought to raid Northumbria from the north. It would seem that he intended to replenish his depleted resources by using the methods of the earlier Vikings in Britain: pick a soft target—rob a monastery. He died after sacking Tyningham in Lothian. This limited operation against the Anglian earldom based on Bamburgh was surely launched from Scotland, rather than York. He is then the largely spent "Anlaf" whose death is pithily recorded in the Anglo-Saxon "E" Chronicle in 940. This agrees with Irish records of the death of Olaf Gudhfridhsson c941. (Beaven p.5)

There was probably another factor that made it impossible for encroachment to be made on Northumbria from out of Scotland on the west side in the years after Brunanburh: namely hostile Vikings. This would not be due to the presence of Erik Bloodaxe, who did not reach the Orkneys until 941 at the earliest (from where he proceeded to dominate the coast-lands and islands further south). It would be Olaf Cuaran (Sigtrygsson) who at that time was using the Solway and its Vikings as a base and eventually as a stepping stone back to York.

Furthermore, it is apparent that Olaf Gudhfridhsson could not re-establish any adequate power-base in Ireland. So there really seems no way that he could have seized the crown at York and then have launched a raid on Mercia, even with help from the Scots. There is certainly no record of these being involved in such operations early in Eadmund's reign. Even if this Olaf did make his way to Ireland immediately after Brunanburh, it is unlikely that such a failed Olaf was the same one as came to York. It has been claimed that the Olaf who was ravaging Irish churches in 938 was Gudhfridhsson. In this respect an annal of 937 recording him as leaving Dublin needs to be emended to 939. This adjustment leaves too little logistical time for any significant armed response to Athelstan's death in the October of that year. It seems more likely that after some attempt to recover his position by looting in Ireland he found refuge with his wife's father, the king of the Scots. The Olaf who started to threaten the lands south of Northumbria in this period has to be Sigtrygsson, whose power was intact.

There is no indication that Olaf Sigtrygsson fought against Athelstan at Brunanburh, so the onus of enmity towards the English would not hang over him, at least as long as that king lived. But he is likely to be the one who, after this event, strove against or allied himself with subsequent English kings for a decade, as well as becoming the rival of Erik Bloodaxe. His claim to Northumbria would rest mainly on the precedent of his father having been accepted as king in York by Athelstan. Indeed, one might take note that before hostilities at Vinheidh it is reported in "Egla" that Athelstan put two "earls" in charge of Northumbria, whose names were Godrek and Alfgeir. The former was killed in a preliminary encounter with Olaf (who the saga recognises as "the Red", rather than "Gudhfridhsson") and is very disparaging about the prowess of the latter of the two earls. One can recognise these as Gudhfridh and Olaf, the sons of Sigtryg Gali. The former represents the Old English version "Godred"; this slain Gudhfridh was not the father of the other Olaf, for he had died in 934. He was rather that brother of Olaf Sigtrygsson who had been driven out of Northumbria by Athelstan in 926. He had an Irish by-name "Cuaran".

While one can recognise that Gudhfridh could have been garbled as "Godrek" in Egla, Olaf Cuaran has been absolutely mangled to appear as "Alfgeir". Egla states that he fled after a skirmish before Vinheidh and reached "Valland" One presumes that this is a Norse representation of Old English *Wealaland* and refers to the Welsh or *Cymry* in some sense, presumably Wales proper, since Strathclyde was part of the opposing coalition.

This identification of Godrek and Alfgeir seems historically reasonable and would suggest that Athelstan had had an unrecorded change of heart about Gudhfridh Sigtrygsson before 937 and had reinstated both him and his brother Olaf to get them on side; but probably only if they acknowledged being his liegemen. According to Egla they fought in preliminary engagements against Olaf Gudhfridhsson, with Gudhfridh (Godrek) being killed and Olaf Cuaran (Alfgeir) retiring in defeat, both at this early stage. The battle against Olaf that they lost may have been at Bromborough, on the Wirral peninsula Cheshire (and perhaps did involve Olaf the Red—*Rauðì*). This was one origin of the battle-name Brunanburh that came to be confused with the subsequent decisive encounter. At any rate it has been claimed that after the defeat at Vinheidh the Irish-Norse army took to their ships from the Wirral and sailed over Dingesmere. (Cavill *et al* pp. 25-38) This name apparently recognises a thingstead on the Wirral and perhaps is the origin of the unlikely marking out of the agreed battlefield with hazel wands and ropes. This could then have been transferred to the later battle of Vinheidh because of the presence of the name Hazelwood right alongside the site of this.

The apparent impulsive behaviour of Godrek and Alfgeir implies that they were anxious to set back the cause of Olaf Gudhfridhsson before Athelstan arrived with his main force: this would have increased their bargaining power with the Saxon king. Not surprisingly this inglorious circumstance has been completely omitted from the English records, especially as it was apparently a purely Irish-Norse affair.

After Thorolf's death in battle at Vinheidh, Egil is said to have put on a huge show of sulking and suppressed anger in the presence of "Athelstan" until he relented and presented a goodly treasure to compensate his kin. The Icelander had held his sword across his lap and kept partially drawing it, This threat gesture would be understood, although it seems highly unlikely that Egil could have successfully committed any violence at the makeshift English court not too far south of Vinheidh and full of victorious warriors. Egil knew his rights and was determined to get them, but could he really behave so truculently towards the triumphant English king?

The site of this battle gives cause for confusion and has long been disputed. It is generally considered to be the same place as the major engagement known as the Battle of Brunanburh that, according to English sources, took place in 937. Your author gives reasons below and elsewhere for Vinheidh (identified as Brunanburh) having occurred on Bramham Moor, Yorkshire. (Pearson pp. 24-39) Others have deemed that Brunanburh is actually Bromborough on the Wirral, Cheshire. The place-name certainly fits, but if the claim were true the proposition would have to be accepted that the names Brunanburh and Vinheidh did not originally refer to the same battle. As already suggested above Bromborough can perhaps be identified as the site of the separate earlier battle between Olaf and the "wardens"of Northumbria in which "Godrek" was killed and from which "Alfgeir" fled. That the two names are so garbled indicates strongly that they were hearsay and hence that Thorolf and Egil were not at the earlier engagement. (For further coverage see Chapter 5)

The circumstances can be provisionally interpreted in the following way. Arinbjörn had also found it necessary to leave Norway: he had indeed already stated that if Egil were forced to leave he would go too. Athelstan got on fairly well with Scandinavians and his court was full of men with Scandinavian names. In the years leading up to 937 he was facing increasing opposition within Britain and useful mercenaries would be welcome to him. It may have helped that Arinbjörn was a North Sea Viking, not a "Westerway" one. As a member of a land-holding family close to the Norwegian royal kin he may have been just the kind of Scandinavian leader that Athelstan was looking for to defend York against the pressure coming from the Irish-Norse kin of Ragnar. It can thus be proposed that while in this capacity he somehow contacted Thorolf and Egil so that they could join him in Athelstan's service. All three could happily apply, for they had never harried in the British Isles and, as far as one knows, neither had their kinsmen. However, it would seem that they remained nothing more than mercenaries and that any power in York came to be wielded on Athelstan's behalf by the Sigtrygsson brothers, Gudhfridh and Olaf (i.e. Godrek and Alfgeir) until their debacle before Vinheidh.

From this point on one can suspect strongly that every time Egil and "Athelstan" are mentioned together in Egla it is Arinbjörn who is meant. Those gold rings and chests that Egil acquired may ultimately have come from Athelstan, but they had surely done so by way of Arinbjörn. This then allows one to believe the saga when it says that Egil was put in charge of a detachment. This may have constituted half an army, but it was Arinbjörn's not the king's. This glorification of Egil's contribution was achieved by a simple swap of names. The same trick was applied to later events, but unfortunately gives the game away in that by this time Athelstan was long dead. It seems doubtful that Athelstan could have appreciated any panegyric poems composed by Egil at court, since they were in Old Norse. One must suspect that they were produced later to "prove" the close links between the two men that were in fact spurious.

From the above one can deduce that the presentation of the sword was not a gift to Harald, but indicates a swearing in ceremony whereby Arinbjörn swore allegiance to Athelstan and accepted conversion. This would be the point where the two names became confused. One can then further deduce that it was in the next year that Hauk dumped Harald's son on him as a fosterling. It may be pertinent to add in this case that Harald's son Erik was Arinbjörn's foster brother. It seems likely that it was Arinbjörn who gave the sword Kvernbit to Hakon. Arinbjörn eventually must return to Norway upon the death of his father Thori, but since Hakon had been sent to England to protect him from Erik he may then have found refuge at the English court and started the rumour that he was Athelstan's fosterling. One can well understand that Arinbjörn would object to Hakon being forced upon him by Hauk in view of his own relationship with Erik. The use of the term "foster" is odd, seeing that Arinbjörn is never recorded as having a wife, but the reasoning seems to be good in that Erik could hardly touch Hakon if he was under the protection of his own foster brother. However, Arinbjörn seems to have retained some resentment towards Hakon and this may have influenced the later relationships between the two.

On Athelstan's death in 939 the already war-weakened Wessex became even more vulnerable. In particular its hold over Danish Mercia looked like being loosened. His successor Eadmund had to annexe it again in 942. Shortly before this the Northumbrians had chosen "Olaf" as their king, despite having made certain pledges.

The upstart had to be Olaf Sigtrygsson. While it is clear that in the time bracket 940-2 Eadmund had to reassert his authority over Danish Mercia after encroachment by Olaf, there is some confusion in the records as to exactly which folk entity it was necessary to take action against. The relevant poem would have us believe that: "Long had the Danes under the Norsemen been subjected by force to heathen bondage until finally liberated by Edward's son". If this referred to some recent invasion the involvement of a "king" hardly applies. There had not been any opportunity for any long term Norwegian domination of the Mercian Danes during the reigns of Edward and Athelstan; before that they had been the dominant force themselves. The reference can be narrowed down to the threat to Danish Mercia from out of the Wirral, namely by Sigtryg Gali. The truth may be that his son Olaf in York had later been making similar noises after Athelstan's demise suggesting aggrandizement ambitions towards the southern Danelaw. Eadmund may not have been fully prepared for military action, but initially found it necessary to move in to confront this situation and to forestall further encroachment. He eventually had to cope with a full invasion out of Northumbria led by Olaf Sigtrygsson.

In order to consolidate his position Eadmund initially established his frontier against Northumbria on a line through Dore *(Dor)* and Whitwell Gap *(Hwitanwylles geat)*. The former place is near Sheffield to its south-west and the latter represents the long north-south ridge forming the watershed between the River Rother and the lower Trent tributaries. (The Dore-Whitwell line is still virtually the modern boundary between Derbyshire and Yorkshire.) Olaf responded to Eadmund's move with an invasion of Mercia and, after failing to take Northampton, seized Tamworth, just north of the Alfredian Anglo-Danish border of Watling Street. He was later caught by Eadmund at Leicester, who besieged him there. After he managed to escape from this it is recorded that Eadmund subsequently became his "friend". (Garmonsway p.111)

Olaf Sigtrygsson had gained a tentative hold on much of the southern Danelaw, including the five boroughs of the Midlands, namely Lincoln, Derby Nottingham, Leicester and Stamford. As a result of the breaking of the siege at Leicester he made a treaty with the English king that left him in control of these north-eastern Midlands territories. The arrangement did not last long. In the meantime his cousin Olaf Gudhfridhsson died while campaigning near the Firth of Forth. Despite the loss of the Midlands, Olaf Sigtrygsson remained. ruler of Northumbria from 941.

The circumstances of these engagements and the establishment of the nationality of the York kings as "Northmen", i.e. Norwegians, has been examined elsewhere. (Mawer pp.551-7; Beaven pp.6-7) Unlike Yorkshire, the Danelaw south of the Humber did not have a significant Norwegian component in its population. However, the suggestion that the subjection of the north-eastern part of the Southumbrian Danelaw (including the "five boroughs") by the kings of York was unwelcome to and feared by the Danish settlers there may simply be a West Saxon view. Mawer argues that the *lange thrage*—"long time"—of their supposed domination is an idiom that cannot be taken literally.

This Olaf at Tamworth and Leicester can only be Sigtrygsson (Cuaran) waging war as king of the Northumbrians against the northern part of Eadmund's realm. Indication of his support in Northumbria can be recognised by Archbishop Wulfstan being with him at Leicester, although he is not chronicled as being baptized until later, when he was sponsored by Eadmund. (He may have gained previous acceptability to consort with Christians by being prime signed.) Rögnvald Gudhfridhsson was also sponsored by Eadmund at baptism.

> While this Rögnvald was a cousin of Olaf Sigtrygsson, one should not be too surprised that the pair were soon vying with each other for power. Yet it is surprising that any brother of Olaf Gudhfridhsson could expect to gain much support in Northumbria—never mind in the wider England—for any power bid; it is nevertheless considered that the Northumbrians on the whole did prefer him.

Despite the conversions and expressions of "friendship", Eadmund soon settled things, at least for the time being. He marched north in 944 to drive both of them out of York and claim Northumbria for the Anglo-Saxon crown. In 945 he seized "Cumberland", but gave it to King Malcolm of the Scots "on condition that he be his ally both at sea and on land". Why did he yield up this land so recently won by force and with such an odd proviso?

After the battle of Brunanburh/Vinheidh (937) Strathclyde had slipped into a terminal weakness and fallen severely under the influence of the kingdom of the Scots to the north, who as a result had virtually absorbed its northern parts; the southern parts, including the eventual Cumberland, were presumably still beyond their grasp, with the Vikings infesting the Solway Firth being among those wanting to keep them at bay. It also seems possible that the Cumbrians (who themselves were part of the Strathclyde Welsh) hoped to revive their fortunes by joining forces with these Vikings. Eadmund showed his willingness to give up these lands north of the River Eamont to the Scots as long as their king, Malcolm, was able and willing to control that province newly subdued by troops fighting for the English. The "at sea" phrase in the agreement suggests that the Solway Vikings were the hostile seafarers in mind. One can infer that the deal included the recognition by the Scots of the English king's absolute right to the lands up to the south bank of the Eamont, i.e. Westmorland, whether or not a sub-king of Northumbria was involved.

Although not stated, the agreement probably also included Malcolm promising to cease making forays into Northumbria on the east side. Any such part of the pact died with Eadmund (946) for Malcolm even reached as far as the Tees in a raid in 949. (Campbell p.92, n.3) Eadmund's reign had been brought to a premature end when he was stabbed to death while trying to save his cup-bearer from being murdered by a well-known villain called Liofa. He was succeeded by his brother Eadred.

The quarrelling between the factions of Olaf Sigtrygsson and Rögnvald Gudhfridhsson was curtailed by Eadmund's assertion of himself as the direct ruler of Northumbria. One might well assume that the reason for his action was an inevitable act of policy; the two were probably being too disruptive and assertive anyhow, perhaps even challenging and insisting upon complete independence. After being ousted Olaf at least probably took refuge near the Solway and this could well be the prime reason why Eadmund attacked that area in the next year and gave Cumberland to the king of the Scots. Indeed, these two events were juxtaposed in the records in such a way as to suggest that the one resulted from the other. (Garmonsway pp. 410-11; Simeon p.89; William of Malmesbury pp.124-25) "Cumberland" may have included some of the British lands in south-west Scotland, as well as that region south of the Solway. The southern boundary of this territory would be the River Eamont, where Athelstan had held his great meeting and which persisted to form the modern boundary between Cumberland and Westmorland.

But Eadmund still needed a sub-king in Northumbria to act as warden: Erik Bloodaxe was available, having probably already helped Eadmund on his Cumberland campaign and with this prize in view. Was Erik then allowed to install himself in York as a reward? The later remarks of his wife Gunnhild at York suggest firmly that Erik up till then had been the king of England's man. [Egla (60) p.157] Olaf Sigtrygsson was the only member of the kin of Ragnar left to wield power around the Irish Sea. It seems reasonable to suppose that he had already clashed with Erik Haraldsson over the question of dominance in the area. The Cumberland affair would cement this enmity into a considerable hatred.

The Scottish claims on Northumberland and Durham were not to be set aside so easily as this. Their kings were destined to make efforts to fulfil them until long after the Norman Conquest. However, Eadmund's conditions did acknowledge that there was a considerable population of Britons as well as Northmen between Solway and Eamont, but relatively few English. The opposite applied in Northumberland and Lothian on the east side.

Chapter 5

The Battles of Brunanburh
and Vinheidh

Introduction

The events covered below have already been touched upon in Chapter 4. In the following the material is examined in more depth, with the aim being to identify better the circumstances and persons involved. An article covering these matters written in 1995 will also be to some extent re-evaluated and superseded. (Pearson 1995 pp24-39) The most reliable fact in evidence is that Athelstan confronted a coalition in battle in 937 and won. Despite its significance, subsequent records have become very confused about its location and the participants. It was nevertheless an important formative event just prior to the arrival in Britain of Erik Bloodaxe.

"Brunanburh" in the Records

The great 10th century battle allegedly fought near a place called *Brun(n)anburh* (Anglo-Saxon Chronicles—937) has given rise to much confusion since earliest times. Other sources give various names for the field, generally beginning with "Brun-". Some are quite different, while others decline to mention a name at all. From this starting point it might seem probable that something is wrong with the name as it appears in the A-S.C., and that this immediately made the place unidentifiable to writers from the 11th century onwards. Such doubt made speculation rife as to the location and scribes tended to be influenced by places they had heard of, especially if containing the element "Brun-" or similar. Following Campbell's reasoning the correct Chronicle form is *Brunanburh* (dative *Brunanbyrig*). (Campbell p60) As a provisional assumption one might feel that the version with "-nn-" is due to Scandinavian influence, resulting from an Old English *burna*—"stream"—being (temporarily) replaced in areas subject to Nordic settlement by Old Norse *brunnr* of similar meaning, a process evident in some place-names, as perhaps Bourne ("Brunne" c 960) in Lincolnshire. (Ekwall p55)

The place is called "Brunandune" by Ethelwerd, "Duinbrunde" in the Pictish Chronicle, "Brun(e)" in the Annales Cambriae and both "Etbrunnanwerc" and "Brunnanbyrig" by Simeon of Durham. Other forms are "Bruneswerc" by Gaimar, "Brune(s)burh" by Henry of Huntingdon and the alternatives "Brunesford" and "Brunesfeld" by William of Malmesbury

Discussion around the name Brunanburh

The variety of endings making an appearance suggests a dominant element "Brun(a)" which could be applied to the site of the battle, and to which others could be suffixed, without any of these necessarily being an actual place-name there. Brunan- presupposes a "weak" noun *(Brun(a)* in the nominative case), whereas *Brunes-* requires the "strong" form *Brun*.

Campbell attributes "Brun(a)" either to a personal name or a river-name and, indeed, the River Browney (Co Durham) had an earlier spelling "Brun". (Ekwall p70) A third possibility is that "Brun(a)" is a hill-name. Elgee indicated that the name "Brown Hill" is quite common among the moor lands of north-east Yorkshire and, with some justification, claimed it to be due to a residual equivalent of Welsh *bron*—"hill". (Elgee pp209, 213) It could hence be true that "Brown" in place-names elsewhere could have the same origin, with early forms of "brown" (Old English *brūn*) being initially confused with "bron". This seems possible with Brown, Somerset, ("in Brunan" 854) which is near the Brendon Hills ("Brunadun" 1204).

> Even so, no matter how one interprets "Brun(a)", the weak form would appear to be more common, while Ethelwerd's "Brunandune" could well refer directly to the Brendon Hills mentioned above, under the mistaken belief that they were near the site of the battle. The "Duinbrunde" of the Pictish Chronicle looks like a Gaelic translation of "Brun(n)anburh", but may rather be due to a confusion of Old English *dūn*—"hill"—with Gaelic *dún*—"fort". The "Brun(e)" of the Annales Cambriae, on the other hand, may go back to some original account.

Simeon of Durham gives us "Etbrunnanwerc vel Brunnanbyrig". He thus equates these two names, the latter reminding one of the various versions occurring in the A-S.C., but the former coming from some other unknown Old English source. His Latin *vel* signifies "or perhaps". He is echoing two sources, one of which was the A-S.C. The "-brunnan-" in the first may have been influenced by the second.

The account of the battle described in the French of Gaimar presents the name "Bruneswerc". This may have arisen through a belief that the battle site was at Burnswark, a hill-fort in South Scotland and perhaps correcting the name from "Brunanwerc". Henry of Huntingdon gives "Brunesburh" as well as "Bruneburh" and William of Malmesbury again indicates a strong genitive with the alternatives "Brunesford" and "Brunesfeld".

The battle is discussed by A. H. Burne, who makes a strong claim for a ridge at Brinsworth near Rotherham, Yorkshire, largely relying on the strategic situation, the use of Roman roads, and the terrain as described for the Battle of *Vinheiðr* in Egil's Saga (see later). However, he fails to note that Brinsworth was "Brunisford" in 1241, which would align it with William's "Brunesford". But the persistent "i" or "e" root vowel of earlier forms weakens this link; Ekwall derives it from "Bryni's ford". (p66) Perhaps the cited local battle tradition is derived from one earlier form of the name coinciding with William's "Brunesford". (Campbell pp.60-67, where all versions are listed and thoroughly discussed; Burne pp.56-7)

Yet was there such a name as "Brunanburh" at the actual battlefield? If one allows that the forms with "-burh" originated in the A-S.C., and in particular in the poem featured therein, then one might propose that there was not. The line in which the name appears goes:

> *ymbe Brūnanburh;*   *bordweal clufan*
> "around Brunanburh;   shield-wall clove"

This was one of the standard alliterative line-types of Old English verse, with the poet achieving two "b-" alliterative lifts in the first half-line, followed by a single "b-" in the second. (The one in *ymbe* does not qualify). In doing so one might well suspect that he has corrupted the name to make it fit better. Thus, and for further reasons given below, the original may have been "Brun(n)anwerc", which would not of course have provided such good alliteration. In early forms many Old English place-names incorporated a preposition (elliptical names), as with *Æt Strætforda,* etc. This seems to make it certain that Simeon, or his source, knew of a place called "Etbrunnanwerc"; in conventional Old English *æt Brūnan-weorce* (or *æt Brunes-).* This is not the same as saying that it was correct for the site of the battle, but the likelihood is clearly enhanced.

> The above suggests that there was a basic form "Brun", relating to an eminence or stream, or even a whole district, to which other elements could be appended.

Vinheidh in the Records

The relevant battle described in the Icelandic *Egils Saga Skallagrimssonar* was named *Vínheiðr* and apparently took place in Northumbria. (Campbell pxii for list of texts; Pálsson and Edwards pp115-131)

The contribution of Simeon is made more valuable, albeit more confusing, by his giving yet another name to the battlefield—"Weondune, Wendune".

Discussion around the name Vinheidh

Campbell would explain "We(o)ndun(e)" away by this being some name familiar to Simeon and by remarking that in manuscripts "n" and "r" are easily confused, and that the name was probably "Weordun", referring to the River Wear. (Campbell p62) Although he does not mention it, there is a hill east of Durham that would fit this description, i.e. Warden Law. This is by the Wear, but otherwise there is no reason to dissociate it from other "Warden" names (from Old English *weard-dūn*—"look-out hill"—elsewhere in England. The argument for Brunanburh being in County Durham would be much more convincing if Warden Law were near to the River Browney; they are miles apart, with Durham city between.

The battle described in *Egils Saga Skallagrimssonar* was named *Vínheiðr* and took place in Northumbria. Even a casual acquaintance with the account suggests a location in Yorkshire and the conflict took place after Olaf Gudhfridhsson shipped an Irish-Norse army over to northern England. He was joined in his endeavours by Constantine and Eugenius (Owen), kings of the Scots and Strathclyde Welsh respectively.

In the past it has even been suggested that the presence of the Skallagrimssons (or Thorolf at least) at a battle in England is pure fiction, designed to cloak them with a glory they had not earned. This is based on the mention at the site of a river called *Vína* and woods called *Vínuskógar*. These features are compared by Campbell with an earlier occasion when Thorolf accompanied Erik Bloodaxe to Bjarmaland and fought a battle there between a River *Vína* (the present Dwina that flows into the White Sea) and a forest called *Vínuskógr*. (Campbell p68) This clearly casts doubt on the Yorkshire river being called *Vína*.

> However, if the battle were fictitious one would have expected the battle name to be *Vínuheiðr* to reflect the other names. Reason demands that *Vína* is genuine, even if *Vínuskógar* were derivative from that earlier event in the saga. However, the reverse may even be true. Provisionally let the proposition stand that "Brunanburh" took place on Bramham Moor and that the name is somehow linked with that of Bramham, while suspending the argument until the mystery surrounding the Battle of *Vínheiðr* has been re-examined.

Egil's Saga and Vínheidh

The battle features in the saga because the tempestuous Egil Skallagrimsson and his elder brother Thorolf had hired themselves as mercenaries to the English king Athelstan. The saga goes on to tell how a certain Olaf had invaded Northern England and defeated the earls of Northumbria, killing one, Godrek, while the other, Alfgeir, fled south to reach Athelstan, who stood by him, despite calls for his dismissal. Athelstan then found himself short of men to resist Olaf, so he re-instated Alfgeir in the north, together with Thorolf and Egil, to keep an eye on the opposition until an army could be mustered in the south. Most other sources make no reference to any preliminary encounter with the Northumbrian earls and, indeed, their names are otherwise obscure.

> Olaf is named as *Ólafr Rauði*, but in reality must have been *Ólafr Guðfriðsson* from Dublin, a member of the kin that had ruled in York for several decades. Athelstan was intent upon ousting them from that

city. The saga erroneously claims that Olaf was killed in the battle. The Annals of Clonmacnois do in fact mention an Awley Froit who died in a battle in Britain and he would be the *Rauði* of the saga. (Campbell p56 - one might think of Olaf Red becoming a sort of Ola Fred in the Irish account.) This example illustrates how the saga, with the exception of Egil, Thorolf and the brothers' henchman Thorfinn Strangi, was written by someone very uncertain about the persons taking part at *Vínheiðr*. Assuming the battle to have been a real event, were then the descriptions taken back to Iceland by a participant, someone among the Northmen's ranks, and whose knowledge of what took place in their own tactics reliable, even if garbling the overall strategy? At the same time one can assume that the contribution of the brothers Skallagrimsson will have been rather exaggerated. Nevertheless there are detailed descriptions of tactics, skirmishes and terrain, and one should take heed of these.

How did Egil's Saga describe the battle and the battlefield? According to it, Olaf was joined by two earls called Hring and Adils who are just as obscure as Godrek and Alfgeir. As already mentioned, Athelstan, having marched north, but seeing himself outmatched in numbers, held a council. A vanguard was left behind while Athelstan returned south personally to conduct a recruiting drive. After a battlefield was chosen on a level heath, this advance party then made a peculiar move: messengers were sent to Olaf stating that Athelstan would "hazel a field" for him at a place called Win-heath beside Wina-woods It would appear that this outlandish custom ensured that once a place of battle had thus been marked out a king could no longer carry on harrying a land without loss of honour to himself.

To the north of the heath was a *borg* (fort) and here Olaf set up his headquarters, apparently recognising and accepting the implications of the "hazelling". He sent some of his men up onto the heath with tents to form an advance guard and to make ready the battle camp. Men who hazelled a field for battle had to choose it carefully and surround it with hazel wands: the terrain must be sufficiently level. There was such a place on the heath: on one side was a certain river, while on the other was a great wood. At a point where river and wood were closest, yet still quite distant, the men of King Athelstan had pitched their tents: they stretched from river to wood, plenty of tents, but thinly manned. The English king's advance-guard erected their tents so that they blocked the view of the enemy and gave a false impression of the numbers they had at their disposal. When Olaf's men came to look at their camp the vanguard stood before their tents and prevented examination by the others, and then lied about their numbers, for the others could not look in to see how many tents there were and were misled about the number of men quartered in each tent.

Olaf's men were camped north of the hazels. Although he was fully prepared for battle, Olaf allowed himself to be drawn into negotiations wherein he refused the initial offer in the expectation of getting better terms, only to find that the delay had allowed Athelstan to get ready and the final terms were quite unacceptable. The time was eaten up by the fact that the English negotiators convinced the others that each exchange would require three days, one to reach the southern fort, a second for consultation and a third for the return to the northern fort. Thus were hostilities delayed for about a week. Adils addressed Olaf and drove the point home that, while they were being fobbed off with offers and promises, Athelstan had been away gathering together his troops. Adils suggested that he and his brother Hring should move onto the attack that very night, so as to retrieve what they could of the advantages which seemed to be slipping from their grasp.

With Olaf's consent Hring and Adils slipped south onto the heath, but failed to make a surprise attack, for in the early light they were spotted by Thorolf's watch, and Athelstan's vanguard hence had time to prepare themselves for battle. The defenders were deployed in two groups; one consisted of the Northmen and the other comprised the forces of Alfgeir augmented by militia from the countryside; Alfgeir's command was by far the more numerous. The two Northmen took up positions near the wood, while Alfgeir was beside the river. Abandoning attempts at surprise, Hring and Adils also had their forces divided into two, with Adils against Alfgeir and Hring against the Vikings. Adils attacked strongly so that Alfgeir must give way, and he soon took to flight. Southwards over the heath he went and far away, with some men with him; it would seem that all the criticism of him had been justified. Adils abandoned pursuit and rejoined the fray, to be confronted by Thorolf who urged his men to make a stand by the wood so that this would cover their backs and prevent them being attacked from all sides. It would seem the Northmen were trapped, with Hring to their north and Adils to their south. When the saga then says that Adils attacked Thorolf it means that he and his men returned from further south and engaged the whole Norse battalion that was commanded by Thorolf from that direction. When we are then told that Egil attacked Adils, it implies that Egil took charge of those turning to face south, while Thorolf continued to engage Hring to the north. One might suppose that, after defeating Alfgeir, Adils wasted precious time pursuing him, for by the time he struck again Hring was already facing defeat and death at the hands of Thorolf. Once the northern party broke, it was then Adils who found himself perilously cut off and came under attack by Egil. It was then that a battle rage seized Thorolf, resulting in him reaching and killing Hring and his banner bearer. Aware of the loss of their leader some flight set in among the "Welsh" and "Scots". Adils, aware of the fate of his brother and the losses they were sustaining, could only rejoin the rest of Olaf's army by fleeing into the woods with his men.

As dusk gathered, Thorolf and Egil returned to camp with their men, just as Athelstan and his army arrived there. Shortly afterwards Olaf and his host established themselves in their camp north of the heath and learned of the defeat of Hring and Adils and the death of the former. A report had reached Athelstan the night before about the fighting which had broken out on the heath, so he had left immediately. Next morning he held council with his leaders to decide how the army was to be divided and commanded. In his own battalion he put those in front who were keenest for the fray and appointed Egil its commander, while Thorolf was to command the other battalion which included the Northmen. He advised them that the Scots fought in loose formations, running about and liable to make an appearance anywhere, but they scattered easily against resolute men. Egil did not like the arrangement.

Olaf too formed up in two battalions, his own positioned opposite that of Athelstan, both being mighty bodies of men, while his second battalion, commanded by Scottish earls and mainly composed of Scots, was stationed by the wood and opposite that of Thorolf. The battle commenced. Thorolf pressed forward beside the wood, intending to outflank Olaf's battalion. Thorolf's men had their shields before them, but with the forest on their right giving them cover. He himself progressed so fast that few could stay with him. It was at this juncture that Adils and his men burst out of the wood into which they had retired the day before, so that the impetuous Thorolf, caught unawares, was hacked at by many and slain. The banner bearer, Thorfinn, ran back to the main body and Adils pressed home his advantage, the Scots letting out great whoops, sensing victory once the leader of the Vikings was slain.

Egil saw the banner go back and came over to the wood. Rallying the men, he cut his way through to Adils and slew him, and soon they were in pursuit of the earl's men, cutting down all they caught. Seeing the flight, the Scots joined it. Egil and his men were now able to attack Olaf's bared flank, just as Thorolf had earlier intended. Athelstan became aware that Olaf was beginning to crack and pressed forward to victory.

He returned to the fort to the south for the night. Egil, however, pursued the vanquished foe, slaying every man he could catch, but eventually returned to the battlefield and sought out the body of Thorolf. A grave was dug for him; they washed the corpse and buried it, together with his clothes and weapons. On each arm of Thorolf, Egil put a gold bracelet; then they piled a cairn over him and covered it with earth. Egil finally quickly put together a couple of verses and recited them over this the last resting place of his brother. Athelstan was drinking at table when Egil rejoined him. The latter is described as huge, ugly and bald, and sat and sulked, half drawing his sword across his lap, until given recompense for the death of his brother and their services in the form of treasure.

The above is a condensed version of how Egil's Saga describes the incidents surrounding the battle of *Vínheiðr*. Certain places are referred to, but not given names. We are told of a *borg* to the north of the battlefield, where Olaf had his headquarters and another one to the south, where Athelstan had his. Likewise there was a place between wood and stream where Athelstan's men set up their tents and another where Olaf's vanguard made camp on the heath, where the land fell away to the north. The only places named directly in connection with the battle are the moor *Vínheiðr*, the river *Vína*, and the woods *Vínuskógar*. Much of this misleads and is indeed designed to do so.

Location of Vinheidh

The battle clearly took place in Northumbria, the *Norðimbraland* of the sagas, and can be identified with the battle of "Brunanburh". We may assume that Olaf had taken possession of York, and that the battlefield was on an approach to the city, in the old West Riding. *Vínheiðr* was a "heath", and it happens that the Roman road from the south (Roman Ridge) crosses Bramham Moor, a low spur of the Pennines, once heath land, but now consisting of fields, with extensive woods nearby.

On the higher ground to the west, towards Leeds, is an area known as Whin Moor This appears to mean "moor where whin (i.e. gorse) bushes grow", but it is more rightly spelt Win Moor and we might allow ourselves to surmise that it was originally applied in a wider geographical sense to include Bramham Moor and carrying the meaning "moor by the river *Vína*" or the like. It thus becomes crucial to identify the stream involved.

> The resemblance to the Went may be superficial, because of the persistent "-e-" of the root vowel in early forms of this, e.g. "Weneta". (Ekwall p506) One could perhaps be misled into thinking that mention of the "river" must imply a major stream, such as the Wharfe or the Aire, but their names are British and well documented; it seems highly unlikely that either could have featured in the saga as *Vína*. The target must be a smaller stream, with a name that could have changed since the 10th century.

Returning to the Bramham area, the Cock Beck has headwaters on Whin Moor, and flows eastwards along the southern edge of the present Bramham Moor to reach the Wharfe just south of Tadcaster.

> While not asserting that the Cock Beck was the *Vína*, its course may be suitable for the situation described in the saga, with Olaf's "borg" more probably being Tadcaster than the vanished Roman fort near Newton Kyme (formerly known as Longborough) and Athelstan's perhaps Castleford, all former Roman stations at important river crossings. (App. 3, Map 7) *Vína* might seem to represent a British river-name. Ekwall did not consider the Cock Beck to be an ancient name. "On the stream is Cocksford. The river-name may be a back-formation from the place-name". (Ekwall p114) Were he right in this proposition the earlier name for the Cock Beck has clearly been lost.

Other place-names in the area add weight to the suggestion that Bramham Moor was *Vínheiðr*. The Old English word *hæth*—"heath"—has generally been replaced by "moor" in the north of England, although its earlier currency is evidenced by names of ancient type. Thus Hatfield, near Doncaster, was "Haethfelth" in Bede and *Hæðfeld* in the Old English translation, i.e. "heath field". Headlam in Co. Durham represents *hæth-lēam*—"heath glades"—while the singular version *lēah* is retained as "He(a)dley" several times in the north. One can give other examples of "heath" being used as a first element, and in Heath, near Wakefield, it stands alone. Of particular interest to us is Headley on the east side of Bramham Moor, the clearest evidence one could wish for, that in Anglo-Saxon times there was a treeless heath there, a place suitable for a battlefield.

If *Vín-heiðr* was named directly from the River *Vína,* the correct Old Norse form would have been *Vínu-heiðr.* The evident lack of flexional ending on the supposed river-name may mean that *Vín-heiðr* was a straight Nordic rendition of an orally transmitted Old English *Wīn-hæth.* The woods by the river are named as *Vínuskógar,* and the area still has extensive woodlands. Even if it did not, there are a number of ancient local place-names giving witness to the former existence of such. Just south of the Cock Beck, near Aberford, is Woodhouse, Old English "house in the wood(s)". An identical name appears on Whin Moor itself, thus weakening perhaps the validity of "moor" for this particular part of it. Just west of Bramham is Wothersome, which represents "wood houses" in the dative plural form. Names of much later flavour occur, such as Woodend Farm. Most important of all is Hazelwood, which like some names mentioned above is one that belies its own antiquity.

If we examine the above facts and then compare them with the description of terrain and events with the section of Egil's Saga dealing with the battle of *Vínheiðr,* then a certain degree of probability emerges that Bramham Moor was where it took place. The topography fits so well that one is urged to believe that the details were handed down in Iceland by one who took part in the events. This is not to say that one must necessarily give the same credence to those events as described. Even were they the truth and nothing but the truth, they could scarcely be the whole truth. The Icelandic observer would know a great deal about what happened to his own company, but rather less about the situation among the main

English forces, and less still with regard to the enemy. In any case, the later composer of the saga was certainly primarily interested in recording events in any detail insofar as they had reference to Thorolf and Egil and their band of Norse warriors.

One extraneous point that apparently made a great impression on our observer was the "trickery" employed by the English to stay Olaf from moving onto the attack before they had gathered together sufficient force. It would seem that the Northmen, as ready-for-action mercenaries, had a grandstand view of all these preliminaries, because of their outpost position north of the River Cock.

Death of a Bishop

William of Malmesbury's account is weighed down with a lot of folklore. However, his statement that Olaf (here Analaf) led an early attack, with the English king being caught unprepared, shines through as probable. Killed during this raid were a bishop and all his men, who had arrived and pitched their tents only the evening before. The doomed prelate had done this even though the king had already received advice to abandon the forward position because of its dangers for him.

This is difficult to reconcile with the saga account of preliminary fighting. One can perhaps make more sense of it by assuming more than one preliminary skirmish before the main battle. A reasonable sequence would be that Hring and Adils had earlier attacked at dawn on Olaf's behalf and using overwhelming force. While the bishop and his men were being destroyed the more alert Northmen were able to make a tactical withdrawal to a place between wood and stream where they made a stand along with the supposedly feckless Alfgeir. Olaf's men were eventually defeated there by the warrior band of Egil and Thorolf. From this one can assume that the forward camp became available again for Athelstan's forces. Hence the king, becoming apprised of the commencement of fighting and final success, decided to march north.

So, if Olaf's plan was to deny their campsite to his enemies it apparently failed. Athelstan and his main forces arrived at the advanced camp, making a formal commitment by both sides of all their resources inevitable the next day. The bishop episode would not appear in the saga because this was only interested in extolling the military virtues of its heroes, and they were clearly not in the close company of any such bishop, and as heathens probably would not have wanted to be, even though the king had insisted that they be prime signed to facilitate association with Christians. (Stephenson p115)

The Location of Brunanburh

There are sufficient similarities between Brunanburh and Vinheidh to identify them as the same battlefield. They were both probably in Northumbria, they both took place in the second quarter of the 10th century, and they both involved King Athelstan of England against a King Olaf. However, while the saga account of Vinheidh gives quite elaborate details of terrain and tactics, and even hand-to-hand fighting, the Old English account does none of this, but is more concerned with glorifying the victors, and describing how their foes must flee the field to make their way homeward to Ireland and Scotland, leaving nobles and kinsmen dead on the battleground. There is no mention of the earlier flight of the Northumbrian earl southwards as far as *Valland*, no mention of Icelandic mercenaries, and certainly no record of the contributions of Thorolf and Egil. The one major clue to the site of the battle is that it was "around Brunanburh". One feels that the poet was a West Saxon whose main concern was to heap praise on his king and fellow countrymen. The poem known as "Brunanburh" neglects to mention the part played by any foreign mercenaries.

On the other hand, the omissions of the saga-man regarding many points to do with the Irish-Norse and Scottish invasions suggests that the material for the saga was passed on by someone who was at the battle, but did not subsequently mingle with the English at court, as Egil is dubiously described as having done.

The men of Wessex were unfamiliar with Northumbria and the place-name as reported may have been mispronounced or mishcard. At any rate this would allow Bromborough, Cheshire, to be considered for the battleground. It was "Brombur" in the 12th century, (Ekwall p68) with the apparent meaning of "fort where broom grows". Even so, while this location may just be possible for the name Brunanburh it is not suitable for Vinheidh. It seems hardly likely that Olaf, already victorious over the earls of Northumbria, would subsequently need to fight on some beach-head on the Wirral. The word "broom" occurs fairly frequently in the West Riding in forms such as Brampton and Bramley, rather than the more usual Brompton, Bromley, etc. Bramham itself has one variant early spelling "Brumham" (1081). (Ekwall p60) However, in all the early sources in which it appears Brunanburh shows no signs of "-m-" and hence, if Bramham is to be related to Brunanburh, some derivation other than from "broom" is to be allowed.

Is there any fortification on Bramham Moor? There are certainly earthworks, the best evidenced of which now are Becca Banks, a linear rampart. The point at which the Roman road crosses the Cock Beck was largely dictated by the river banks, which are steep on the north side west of Aberford, and on the south side to the east. The earthworks reinforce considerably this steepness. Becca Banks is the name given to the earthworks west of Aberford, while those to the east are known as The Rein, which follows the south bank for a short distance before diverging from the river over the fields. In order to avoid these hindrances north-south travellers would be funneled into the crossing at Aberford. However, these earthworks being linear, rather than enclosing, might qualify as a *werc* rather than a *burh*, and in any case would seem to be a bit too far south for Brunanburh/ Vinheidh. But there have in fact been earthworks on Bramham Moor itself. Leadman describes one, as approached from Tadcaster in the east. "Turning up the Bramham Road (north) the traveller will cross Bramham Moor, at one time an unenclosed common. A little further on is Camp Hill, where an entrenchment formerly existed, but of which the plough has destroyed all traces". (Leadman) This site might hence be thought of as Brunanburh. (Roadworks have since further damaged much of this landscape.)

The saga makes Adils and Hring earls in Wales and tributaries of Athelstan. These names are not Welsh, but Norse, and would normally belong to Scandinavians. There is no evidence that the Welsh of Wales were involved at Brunanburh, but the Britons (Welsh) of Strathclyde were under their king Eugenius (Owen) who, like Constantine of the Scots, is not mentioned in the saga. Nor are there any Celtic names at all in this source, even though "Welsh" and "Scottish" detachments feature largely in the fighting.

While the saga is thus vague and unhelpful with regard to personalities, there is no need to assume it equally so when dealing with places and events. As a general rule, geographical situations can be shown to be quite reliable throughout its length. and it is only unhelpful in this case in its sparseness of information, and in that the "Vin-" names have no indisputable modern counterparts. However, we must take note as to how well the situation of the battle of Vínheidh is described. This information cannot be fabrication, it is too commonplace, and it must have been conveyed to Iceland by an eye-witness, wherever it took place. One may also take note that there are no grounds for the English "trickery" to be included unless it is basically true, even if thought to be borrowed from some other battle tradition. Thus, allowing for some bias showing Thorolf, Egil and their Northmen in a glorious light, especially in contrast to the implied incompetence of Alfgeir, there is otherwise no reason for doubting that events, while not all being covered equally, are as accurate as the memory could manage.

Of the many earlier writers who have contributed ideas in connection with the battle of Brunanburh and its location, A. Campbell is predominant. If one must quibble at his work, it is to the effect that he seems to have set out to prove that the site cannot be found.

The Participants

A reassessment of the evidence is now possible as summarised and commented upon by Campbell, and in the light of suggestions made above. Of all the information derived from the sources, the one certain fact to emerge is that Athelstan, king of Wessex and England, was involved in the battle. There also seems no reason to doubt that his brother Edmund was present, even though scarcely older than sixteen. His presence is noted in the Anglo-Saxon Chronicle and in Simeon.

Egil's Saga tells us that Thorolf, Egil and Thorfinn Strangi took part in the battle of Vinheidh. One can safely assert that they are not referred to in any other account; this in no way indicates that they were not there, but implies that their contribution to the conflict has been grossly exaggerated by the Icelandic narrative. Also on Athelstan's side there are the two otherwise unknown earls of Northumbria, named in the saga as Godrek and Alfgeir, and set up by the king to guard his northern frontiers. Presumably they were appointed wardens after Athelstan's earlier punitive expedition against the Scots, (A-S.C. 934) and lasted three years as such. They have already been identified above (Chapter 4) as the brothers Gudhfridh and Olaf Sigtrygsson, temporarily driven out of Northumbria by Athelstan in 926. As already suggested in Chapter 4 Olaf probably took refuge either in Wales or beside the Solway.

Campbell points out that Hring and Adils were Scandinavian names of legendary flavour, especially the latter. Because of this he casts doubt on their reality. (Campbell pp44, 71) In the saga they are said to be Welsh, and their impetuosity in attack and the use of the wood by Adils, both to escape and to launch a surprise assault, seem more in accordance with Celtic than Nordic attitudes to fighting, and may be linked to advice given in the saga about the peculiarities of the Scots in battle. It may just suggest itself that the two earls were British chieftains who had been given names not appropriate to them because the saga-man wanted to name them, and either had no names, or corrupted their Celtic ones into Norse ones.

Against this one might argue that the saga-man was shy about identifying opponents of Thorolf and Egil as Scandinavians. He seems to press the point excessively that their opponents were Welsh and Scots. In another source it is suggested that Hiring, the king of Denmark's own son, was killed at the battle. This could well identify him as Hring. In the various accounts of Simeon five kings and seven dukes are reported as fallen, while Olaf is said to have come in 615 ships and to have entered the mouth of the Humber, and that his allies were Constantine of the Scots and Owen of the Cumbrians. This lacks sense if he came from Ireland, except that some of his support may have landed in the east. Perhaps the reported death of "the king of Denmark's own son" on his side is relevant to this. Adils and Hring could well have been leaders of a Viking force from Denmark who were eager to acquire loot as well as to reverse the growing dominance of the royal house of Wessex.

Bramham Moor:
Comparison of Place-names

In the general Bramham area, note can be taken of a feature lying between Barwick-in-Elmet and an arm of the Cock Beck, and called Wendel Hill.

> Could this be the Wendun of Simeon, (Stephenson J. p482) with "Wendel" being due to the assimilation of the "-l" with the final sound of "hill" and Wendon Hill thus becoming Wendel Hill? "Weondun" has been compared with the "Vin-" names of Egil's Saga in the past, although Campbell did not think much of the idea. (Campbell p62) Nevertheless, interpretation of "Weondun" as "hill by the River Weon or Win" is attractive enough, and might strengthen the suggestion made above that either the Cock Beck or the Bramham Beck once bore this other name. That "Weon" could equate *Wīn* in Old English can perhaps be illustrated by the afore-mentioned River Wear. The "Wirus" of Bede became *Wiire thære ēa* in the O.E. translation, but in the "Historia de S. Cuthberto", however, we come across forms like "Weor" and "Weorra".

If one accepts the Bramham Moor area as the location of Vinheidh, one can put Hazelwood within the compass of the woods referred to as *Vínuskógar* and Headley as locating the heath where the battle took place. A difficulty arises, however, when one tries to reconcile the Cock Beck as the stream near which the English forces camped and which guarded their left flank in the fighting. The tents were pitched where the woods came closest to the stream, but were still quite distant, and placed in such a way that the enemy could not look over them. It is hard to visualise how these conditions could be fulfilled at a point just north of the Cock Beck at Aberford.

Near the Bramham Cross Roads a diagonal stretch of the Roman Ridge has fallen into disuse: this may indicate that at some time it became overgrown by Hazel Wood. A camp here, between the wood and a branch of the Bramham Beck (Openrakes Beck, in a ravine) would better suit the situation as described, even though the stream is small. If this suggestion is just, then one can pinpoint the battlefield as being south-east of Bramham, indeed close to where Headley Hall now stands and virtually the same site as the one marked on maps for the Battle of Bramham Moor in 1408. In this way one can link the

Battle of Vinheidh more closely with Brunanburh and Bramham, but any connection with the Cock Beck is weakened. Bramham needs to be examined more closely.

Most names in "Brom-" or "Bram-" are considered to refer to the plant called "broom". The frequency of this plant-name in place-names may strike one as excessive and leads to the suspicion that some such names might be found to have other roots, were early enough forms available. Clearly, if Brun(n)anburh, Brun(n)anwerc, etc., were thought of as relating to Bramham Moor, then "broom" could not be involved, but a name "Brun(a)" as discussed above emerges, and one candidate for this title is Bramham Beck. Bramham would then be from a theoretical *Brūnan-hām* to give "Brune-ham" and hence "Brum(e)-ham" by assimilation to the "-m" of "ham". This then allows Brunnanwerc or Brunanburh to refer to an earthwork above Bramham, such as the Camp Hill referred to earlier. Yet it is odd that the name Bramham does not appear in any of the sources. Perhaps the present settlement was alternatively called "Bruneford" or "Brunanford", with "Bruneham" embracing the whole estate as well as the settlement, for if these deliberations were correct Bramham Beck could have been called "Bruna", virtually an identical name to that of the River Browney in Co. Durham.

If Bramham Beck was the "Bruna", could it also be the "Vina" of Egil's Saga? There is certainly nothing to suggest that *Vínheiðr* is not a genuine name, a view supported by evidence presented above, while the name *Vína* is not without a degree of probability; only *Vínuskógar* as a name for the woods may be artificial and named by analogy after another forest lying by the arctic Dwina. That "Vina" or "Wina" is possible as a stream name in this part of Yorkshire is indicated by a watercourse not all that far away called Wine Beck, near Addingham in Wharfedale. In the saga, Egil names the Vina as the stream by which his brother was laid to rest. The Cock Beck was probably a good way to the south of the battleground, which makes it less likely as the Vina, since the impression is received that Thorolf was buried near where he fell.

The saga makes it clear that Athelstan divided his army into two battalions and that the Northmen were not in the one directly under his command. The point is also made that the brothers were parted, Thorolf leading one battalion and Egil the other. This is certainly gross exaggeration of their roles, in order to award the maximum glory to the two heroes. It may, of course, have been true that Athelstan was short of really good guards and put Egil into some unfamiliar group, rather to his disgust. As in the earlier skirmish, Thorolf and the Northmen were stationed facing north, with the wood beside them on the right. Athelstan's battalion was to the left, with the stream on its left. Facing Athelstan was Olaf and his Irish-Norse, while Constantine and his Scots confronted the other battalion.

However, while mentions of "Athelstan" in general can be taken as right, where he is mentioned in connection with Egil one can assume that "Arinbjörn" is really involved.

There are separate accounts of both Thorolf and Turketul advancing too far and needing to be rescued. Campbell (pp78-80) justly rubbished the comparisons of nomenclature made by Whistler in the accounts of Turketul at Brunanburh and Thorolf at Vinheidh. The battle was so huge that the presence of the Icelanders, even if forming a band 360 strong, can hardly have been hugely significant. (Could the Skallagrimssons really have arrived in England with such numbers? This is much more likely to have been within the capabilities of Arinbjörn.) One must discount the personal names, yet not discard the events as far as they go. One might prefer that it was Turketul leading the right battalion against the Scots, but after initial success found himself in peril; but was rescued by Singin. There seems no reason to doubt that Thorolf also took part in this advance and was killed. In the saga he has usurped the role of Turketul, this perhaps being suggested by the two names, i.e. in Old Norse *Thorketill* and *Thórólfr*. Egil did not rescue Thorolf, so comparison with Singin is unnecessary.

While Thorolf was hoping to outflank Olaf, we are informed by the saga that the wood was not the protection of his own flank he had supposed. There seems no need to doubt that Adils's attack out of the wood was successful in trapping Thorolf, and that Egil took part in a counter-attack which was too late to save his brother. But the saga in its heroic approach has Egil rallying the Northmen, slaying Adils in single combat, putting the Scots to flight and turning Olaf's flank.

He thus practically won the battle of Vinheidh single handed and, believing this, one can understand that Athelstan was encouraged to find the opposition cracking. Egil is also presented as the chief pursuer of the vanquished, while Athelstan enjoyed the luxury of retiring to the borough south of the heath.

It is far more likely that Arinbjörn was the one in a position to appreciate Egil's performance. So, if one takes into account the contents of Chapter 7 one can see the roles of Thorolf and Egil in the main battle rather differently. It was Arinbjörn who put Thorolf in charge of one of his detachments, while he kept Egil by his own side. Likewise, after the battle it was Arinbjörn who was chivvied into recompensing Egil with treasure and for whom the latter composed a poem. It seems unlikely that Egil was ever even in Athelstan's presence.

The Battle Site Revisited

The above descriptions of the battle all make great sense if we take the site of the English tents to be the Camp Hill mentioned earlier. This lies beside Spen Farm, between the Bramham Beck system and the forest called Hazel Wood. On the farmhouse site, towards the north-east and facing Headley, it forms a low scarp, but it is quite obvious that if Athelstan's camp was here, and Olaf's near Headley, the English had certainly got the strongest position. If the tents were arranged along this scarp, no-one to the north-east would be able to overlook the camp to find out their true number, nor the real strength of the force thus ensconced. This low hill in the middle was passable on either side, but especially by the stream. This may explain the prominence given to the fact that the English forces, at the start of the engagement, were deliberately divided into two, and then matched by their opponents; it was better to defend these two passages. This Camp Hill, again, might have been the "Brunanburh" around which the battle raged and where the shield-wall was cloven. Yet any earthworks, now ploughed out, may even then have been very old, and not significantly contributing to the defensibility of the position.

When viewed in accordance with the terrain at Camp Hill, events as related become much clearer. We may well doubt that the battlefield was marked out with hazels, although there are several instances in Norse literature of this happening at various types of meeting. The saga-man may have been confused by some other mention of "hazels". Campbell discusses at length suggestions by earlier scholars that the words *hæð*—"hill"—and *heiðr*—"heath"—have led to confusion in the manuscripts, but discounts this. (Campbell p69) However, if we apply what has been discussed above about the site of the battle, Campbell's comments may seem to be undermined, and the earlier views to some degree justified. In the case of Olaf's force, he is probably right in asserting that it was *norðan höslurnar*—"north of the hazels"—rather than *neðan hæð*—"below the hill"—although either description would suit the site at Headley, which is proposed as being near Olaf's camp. By "hazels" here, of course, reference would be to Hazel Wood, not the dubious "hazelled field".

Very important, to this discussion is the reading:
Skamt frá ánni var hæð mikil en á hæðinni tjollduðu men Aðalsteins konungs—"Not far from the stream was a big hill but on the hill tents were pitched by the men of King Athelstan".

Campbell claims that á *hæðinni*—"on the hill"—should read á *heiðinni*—"on the heath"—but, be he right or wrong, anyone looking at Camp Hill can see that it is indeed a hill on a heath near a stream (Openrakes Beck), while common sense dictates that any armed camp thereabouts would preferably be on it. As with anyone without a particular site in mind, the words of the saga would not allow Campbell to realise that there was a heath with a hill on it, but one can agree with him when he stated, "It is impossible, therefore, to agree with Neilson that the 'heath' is from the whole context a hill-top", (Campbell p69) for this writer too was concerned with demonstrating that there was a "hill" or a "heath", the terms being synonymous. The eminence in question may not seem to merit the description "big hill" judged by Icelandic standards, but what it lacks in height it makes up for in area.

The use of Norse *heiðr* with reference to Bramham Moor is found in Monk Hay Stile. Medieval spellings such as "Munek(e) heth" (1268), "Munkheyth" (1246), etc., indicate -*heiðr*, and indeed the name relates to Spen Farm and Common, as in "Munkehaithespen" (1240). The "Mun(e)k(e)" spellings suggest "monk", but any indicstion of monastic associations is elusive.

Athelstan's headquarters were at a *borg* to the south:
Borg þá, er var sunnan undir heiðinni
"the fort then, that was southwards under the heath".

"Under" here must be taken as meaning "at a lower elevation than" and the heath as being the whole upland area surrounding the courses of the Cock and Bramham Becks, to make it the original Whin Moor or *Vinheiðr*, which then allows this "borg" to be Castleford.

One can stand on Camp Hill and look over the level ground towards Headley and observe how, even today, this justifies:
Stóð konungs fylkinga viðlendit til árinnar, en þórólfs fylking fór et ofra með skóginum
"stood the king's battalion on the plain towards the stream, but Thorolf's battalion fared higher up by the woods".
Even today Hazel Wood fills the skyline to the east, with the land sweeping somewhat up to it.

When Adils drove after Alfgeir, south of the hill, he would have disappeared from the sight of Thorolf and his men. Having passed west of it on the old line of the A1 road through Aberford, his force would, to their discomfiture, reappear behind the Northmen and force them to fight with their backs to the wood.

It is not of course intended to imply here that Camp Hill got its name from having been Athelstan's camp, for the name presumably refers to the vanished earthworks of the more ancient "camp" on it, this word often being applied to such ancient enclosures. Even though the battleground is twice referred to as *campstede* (Campbell p94) in the Old English poem, one must still doubt that there has been preserved a folk-memory of the battle (or even battles) fought here (Old English *camp*—"battle") for this can in no way be proved. The same applies to seeing in Vinheidh and Whin Moor some reference to Old English *winnan*—"to fight"—unless it lay behind the choice of "-i-" or the shortening of it in Old English sources.

Is the claim that the period of three days allotted for riding to and fro between the two headquarters nonsense? The ride was not between the battle-camps, and the second day was set aside for discussion. One day's ride each way may seem reasonable enough if Athelstan was at Castleford and Olaf at Tadcaster, or even York. (Tadcaster to Castleford is at least 20 miles.) There seems little reason to doubt that Athelstan, faced by the huge forces at Olaf's disposal, tried to buy him off. One may, however, feel less certain that it was a deliberate ploy to play for time.

To recapitulate, the battlefield called Vinheidh in Egil's Saga can be identified as the Brunanburh of the Anglo-Saxon Chronicle, but neither name has left a clear impression on later nomenclature. Vinheidh can be taken as the whole upland area associated with the becks, but with the battleground itself being on the present Bramham Moor, while the original name has a reduced currency now as the present Whin Moor, an area north-east of Leeds.

Brunanburh was a hill on a heath with ancient earthworks and now known as Camp Hill. The name Brunanburh may have been a convenient West Saxon poetical form of Brunanwerc, the real name as recorded by Simeon, who also used the name Weondun or Wendun, perhaps for *Wīn-dūn*, which again may have been elliptical for "hill on *Wīn-hæth*", or the like. The present Wendel Hill, near Barwick-in-Elmet, a different feature, may have some relationship with the other "Win-" names. However, Ekwall derived *Wēondūne* (dative) from a nominative *Wēodūn*—"holy hill". (Ekwall p507) *Hæth-lēah* (now Headley) is a settlement on Bramham Moor. *Vín(u)skógar* refers to the woods by the River *Vína* in an Old Norse form. An English name for one nearby forest is (and long has been) Hazel Wood.

However, the ancient name for the Bramham and Openrakes Beck system may really have been *Wína* or the like in Old English, even if ultimately of British origin. An alternative English name for these woods would be *Wīn-wudu;* but this is not in direct evidence.

It can never have been a British or English custom to "hazel a field"—*hasla vǫll*—before a battle. Yet it might have been done with such as Arinbjörn, Thorolf and Egil in the advance camp. However, one feels that it could only have been worth while in the realisation that Olaf, in spite of what the saga says about him, was also a Northman, and not king of the Scots.

The Flight over *Dingesmere*

The poem in the A-SC dealing with Brunanburh describes how, after defeat, the Northmen fled to Dublin in their ships. They are said to have done so "on Dingesmere" and "over deep water". This referred to Olaf's army.

The problems of this passage have been much discussed. (See Cavill *et al.* pp25-38) The debate is largely about what *Dingesmere* means and where it was. There is no point in going over all the EPNS arguments again. As far as "Ding" is concerned it suffices to accept that this refers to Thingwall on the Wirral peninsula, Cheshire. However, the "mere" is a different matter. It might seem perfectly reasonable to accept this as Old English *mere* (now "mere, lake'") in senses stretching from "ocean" to "wetland", but it is this identification that leads to all the problems.

Identifying the feature is made much simpler is one rejects *mere* and takes the word to represent Old English *mære*—"boundary". The West Saxon poet may have been put off by not recognising the northern form of his own *gemære*—"boundary". In northern place-names *mære* is usually spelt "mer" in texts. This has created confusion. In some old spellings Westmorland appears as "Westmeringaland" rather than "Westmoringaland", thus implying "land of the folk of the west border" rather than "… folk west of the moors". Marton usually signifies the presence of a lake, but East and West Marton are on the Yorkshire-Lancashire border, thus suggesting *mære* rather than *mere*.

Thingwall is Old Norse *Thingvöllr*—"assembly plain"—and is centrally placed in the Wirral. Directly across the Mersey there is another Thingwall in Lancashire. The "things" at such places were jurisdictional centres of Scandinavian type. Over much of northern England the area covered by such a one would be called a wapentake. The two things here are separated by a very old and important boundary, the estuary of the Mersey. This name itself represents Old English *mæres-ēa*—"river of (the) border"—once serving as the boundary between Northumbria and Mercia, but later between Lancashire and Cheshire.

It can hence be asserted that Dinges-mere was a poetical name for the Mersey and carried the sense "thing's boundary". The EPNS article points out that the poem's *on Dingesmere, ofer deop wæter* includes a convention of Old English verse. In this the same feature is usually referred to twice, so that "on Dingesmere, over deep water" is all about the Mersey, especially the estuary. It is then clear that Olaf had to come back here to escape because this shore was where he had left his invasion fleet.

The one point obviously requiring attention is that found on the Mersey shoreline and quite close to Thingwall is Bromborough. The argument that this could not be the site of the Battle of Brunanburh has already been made above and later will be taken further. So why does a candidate for the battlefield appear to be on the Wirral? The confusion must have arisen in the mind of the poet. An event may have occurred to cause this. Egil's Saga relates how Olaf was confronted by the Northumbrian earls Godrek and Alfgeir. That this encounter took place at the main battlefield is an assumption. One might rather claim that the earls tried to stop Olaf at his beachhead (at Bromborough?), but failed disastrously. Bromborough has never included "Brun", but may have suggested the otherwise vague name Brunanburh.

Chapter 6

Erik in England

After succeeding Athelstan in 939, Eadmund found that Olaf Sigtrygsson was intent on exploiting the perceived weakness of the English realm and had taken to the warpath. He had already subdued Northumbria and now was heading south to face Eadmund in the Midlands. It would seem that the men of Yorkshire had willingly accepted him as their king, despite pledges to the English ruler. He stormed and sacked Tamworth, but was finally besieged by Eadmund in Leicester.

> There is an Icelandic saga claim that Eadmund wanted to replace Erik by "Olaf", with this being associated with Erik meeting his death in battle. (Holtsmark p.84) Yet this cannot be true, since it is as certain as one ever can be that Erik fell later, during the reign of Eadred. Still, any reference to "Eadmund", whether correct or not, must relate to Erik having a period of rule in Northumbria in the years following Athelstan's death, although hardly in 939-40 as discussed and rejected below. There are however problems. If Erik were indeed king for a while so early on, under what circumstances did he get to York at that time and why did he then soon leave?

A meeting between a certain "Erich" and St. Catroe has been used to support the claim that Erik ruled twice in York. (Woolf pp.189-93; Wood pp.457-58; Stanton p.361 n. 2) The argument accepts a revised chronology within Eadred's reign (as proposed by Sawyer, see below), but maintains that Erik had ruled previously in York, namely well before Eadred's accession. This is based on an account in the "Life of St. Catroe" in which the saint is conducted to Erich at York in the reign of King Eadmund, i.e. 939-46. Erich's wife is said to have been a kinswoman of the British saint. From a review of the sources the conclusion is reached for a "window of opportunity" to exist that would allow King Erik to have received St. Catroe between late October 939 and Spring 940.

Certainly in the weakness immediately following Athelstan's death it might seem credible that Erik was able to seize power in York (having perhaps earlier established himself near the Solway), although soon to be replaced by an Olaf. Yet, while there seems to be no reason to doubt that Erik had two reigns in York, and without denying that Catroe visited a Northumbrian king about this time, reasons are given below for Erich to be regarded as a misnomer. The following arguments lead one to discount any date for Erik in Northumbria as early as suggested above.

The Battle of Vinheidh in Egil's Saga (Egla) has every indication of being the same action as Athelstan's victory known as Brunanburh. According to Egla, Egil (whose brother Thorolf had fallen there) reluctantly parted from "Athelstan" the next year, while suggesting he might be coming back. He went to Norway that summer and visited his friend Arinbjörn. That was in 938. Having married Asgerdh, his brother's widow and having been warned against staying in Norway because of the power there of Gunnhild, Erik's queen, he made preparations the next spring and reached the family home at Borg in Iceland by autumn 939. He is said to have stayed there for several years. This would make it impossible for him to have found Erik in York in that same winter as St. Catroe came there, i.e. 939-40, or for some time later.

The saga's "several years" hence creates difficulties. Could it be so wrong? Yet even with a short stay in Iceland Egil could not have reached York by the spring of 940 to meet Erik there and then. But still, could Erik even have been installed there so early and remained long enough for Egil to have visited him at a later date? Well, it is not just that the years do not add up, but there are far too many events to the contrary and to squeeze into too little time. To this effect one can note most conclusively that Hakon did not leave England till 944 and that it is only thereafter that he drove Erik from the Norway that up till then had absorbed all his energies.

So in 927 Egil Skallagrimsson had sailed to Norway and then made his way back to Iceland in 939 after 12 years abroad. He spent that first winter at Borg, along with his father Skallagrim and Thorfinn Strangi.

In order finally to reject any idea of a meeting between Catroe and Erik it is necessary to dispose of the mentioned Erich; this name is the only reason for allowing the event. The secure date here is that of the Battle of Brunanburh, i.e. 937. After it Egil visited Norway twice, involving several years, and the second time confronted Erik Bloodaxe who was king there; this alone makes it difficult for Erik to fit in with the chronology of Catroe's visit to York. This improbability becomes an impossibility when Hakon's intervention and Erik's departure for the Orkney's are considered. Erich may have been a misconception and added orally and retrospectively from the misplaced use of the later situation: "King? The king there is called Erik".

Now Erik proper is said to have replaced an "Olaf" as king in York, who is much more likely to have had a wife related to Catroe. Probability demands that it was Olaf Cuaran who received the saint.

Such an early event involving Erik hence will not work. He can be discounted until at least 944, when Eadmund drove Olaf Sigtrygsson and Reynold Gudhfridhsson out of Northumbria and took over the rule himself. (Garmonsway pp. 110-11) William of Malmesbury suggests that Reynold was the son of Gurmund (*Gudhormr*, who Alfred defeated and made king of East Anglia after accepting conversion). This seems unlikely in view of other sources and the time gap, even though Guthrum's comrade Halfdan was the first Scandinavian king in Northumbria. Otherwise, was this Reynold (Guthrumson?) the one who descended on Northumbria c914 and made himself king in York in 919 (and soon to be succeeded by Sigtryg Gali)? It is best to assume provisionally that Guthrum is irrelevant to the contemporary history of Northumbria and that Malmesbury's "Gurmund" is corrupt and has been confused with "Gudhfridh". (Stephenson p. 116)

The problems of the period immediately after the accession of Eadred can be viewed from two different standpoints, namely from that of the West Saxon dynasty (English) or from that of the contemporary Northumbrian one (Norwegian).

The reigns of both Athelstan and Eadmund illustrate how they had great difficulty at times in keeping control of Northumbria. Was the same true of the third brother Eadred?

The Anglo-Saxon "D" Chronicle need hardly be doubted in any detail when it states that Eadred came to Tanshelf (near Pontefract). He had summoned Wulfstan and the councillors of the Northumbrians there to receive their pledges. Yet no sooner had he departed than they were false to their oaths; they maintained their support of Erik "Bloodaxe" Haraldsson and took him as their king. So in 948 Eadred mounted a punitive expedition which by-passed York and culminated in the burning down of Ripon cathedral, which was found to the west of Dere Street and well to the north. This was clearly meant to hit Wulfstan where it hurt. It would seem that Eadred at this stage feared for his safety and did not feel up to a direct confrontation with Erik and his hardened warriors. Such fears were justified, for the action provoked the army in York into coming out to attack and eliminate Eadred's rearguard troops stationed at the Aire crossing at Castleford, just north of Pontefract. Being forced to withdraw to the south, wrathful Eadred threatened to return and devastate Northumbria the next year. (Garmonsway p.113; Stephenson p.89; Holtsmark p.84) The Northumbrians took this message seriously; they abandoned Erik.

Archbishop Wulfstan resented the prospect of Northumbria being ruled by a southern king. His aspirations presumably involved the establishment of an Anglo-Norse kingdom based on the Danelaw and with its capital at York. His vision would then include an archbishopric based on that city and less subservient to Canterbury. In 943 he had been present at Leicester when "Anlaf" (i.e. Olaf Sigtrygsson) was besieged by Eadmund. But they came to an agreement and Eadmund stood sponsorship for both him and Rögnvald Gudhfridhsson at baptism. After this Olaf and Rögnvald appear to have temporarily become joint or rival kings in Northumbria. Whatever their views of each other they apparently jointly denied overlordship to Eadmund, so he must come and drive them out of York in 944. Their ensuing absence left a vacuum in the north, a gap that Erik could easily slip into.

Eadmund died in 946, but Erik did not intend to acknowledge his brother Eadred as his overlord. The subsequent raid and deliberate burning of Ripon cathedral must be seen as a dire warning to Wulfstan to toe the line and advise Erik to yield to Eadred's demands. Erik would have none of this and made his sortie out of York. But he had gone too far and the nervous Northumbrians withdrew their support. This allowed Olaf back in with Eadred's approval and Wulfstan's compliance. The Anglo-Saxon Chronicle dates this as 949, yet it seems that there were three entries that should all have been for 947, but were spread over to 948 and 949 because these two subsequent years were otherwise without entries.

Simeon of Durham chronicled Erik's confirmation as king in Northumbria thus:

A.D. 949. Wlstan, archbishop of York, and all the Northumbrian nobles swore fealty to Edred, the illustrious king of the Angles at the vill called Taddena's-cliff; but they did not keep it long, for they placed over them as king a certain man of Danish extraction, named Eyric.

The spelling used reflects the Old Norse form *Eirikr*. "Taddena's-cliff" is erroneous, being really Tanshelf—*Taddenes-scylf*. The date illustrates the two year time slip and should be 947. (Stephenson 1987 p, 90)

Wulfstan and his council appear to have been convinced that Eadred could and would fulfil his threat. Eadred may thus have been put to the test soon after becoming king and eventually, like his predecessor Eadmund, gained some control by playing one pretender to the Northumbrian throne off against the other, although with reversed preference. Olaf will thus have taken Erik's place with Eadred's consent, but no earlier than 948. He may have been more tolerant of Olaf's presence in York seeing as Sigtrygsson was already a convert to Christianity. He had indeed been sponsored at baptism by King Eadmund, but perhaps more importantly he was showing a readiness to accept the role of under-king to Eadred.

However, according to an amended chronology, Olaf had already been allowed to return to Northumbria in 947 as a sub-king of Eadred, The last point can hardly be totally correct. He may indeed have returned to the north of England then, but there is no mention of him being accepted as king by the Northumbrians at this stage. His subservience to Eadred would not be to Wulfstan's liking, so persuasion, first by word and then by threat from the English king was required to persuade the prelate. Yet not being initially strong enough to take on Erik alone, Olaf lurked and plotted—probably in north-west England—until the opportunity arose in 948 officially to succeed the departing Erik.

That King Eadred arranged to meet the Northumbrians of Yorkshire at Tanshelf seems to imply that he was accepting (yet insisting) that the Aire was now the northern limit of his direct rule and indeed the incidence of Nordic place-names is much less in the county south of this river. This would be accepted only under duress by the Anglo-Scandinavian northerners, and it seems only to be expected that they would look for and find some strong leader who could assert their rights both to full independence and to the traditional border of Northumbria being further to the south. Such a man had previously been put in place by Eadmund—Erik Bloodaxe—an ambitious would-be king still looking for a decent realm to call his own. Among his fighting men was an initially loyal kernel from Norway, including Arinbjörn Hersi.

The reasons for the apparently quiet departure of a formidable warlord like Erik because Eadred had made threats may not seem absolutely clear. There would certainly be factions in Northumbria who would want him out and, despite his successful defiance of Eadred, significant ones probably withdrew their support as a matter of expediency in the face of Eadred's hostility. This may have fostered doubt or even dissent among the ranks of his own men, including those led by Arinbjörn. Olaf was also still lurking as a considerable threat. As happened in Norway, Erik was not one to fight for a crown when the odds were stacked overwhelmingly against him. Whatever else he was, he was a survivor.

Eadred may have thought he had solved the Northumbrian problem, with himself established as king of the whole Anglo-Saxon realm. But the Northumbrians still had other ideas; as always they were reluctant to be ruled by any king from south of the Humber. That persistent Irish-Norse pretender from Dublin, Olaf Sigtrygsson, came back, made himself available and would seem eventually to have been imposed on the Northumbrians. He seems to have departed quite soon, namely when Erik returned, this time clearly with sufficient support, political as well as military, to reclaim his Northumbrian throne.

The timing of these events from 946 to 954 is very difficult and some of the Anglo-Saxon Chronicle dates must be held to be dubious. A time slip has been suggested so that some dates should be taken back two years. (Sawyer pp. 39-44) Apart from the documentary arguments this revised chronology does make more sense. It seems highly unlikely that when Eadred came to the throne in 946 he would take three years to remove Erik "the over-ambitious" and replace him with the favoured Olaf. Erik appears to have been reasonably content as an under-king of Eadmund, but the reported remarks of Queen Gunnhild in Egil's Saga indicate that she had become far from happy, although this may reflect the situation soon after Eadmund's death.

Chapter 7

Erik and Egil at York

In the previous Chapter the period of Erik's first rule in York was examined as it is covered by the English records. This can be compared with the Scandinavian accounts, namely the same and other contemporary events as they have featured in Icelandic sagas.

Hakon the Good's Saga is quite in error when it states that Erik was invited by King "Athelstan" to the Northumbrian throne. It is probably correct, however, in claiming that Erik and Gunnhild, once installed, let themselves be baptised by a bishop. This would certainly be a condition for support by the Northumbrian and English establishments. The (Arch)bishop was Wulfstan, who was the leader of the Northumbrian delegation at Tanshelf. It is also near the truth when it states that Eadmund (actually Eadred) did not like Northmen, was antagonistic towards King Erik and wanted to set another "chief over Northumberland", and also that he eventually appointed someone called Olaf as "warden" there. Eadred must have favoured Olaf Sigtrygsson, who was apparently more pliable and whose ambitions would be restricted to Northumbria, whereas Erik thought of himself as a king on a par with his father Harald and hence posed a threat to the English crown itself. The first punitive expedition did not work, although Eadred (probably with too small an army and surprised and worried by the mettle, if not the magnitude of Erik's troops) managed to take the drastic step of burning down Ripon Cathedral as a warning to Archbishop Wulfstan. He clearly did not subdue York and the troop that came out of there would be sent or led by Erik and slaughtered the force left by Eadred to guard the Aire crossing near Tanshelf.

Sometime during Erik's rule he received a visit from someone he would hardly have expected to seek him out at his court. At York Erik had as his queen his wife Gunnhild, while one of his closest henchmen there was Arinbjörn Hersi, his foster brother, who had left

Norway with him. The visitor was Egil Skallagrimsson, who had been Arinbjörn's best friend, but Eriks declared enemy.

In Iceland Egil had spent two winters at Borg after his father's death, but was feeling ever more disgruntled with his lot. The unsatisfactory manner of his last departure from Norway was clearly bothering him and it so happened that during the summer in which Erik and Hakon were disputing Norway a ban had been put on ships going to Iceland. This action would have an impoverishing effect on the island, as well as restricting the passing on of news. Icelanders at the time were not welcome in Norway, but they could sail to other shores, the most convenient being those of the British Isles. The next summer he could bear it no longer and got a ship ready with the intention of sailing to England to see Athelstan - although this king was in reality long dead - to remind him of the promises he had made after the Battle of Vinheidh. He left his wife Asgerdh behind to run the farm.

> Here can be seen the continuation of the myth embodied in Egla that Egil had a special relationship with "Athelstan". Henceforth all tales of Egil continued to be modified in order to preserve this untruth, no matter at what cost to the real story,

However, it was said that Gunnhild had worked a spell against Egil, making it impossible for him to live in peace in Iceland until he had come to her so that she could look upon him.

> This can be interpreted as the saga man's way of suggesting that there had been some communication between Borg and York. The implication is that Egil knew full well that Arinbjörn was at York with Erik.

Coming to the Orkneys from the north, Egil and his crew of thirty made no landfall there, but sailed past for fear of Erik's power in these and other isles. They sailed down the east coast of Scotland and northern England, buffeted by the winds. Eventually they were shipwrecked in the Humber estuary; the ship was lost, but all men and most of the cargo were saved. Egil learned that they had come ashore in the realm where Erik and Gunnhild were installed close by, namely in the borough called York, and that Arinbjörn Hersi was there too, who was well thought of by the king. Egil considered his chances of escape from his predicament to be meagre; in any case, to be taken in flight was the hallmark of the "little man". Obtaining a horse, he rode alone to York, reaching it that evening and then sought out his friend. The crew was left with the ship to guard its cargo.

The saga account makes out as though Egil was surprised to discover that he was stranded where Erik ruled and that Arinbjörn was with him. This can hardly be true. The shipwreck had forced pretence of a different destination. Yet his intention may have been boldly to contact Arinbjörn, but the plan had to be changed due to that mishap in the Humber. In the event he would appear to be stranded since it seems evident that his friend was initially unable to provide him with a replacement ship and a humiliating confrontation with Erik became inevitable, especially since the latter became aware of Egil's presence. It seems certain that Egil's visit was during Erik's first period of rule in York. Could it really be the case that Egil was trying to reach the south of England with goods? If he had known about Athelstan's death, he would have expected to find Eadmund enthroned; but had this ruler yet met his untimely end? Egil's Saga states that "Athelstan" gathered an army to meet Erik (Pålsson 1976 p151). But this must refer to Eadred and the events described above,

Whatever foreknowledge Egil had, he would now be faced by the truth of Athelstan's death. While that king had been able to get on with Northmen, Eadmund may have been tolerant towards them, although Hakon's Saga says he did not like them; here Eadred is certainly meant. There is clear cause to believe that two years after Erik was installed in York, Eadmund was murdered and replaced by Eadred, who objected to the arrangement made with Erik. His hostility was justified by Erik having himself declared king and backing it up by conversion to Christianity. By the 10th century it was not possible to be widely accepted in Europe as a rightful king without accepting the faith. One can perceive in Eadred's burning down of Ripon Cathedral and the eventual imprisonment of Archbishop Wulfstan tokens of his rage because Erik, a Christian of convenience, claimed to be a king of equal standing to himself, even in the eyes of God,

Arinbjörn and his men armed themselves and together they all made for the king's quarters. Twelve went in to see Erik, including Egil and Arinbjörn. The latter made a conciliatory speech on Egil's behalf. The king, however, was amazed that Egil had dared to come into his presence after what he had done in Norway. Being in dire straits, the big Icelander rather uncharacteristically clasped the king's foot and recited an appeasing verse. Erik reminded him of his crimes against the royal kin, anyone of which should warrant his death.

Gunnhild proceeded to emphasise to Erik the kin and friends that Egil had butchered and demanded that he should be executed, and immediately; no one should be allowed to injure a king thus and get away with it. But Arinbjörn again spoke up for Egil and suggested that if he had in the past spoken ill of King Erik, he could make up for it now by extolling his many excellent qualities. The inexorable Gunnhild would have none of this, insisting that her husband take Egil outside at once to hack him down. Arinbjörn made reply to this by warning the king against being swayed by such dastardly advice, because such "night-slaying" could be deemed as nothing short of murder. Erik typically deferred decision until the morrow.

Thanking the king, Arinbjörn tried to make further capital for Egil by reminding Erik of how his father Harald came to take the life of Egil's uncle, Thorolf, through listening to the falsehoods of evil men. Furthermore, Erik himself had broken the law when acting against Egil for the benefit of Bergönund and had since continued to persecute him.

The confrontation in York gives an insight into conflicting loyalties. Arinbjörn was torn between the loyalty he owed to his overlord Erik and his friend Egil. Erik was torn between the deference he apparently must show to the views of his wife Gunnhild and the stance of his lieutenant Arinbjörn. Her continual presence at court and her influence over Erik's decision-making was quite extraordinary and must have added fuel to the flames of her reputation for exerting witchcraft over him. In spite of all his faults, there is no cause to think of Erik as an absolute brute; although a war leader, it might seem that he had no stomach for cutting down a man in cold blood, unlike Gunnhild, who was all for it. This was apart from the prospect of falling out with Arinbjörn, which would itself be disastrous. Gunnhild was so incensed against Egil that she seems to have been quite oblivious of such a quarrel making their position in York even more precarious than it already was. It is easy to see that Erik, though furious that Egil had arrived, wished above all that he would go, and grasped at an excuse to let this happen. Hence the long and immensely flattering poem by Egil. One gets the feeling that Erik was so desperate for support that Arinbjörn had believed that Egil could patch up his quarrel with him, given the right approach: if so, such aspirations were soon dispelled by Gunnhild. Egil's intention had almost certainly been to repair his relationship with Erik sufficiently that he could at least feel secure enough to join Arinbjörn's household in York. This would mean ultimately that he had been accepted into Erik's service.

The party left the royal presence and returned to Arinbjörn's lodge, the host telling his guest that he believed the king had softened his attitude towards him and, if he were to compose a poem of twenty verses, it might save his head, for thus had a kinsman of Arinbjörn retained his under similar circumstances. Egil, a poet of ability, agreed to try; so he went and sat alone in a loft. Arinbjörn drank with the others until midnight, then went up to the loft to enquire how the composition was going. Egil had in fact been unable to start on the poem because of the twittering of a swallow outside the window that was distracting him. Arinbjörn therefore decided to sit out the night outside that window and in doing so at one time noticed a form drift away from the house. One would presume that this was supposed to be Gunnhild, exercising her sorcery.

It is of interest that Egil sat up the night in a building with an upper storey and a window. The distracting twittering outside the window is quite feasible if house martins were nesting there. These details have only been recorded in the saga to provide an example of Gunnhild's dabbling in sorcery. One can discount the "shape" that left the scene as the product of an overactive imagination, to be placed in the same category as Gunnhild's casting of a spell to lure Egil to York. The confrontation will not have taken place in the industrial zone down by the River Foss, where the York Viking Centre now exists in Coppergate. Erik was installed at the *Konungs-garðr*—"king's enclosure". (Gordon 1927 p108) This was perhaps a reference to part of the remains of the large Roman legionary fortress at York which lay in the northern angle of the later medieval walled city. It more probably was a reference to Erik's seat, a surviving edifice where he held his court. One can compare examples like Danish *herregård,* meaning "stately home", without "enclosure" necessarily being inferable. Perhaps Arinbjörn had quarters at one of the gate-houses in the wall, where the possibility of an upper chamber with window visible from outside would exist, in a manner that cannot be envisaged with contemporary vernacular buildings. This suggests that Erik was probably stationed at another gateway, with guards ready at all four gate-houses, a sensible arrangement one would think, (Ref, discussion on York in Viking times, App, 4 and Photos, 38 to 42, App, 5)

Appendix 4 of this work strays exceedingly beyond the immediate time-span of Erik Bloodaxe's presence in York, but is intended to paint a rather broader and clearer picture of the period into which he fitted than at present available. While the accompanying discussion does not enable one to pin-point the building with an upper storey occupied by Arinbjörn, it allows one to propose that the Northmen under arms in Erik's time occupied the decaying Roman defences. With Erik presumably installed in the King's Square gate-house, Arinbjörn would be in one of the other three. One can perceive that in the early Medieval Period, without bridges over the Ouse or even the Foss, York would lie somewhat isolated from all folk without boats, except from the north and north-west, This is then of interest with regard to the arrival of Egil Skallagrimsson on horseback. Both rivers would be much wider at York than they are at present, and he probably had to cross the Foss further upstream, perhaps even as far north as Huntington.

The morning after the night Egil spent composing his poem, Erik was at table with his men when Arinbjörn and his followers arrived. He and Egil went in with half the men, while the rest stayed outside. Arinbjörn addressed the king on Egil's behalf, pointing out how he himself had stayed with and supported Erik when others had forsaken him, even to the extent of abandoning his own lands, kinfolk and friends in Norway. Arinbjörn had apparently supported Erik against Hakon and they had left the realm together.

It was Gunnhild who then made reply, claiming that her husband had amply repaid Arinbjörn for his support and that his duty clearly lay with the king, rather than someone like Egil. After what had been done, he should not presume to ask that Egil get away unpunished. Since it now appeared that the king, as well as the queen, was becoming irreconcilable, Arinbjörn besought at least that Egil be given a week's grace, with safe conduct out of Erik's realm, since after all, he had come there of his own free will. Gunnhild then turned on Arinbjörn and accused him directly of favouring Egil above the king. Given a week, Egil would reach King Athelstan and Erik was fully aware that as far as kings went, he was now a lowly example. Not so long ago no-one would have expected King Erik to hesitate to take vengeance on the likes of Egil.

Arinbjörn countered by pointing out that there would be no honour in Erik slaying a mere farmer's son, an expatriate who had quite voluntarily given himself up. But if he insisted on achieving "greatness" in this manner, Arinbjörn would see to it that the deed would be worth retelling, for he was going to stand by Egil, whose life would be bought dearly over the bodies of Arinbjörn himself and his men. Well, Erik was indeed loathe to fight with his henchman, yet claimed cause enough against Egil. So, in the end, Egil did come to recite his poem, which heaped praise on Erik as a warrior (but with no mention of an axe, bloody or otherwise). Whether the flattery worked, or simply gave Erik the excuse he needed to back down, Egil won his freedom thereby. But Erik still made his customary parting threat, that he should not show his face again; or else! One can understand it as a mere reprieve, for the blood feud between Egil and Erik was clearly still unresolved.

Arinbjörn and Egil left York on horseback, together with "a hundred and twenty" other riders, and came to Athelstan, the English King, by whom they were welcomed. He enquired about the encounter with Erik and invited Egil to stay. Before he parted from Arinbjörn, Egil presented his friend with the two rings given to him by Athelstan after the death of his brother Thorolf at Vinheidh. In return Arinbjörn gave Egil a sword that had once belonged to Thorolf Skallagrimsson and was glorified by the name *Dragvandill*. It had been passed down through other leading members of the kin. Arinbjörn then returned to Erik in York. Under his auspices Egil's crew, who had been left in the north, were able to sell the salvaged cargo and that winter rejoined their leader in the south of England.

It was quite impossible for Egil to go south to see "Athelstan"; he had been dead for a number of years. He may of course have sought out one of his successors, either Eadmund or Eadred. But one can well imagine them asking "Egil who?" The most fruitful view is that he did nothing of the sort: The offered reason for the journey was intended to further the myth of Egil's supposed special relationship with Athelstan. This does not discount that a journey was made and that he was in the company of Arinbjörn and his troop. If so, what was going on? The size of the troop is ridiculous as an escort for Egil. It seems far more likely that Arinbjörn had cause to ride out of York and that Egil went with him.

It would seem that Egil arrived in York just when Erik and Gunnhild were faced with difficult circumstances, while Arinbjörn's loyalty was being severely tested by the deteriorating situation and Gunnhild's attitude towards him. This was the period when King Eadmund was murdered, his succeeding brother Eadred had marched north and burnt down Ripon Cathedral and Erik's army sortied from York to destroy the English King's border guard at Castleford. Egil's arrival not only increased the deep seated tensions between Arinbjörn and Gunnhild, but also caused a clear rift between Erik and his henchman. Gunnhild's remarks suggest that the current English king was hostile, so Eadred can be inferred.

The possibility then arises that Egil's ride with Arinbjörn was actually coincidental with the raid on Castleford. If so an important skirmish has been suppressed simply to preserve the "Athelstan" myth. Yet it seems very unlikely that the saga would ignore Egil's participation in such an encounter. Furthermore, one would expect that Erik himself would have been in command. The preferred solution here is that "Athelstan" and "Arinbjörn" have been confused and it was indeed the latter who offered to Egil the chance to stay in England as a member of his army. Events indicate that Arinbjörn had his own following of armed men, quite separate from those of Erik. Far from riding to the south of England, they had left York to stay at some place where Arinbjörn was at home and where Egil could be kept safe. The confrontation in York had clearly exacerbated existing differences between Arinbjörn and Gunnhild, which was even putting his relationship with Erik at risk. They were all under stress because of the rage and hostility of King Eadred after the Castleford raid and the supposed consequent dwindling support of the Northumbrian council, Arinbjörn probably left York to cool off, and eventually returned. In the meantime he had arranged for the sale of

Egil's cargo. After this the crew could rejoin their leader, but not in "the south of England"; a location in the south of Northumbria is far more likely to be true. So for the time being Egil and his companions sojourned at Arinbjörn's English country seat.

In the previous autumn news had reached England from Norway that a certain Eirik Alspak, a landowner in the Vik (around the Oslo Fjord), had died and his estates had been seized by King Hakon's bailiffs. This Eirik had once been married to Thora, daughter of Thori Hersi and sister of Arinbjörn and they had a son called Thorstein Thoruson. He, having been fostered with his uncle Arinbjörn, came to England with him. The time was ripe for him to return to Norway, so in the spring he went south to Athelstan in London. Because of his association with Arinbjörn and Egil, Athelstan was well disposed to intercede with Hakon on his behalf. At the same time Egil announced that he too would return to Norway to see to the land he had been robbed of by King Erik and Bergönund and now in the possession of Atli, the latter's brother. Thorstein too sought support from Athelstan in his affairs. The king expressed preference that Egil stay with him to be warden of his land and leader of his army, which would be a lucrative occupation. While Egil appreciated the offer, he explained that first he must return to Iceland to look to his wife and estates there.

Athelstan gave Egil a good merchantman furnished with ample cargo, among it wheat and honey. Thorstein Thoruson joined him and together they set sail for Norway, with Egil and Athelstan taking leave of each other in great amity. The voyagers had reached the Vik and Thorstein went north into the hinterland where his inheritance lay. He disputed his case with the king's bailiffs and found support among the local people, among whom he had many kinsmen. The upshot was that he gained possession, though not exactly full right of ownership. Egil and a company of twelve then joined him there, taking along wheat and honey. The pair spent a pleasant winter together.

Here again the history can be worked out by assuming a confusion of "Arinbjörn" with "Athelstan". This being true, it was indeed Arinbjörn who had at first offered to Egil the chance to join him, but then had provided him with a ship. That Egil could have asked his friend to intercede with Hakon on his behalf then suggests that Arinbjörn had even already been tempted to desert Erik and also return to Norway. (This last was something that Erik certainly could not do.) Instead of Thorstein going south to visit Athelstan in London one can deduce that he went south from York to visit Arinbjörn at his seat. Even the mention of "London" is suspicious. While it was a place of growing commercial importance, London was certainly not the capital of the West Saxon dynasty. As it happens, about half way between York and Brough-on-Humber there is a village called Londesborough. Brough was the site of a Roman fort on the north bank. Just north of there the Roman road forked to provide routes to either York or Malton. The latter route followed the edge of the Wolds. The former is at lower level to the west. Londesborough lies on the higher route and hence was in a good position to guard one road and oversee the other. Hence one can propose that Londesborough is the "London" of the saga, whilst also laying claim to it being Arinbjörn's seat.

Whether Londesborough has an earlier history is uncertain, but in its modern form the place-name is Norse. *Loðins-borg*—"fort of Lodhen"—with the personal name being a Nordic nickname meaning "hairy". In modern Danish the adjective *lodden* means "covered with thick hair". The prospect then looms that the "Lodhen" of the name actually was Arinbjörn Hersi. This would then indicate, either that he was exceptionally hairy, or that the nickname reflected the "bear" *(björn)* in his name, with this being reinforced by a pun on the unfamiliar Norwegian title *hersi* (not to mention Latin *hirsutus*). The likelihood is that the nickname was applied by Danes. If the proposition is just, then one can further assume that Londesborough was the seat of his personal estate, from where he could keep an eye on the southern frontier of Erik's Northumbria, i.e. the shore of the Humber. Londesborough Park still exists attached to the east. To the north-east there is Londesborough Wold in the area where once was a lost place-name "lothenhaues, lodhenhawes" lying on the boundaries of Londesborough and Middleton on the Wolds. The "-a-" suggests that "howes" (i.e., burial mounds) were not involved, but rather that the name marks a pass. It would involve the same element as found in Hawes, Wensleydale, namely Old Norse *háls*.

Since Erik and Gunnhild were no longer in Norway, Egil could take advantage of the opportunity to return there in order to take care of his unfinished business. However, he was going to claim the support of his friend Arinbjörn, who had left Norway with Erik, but without actually taking part in hostilities towards Hakon. He apparently decided not to leave England with Egil and Thorstein, choosing instead to stay with Erik for the time being. However, Arinbjörn did eventually make his way separately to Norway, i.e. to his home in The Westland. As for Egil, the salvaged cargo from the Humber had no doubt eased the provision of a seaworthy ship and a cargo of exotic English goods for him and his companions, including flour and honey.

Other points can be added. An initial attempt could well have been made by Arinbjörn to recruit Egil and his party, which some of them may have accepted. This would be in view of Erik's precarious position in Northumbria. Eadred would be showing clear signs of reversing the policies of his brother, e.g. in favouring Olaf Sigtrygsson, who Eadmund had driven out. In the same way one can perceive that Eadred wanted to get rid of Erik, who, it is claimed here, had been favoured by his brother. Arinbjörn was caught up in all this and, after witnessing Gunnhild's attitude towards Egil and indeed himself, may have been sorely tempted to part from Erik. Yet if he did rejoin him in York, his staying with Erik may have been facilitated by Erik's departure from Northumbria and seeking adventure elsewhere—in a man's world, without Gunnhild. Apart from having little choice, this was the Viking life-style that would appeal to Arinbjörn, especially as it held promise of replenishing his own fortune. Well, the relationship between Erik and Arinbjörn had been damaged and at some point the latter broke away and returned to Norway.

There may indeed have been some truth in the English claim that Erik left his kingdom because the Northumbrian's abandoned him due to Eadred's threats. On the other hand Erik may have had no choice, because his position had been weakened by threatened defection among his own folk, including Arinbjörn.

The saga details of the whole York encounter would seem to have been embellished for effect, namely to salvage Egil's reputation from what otherwise had been a totally humiliating experience. Gunnhild may well have been much more hostile to Egil than was Erik, but the dialogue—even allowing for Egil having a prodigious poet's memory—must to some extent be paraphrase. It was designed to illustrate her prolonged irrational and implacable hatred of him and the portrayal was furthered by persistent references to her use of sorcery. In the same tampering vein the saga contributor (probably Egil himself) was intent on enhancing the hero's prowess and competence and especially to emphasise and perpetuate his claimed (yet spurious) special relationship with Athelstan.

The details of the journey to York can be seen in this light. Seeing as he left Iceland late in the year, one can well believe that the going was stormy. He avoided landfall on the Orkneys because he was apparently aware that they had fallen to Erik Bloodaxe. The fact that Egil happened to enter the Humber does suggest that he had acquired foreknowledge that Erik was established in York and that Arinbjörn was his man there. It may have been awareness of his friend's presence that drew him to risk landfall near the Humber. Otherwise his shipwreck in that estuary was a strange coincidence; the story of him being unwillingly blown in and deliberately grounding his ship could have been invented as a travesty of the truth, because Egil could not abide his seamanship appearing to be wanting, The certainty is that without his ship he was "sunk" in another sense and badly in need of help and protection for both himself and his goods.

When Egil was first shipwrecked he is said to have obtained a horse and reached York that evening. The distance and unfamiliarity with the route is against this being possible. More feasible is that Erik first walked to Londesborough, where Arinbjörn had his seat. Except for the loss of his ship, it would seem unlikely that Egil would have needed to go to York. The visit there was specifically to admit Egil's presence and get Erik's approval for Egil to join and remain with Arinbjörn's troop. Gunnhild put a stop to this, even though Erik could have done with another good man.

If the "twittering swallow" story can be relied on, then Egil had already spent the winter somewhere before risking a visit to York. One would presume that this had been at Londesborough with Arinbjörn and it was here that he was eventually provided with a riding horse. Arinbjörn was apparently anxious that he arrive discreetly, for he asked him if anyone in the city had recognised him. It is hence not true that Egil sought service with any English king, but most certain is that Erik outlawed him, so that getting out of York under protection and finding permanent refuge became imperative. The fact that Thorstein Thoruson wanted to return to Norway seems to have offered an escape route. The date suggested for Egil'ns visit to York is 947.

Egil was presumably helped to acquire a ship from the proceeds of his cargo. Yet how could he have collected a cargo in Iceland that would have attracted buyers in England? Seal skins may have featured, but otherwise its mainstay must have been the loot he obtained at the time he killed Bergönund, with weapons probably featuring largely among this gear. The reason he had felt obliged to risk the journey from Iceland was nothing to do with Gunnhild's magic, but everything to do with Egil being impoverished and sitting on unsentimental trophies and goods that were of no use to him at home. He simply had to go and seek his fortune abroad once his father died, the latter having just maliciously and untraceably hidden his own considerable wealth in a bog. There would seem little doubt that Egil's cargo would have found a ready market in York, while Arinbjörn might well have been glad of any weaponry.

Erik's fortunes had changed for the worse with the death of Eadmund. He probably initially saw it as an opportunity to further his ambitions in England. But then Eadred succeeded and wanted him out. After this king had been severely provoked, the Northumbrians promised to withdraw their support of Erik, but did not; the new king must insist.

Egil eventually returned to Iceland. Erik's next movements become more obscure. He apparently departed from York without a struggle. It would seem that he no longer had the proper means to maintain himself there. He would only have been able to remain with the support of the "Northumbrians" of whom Archbishop Wulfstan was the leader. This prelate gives the impression of being a northern patriot who wanted a Northumbrian state independent of that ruled by the Wessex dynasty and, one presumes, with the archbishopric of York being of a status nearer to that of Canterbury, It was presumably Erik's direct descent from the royal house of Norway and his royal Danish connections that originally caused him to be considered by the Northumbrians to be a more suitable candidate to wear this crown than any Irish-Norse member of some other kin, such as that of Ragnar

Chapter 8

Egil Skallagrimsson's Return to Norway

By simply returning to Norway, Egil Skallagrimsson achieved something that his arch-enemy Erik Bloodaxe was never to manage again. However, the effects of his relationships with Erik, Gunnhild, their kin and their friends were still lying in wait to confront him.

Once the winter waned Egil and Arinbjörn's nephew Thorstein travelled together with nearly thirty men overland through Opland and over Dovrefjell to Trondheim, where Hakon had been quartered for the season. The king proved to be well disposed towards Thorstein and he obtained his inheritance. Then it was Egil's turn to plead his case, mentioning the backing he had from Athelstan (i.e. Arinbjörn) and restating the unlawful acts against him at the Gulathing, when his claim to the legacy of Björn for himself and his wife Asgerdh had been lost on account of King Erik's powerful opposition, aided and abetted by Gunnhild. However, Hakon deemed not to be helpful, despite his past differences with Erik and suggested that Egil would do very well if he, the king, indeed took no action at all against him for misdeeds.

Egil then appealed to his sense of law, maintaining that he still had strength of kin in Norway to uphold his claim against that of Atli. He also offered his services as a warrior to Hakon, suggesting that he could be clashing again with Erik before long and, even if not, Gunnhild had many sons to follow their father. Hakon turned him down flat, for he had in mind the depredations the kin of Egil had made on his own family and advised him to return to Iceland, where he would be safe; otherwise Egil might also find himself in peril from Hakon's kin. Still, for the sake of King Athelstan (rightly Arinbjörn) Hakon granted Egil the right of peace if he chose to stay in Norway.

The reference to the threat of Erik's sons has all the signs of insertion into the saga using the benefit of hindsight. The future King Hakon the Good had left England while Eadmund was still on the throne there. So he would have been well aware that Egil could not have been backed up in these matters by Athelstan, who had died years before. Again one can replace this name by "Arinbjörn". At this point Hakon was still feeling fairly tolerant towards Arinbjörn and his family, but not towards Egil, who had spilt the blood of the royal kin. It has already been argued above that Arinbjörn was actually Hakon's foster father, albeit reluctant.

There is a certain irony about the different treatments of Thorstein and Egil by Hakon. Despite Thorstein being a nephew of Arinbjörn Hersi, with him likewise having been with Erik in England, one might have expected that his application would also be refused. Egil was indeed a friend of Arinbjörn and the enemy of Hakon's former foe, namely Erik. Yet there was the crucial difference relating to kinship and vengeance. Both were apparently relying on the fact that Hakon had returned *oðal* to folk who had been deprived of it by Harald and Erik. It was however too late, for once in power Hakon did not need to grant boons of this sort, at least in the Westland. His decision contained an element of expediency; Thorstein's land was in the Vik, where Hakon's position was perhaps less secure and he needed friends.

It is clear that Bergönund's brother Atli had not left Norway with Erik and, since he was still installed at Ask, his status had presumably been confirmed by Hakon; he would neither want to go back on his word nor make enemies unnecessarily, at least not just to please Egil. Hakon's great ambition was to convert the Norwegians and get rid of the old heathen practices. Here he met with stiff opposition, especially from the farmers of the powerful Trondelag earldom. Arinbjörn and Thorstein must both have been nominally converted in York along with Erik and Gunnhild; this could have put them in good stead with Hakon. Yet crucial in Thorstein's favour was that his father Eirik had been King Hakon's man before he died. Egil, on the other hand, was still a heathen, although he had been "prime signed" as a matter of convenience before the Battle of Vinheidh. He also seems to have misjudged Hakon's attitude towards Erik, who was after all kin, and who had given way to him without blood being spilt. Egil could not have blustered untruthfully to Hakon that "Athelstan" had recently offered him a command in his army. So Egil failed to impress with Hakon, who saw no immediate threat from Erik, and in the big Icelander only a trouble-maker who had butchered members of his kin and their friends. Still, he gave Egil the right to remain in Norway without being regarded as an outlaw, and no doubt with the proviso that he kept the peace. Some hope! As already discussed above the departure from England of Thorstein with Egil had taken place in circumstances that tended to undermine Arinbjörn's commitment to Erik's cause there. Egil was also going to compromise Arinbjörn's fragile relationship with Hakon.

While neither Hakon nor Egil were ever to set eyes on Erik again, his shadow was still hanging over Norway; but this had not helped Egil. He and Thorstein left Trondheim, the one satisfied and the other highly dissatisfied. They retraced there steps over Dovrefjell and then parted, Thorstein ever southwards to claim his estates, and Egil westwards to the coast at Romsdal. On the island of Hodh a newly widowed sister of the expatriate Arinbjörn Hersi, Gydha by name, was being threatened by a Swede called Ljot. He was challenging the masters of households to "holmgang" duels. After winning he would claim any property involved. Gydha's son was a callow youth, so Egil took his place. He maimed Ljot in the fight and thus considered himself in a position to lay claim to all his other ill-gotten gains.

Thus did Egil immediately engage in strife, even though as described the cause appeared to be a quite worthy one. Yet was he being far too bold in claiming for himself the properties that Ljot had won for himself? Ljot may even have been operating on the king's behalf to deprive of their land those Hakon did not like or trust. Otherwise how was he getting away with it? This could explain why he homed in on Arinbjörn's kin, why Egil visited the place at all and why Hakon was soon to make a point of denying to Egil possession of Ljot's other seizures. These farmers in The Westland thought they were still occupying odhal; Hakon had other ideas.

After this Egil made his way to Aurland on the Sognefjord, the home of Thordh, Björn Brynjolfsson's brother. He reported the dealings he had had with King Hakon.

Thordh was the "hersi" in Sogn after his father Brynjolf. Egil would need to inform him that he had been given the king's blessing to stay in Norway, although this had clearly now been compromised. Thordh would hence need to assess the risk in harbouring the wayward immigrant. Egil was trying to use Thordh as a shield in the same way as he used to use Arinbjörn. But he had no intention of staying in Norway without a rightful seat, nor of returning to Iceland without resolving the problem posed by the denial of his rights.

Later Egil together with thirty men took a rowing boat and went to the island of Fenhring (now Asköy) in Hordaland, the place occupied by Atli, brother of the late Bergönund. The two men fell into discussion, each with his own armed band in attendance. Atli would refute Egil's reiterated claim to the legacy of Björn by reminding him of the judgement of King Erik, and added that he had not had recompense for the deaths of his brothers and the ensuing sacking of Ask itself. The upshot was that Egil summoned Atli to attend the Gulathing and then returned to Aurland. The thing duly assembled and Atli pleaded his case, but Egil answered him by a challenge to holmgang. Atli accepted and lost his life thereby, so that Egil then considered that he had finally won those estates he claimed through his wife Asgerdh. After visiting Thorstein in The Vik, he returned to Iceland, now wealthy and respected, and remained there for several years.

Yet he must have been well aware for some time that he could not hang on to his wife's legacy. Even so, he could not rest until he had established by fair or foul means, and at least in principle, that the estate was his by right to be disposed of as he wished. In Egil's view, the killing of Atli was a matter of righting a wrong in law, when all other means had been exhausted. As he was getting older he became less rash and more willing to settle disputes by reference to the law. Only when he saw himself as losing by unfair treatment did he resort to violence.

As an old man in Iceland he became involved in a dispute between his son Thorstein (who was by then the landed man at Borg) and a neighbour over grazing land. They agreed to allow Egil to adjudicate at the thing. Although Önund had long been a friend, Egil came down harshly against him and his son, even going so far as to declare their right to their own land void. Egil was full of bitterness.

After the slaying of Atli, Egil in his own mind considered that the lands of both Ljot and Atli were now his, but did not hang around to have this confirmed. He did after all have land and a wife in Iceland. It is stated that he returned to Borg a very wealthy man. This could hardly refer to the winning of the disputed land, for such wealth was hypothetical. But one reason why he first revisited Thorstein in The Vik—after he had been to Sogn "to make arrangements about the property that was now his"—may have been to pick up any gear he had left there, and especially the ship he had brought from England, which he would need to transport any extra loot that he was going to lift from his dubious gains in The Westland.

Chapter 9

Erik's Bane

One Anglo-Saxon Chronicle entry records that Erik Bloodaxe returned to rule again in York a few years after being driven out, but under such circumstances that various enemies were soon gathering around him. According to a saga statement Olaf had been appointed "warden" and one of his duties was to keep out "Vikings". This would be in particular aimed at any led by Erik. The date was c948. Eadred could have compromised Olaf's claim to Northumbria proper, in that he may have been forced to accept the Aire boundary. Yet there were clearly those in the land who preferred the top-ranking Erik, for the Anglo-Saxon Chronicle tells us that the Northumbrians before long drove King "Anlaf" out and accepted Erik. (Garmonsway p113)

The means by which this was accomplished are not immediately evident, but one might presume that the event was accelerated by news that Erik and his army had returned and were looming nigh to the realm and that Olaf would not be able to stay in charge there without a military confrontation. Erik's whereabouts during his absence of two years are vague, but this may be because he eventually did organise an expedition to Spain and the Mediterranean. (Wood 1981 p168) He had left Northumbria because he was short of power, and this could be increased by amassing wealth. It does seem feasible that Erik returned from an adventure in the south loaded with loot and ready to reclaim his chosen realm. Arinbjörn's apparent absence from Norway at this time makes it possible that he was still with Erik.

William of Malmesbury only mentions Erik as the reason for Eadred's action against Northumbria:

"(Eadred) . . . ; for he nearly exterminated the Northumbrians and the Scots, laying waste the whole province with sword and famine;

because, having with little difficulty compelled them to swear fidelity to him, they broke their oath, and made Iric their king. He for a long time kept Wulstan, archbishop of York, who it is said connived at the revolt of his countrymen, in chains; but afterwards, out of respect for his ecclesiastical dignity, he released and pardoned him". (Stephenson 1989 pp, 127-8)

> William's remarks seem to conflate Eadred's earlier punitive invasion of Northumbria (resulting) in Olaf Sigtrygsson being installed) with the imprisonment of Wulfstan after Erik's demise. Everything between is ignored. The reference to "Scots" is enigmatic Eadred has apparently managed to arrogate to himself all military prowess and victories, while failures and defeats are overlooked. It seems an irony that the sagas have for some reason cut him out completely. At the same time they attribute to Athelstan and Eadmund events that happened after their deaths.

> One might wonder if any legitimacy could lie behind Erik's claim to a realm based on York. Such may have been strengthened by him being considered to be "Danish". Yet why could he be thought of so, since he was the king of Norway's son?

Erik was of Danish extraction on his mother's side, she being the daughter of a King Eirik of Jutland. Erik's wife Gunnhild was herself Danish, being the daughter of King Gorm the Old and sister of King Harald Bluetooth. This dynasty also appears to have regarded Jutland as its home territory and both Gorm and Harald let impressive rune-stones be raised at Jelling there. There is an account that Gorm came to Jutland from Norway, whereafter he quelled and subjugated its petty kings and caused such irritation on his southern border that the German Emperor found it necessary to retaliate. So Gorm appears to have had roots in Norway. His wife Thyra was the aunt of Ragnhild, Erik Bloodaxe's mother. (For genealogy see App. 2) Thus were both Erik and Gunnhild descended from King Klakk-Harald through his daughters Thyra and Thyrne. By this reckoning Gunnhild was also aunt to Sweyn Forkbeard, the later invader of England along with his son Knut, i.e. the eventual King Canute the Great of both England and Denmark. In a way Erik and Gunnhild, despite their disastrous episodes at York, contributed to the royal ambitions in England that continually dwelt in the collective consciousness of this dynasty.

In a saga account Erik had originally been invited by King Athelstan to accept the realm of Northumberland as his vassal, and to defend it against foreigners. Erik and Gunnhild are also reported to have been baptized, which does seem likely as a political expedient. He had many men about him, including most of the Northmen who had sailed over with him, plus many friends who had arrived later from Norway. But his realm was not large and in the summertime it was his wont to go raiding around Britain, and thus he acquired a deal of wealth.

When King Athelstan died he was succeeded by his brother Eadmund, who did not like Northmen. This would include Erik, who he planned to replace with someone called Olaf. Erik's response was to sail off around the westerway of Britain, gathering men to his cause. According to Hakon the Good's Saga, after he had been to the Orkneys he moved south to the Hebrides and Ireland, gathering as many men as he could and, bolstered by this force, then harried and attacked lands further south, namely Bretland (either Wales or Strathclyde) and England. Eadmund put Olaf in charge of defence and, having assembled an invincible army, he attacked, defeated and killed Erik, together with five other kings and many others. Some who escaped took the bad news to Gunnhild, who was in Northumbria with her sons.

The truth has been both compressed and distorted in this saga account. The main point to note is that the names of the relevant English kings are used quite wrongly. The statement about Eadmund succeeding Athelstan is right enough, but not in this context; one should understand here that Eadred succeeded Eadmund and this sequence should replace "Athelstan" and "Eadmund" above. The kingships of both Athelstan and Eadmund illustrate how they often had great difficulty in keeping control of Northumbria. Was the same true with Eadred, the third brother? It is possible that Arinbjörn was among the survivors who took disastrous news back to York.

It would seem that Erik's final battle took place on the bleak upland crossing of the Pennines used by the Romans and known towards the west as Stainmore. It is reported that Erik was betrayed by Oswulf, earl of English Northumbria and finally slain by a certain Earl Maccus, son of Olaf. In the end it had been shown that Erik was no more welcome in England than he was in Norway; but after his death he found a place that did welcome the likes of himself. A poem was composed in his memory. In it one can recognise how shallow any conversion to Christianity must have been, for his lifestyle and end, at least in the view of the poet, had made him a very suitable candidate for a place in Valhalla, where he eagerly entered to be greeted by those who had beckoned him at the gates.

> King Erik did indeed meet his death in battle in England, but the English king at the time was Eadmund's brother Eadred. While Erik could not have been installed by Athelstan, it is feasible that Eadmund did so not long before being killed. But the saga statement that "Eadmund" did not like Northmen then has to refer to Eadred. Eadmund could well have seen Erik as someone powerful enough to keep the constantly belligerent Scots, Britons and Irish-Norse at bay. (Such installation as Northumbrian ruler before the death of Eadmund does not feature in the chronicles.) He was appointed to function as a warden on Eadmund's behalf, but would actually be quite dissatisfied with this limited status and soon was showing his mettle as a Viking and brutally exceeding his remit. Then Eadmund's untimely death caused the onset of a crisis. The murder will have been recognised as an opportunity rather than a setback by Erik, who was just waiting for the chance to reveal himself in his true colours, namely as a land- and power-hungry reviver of the old kingdom of Northumbria, with the backing of the church in the form of Wulfstan, Archbishop of York. As already described above, Eadred would not stand for this and took the steps described on previous pages that would end with Erik's departure.

> Under these circumstances Olaf Sigtrygsson could be tempted to come from Dublin (or the Solway), or even be summoned, and he would be a better alternative for the new English king, especially if one presumes that he was at least willing to swear allegiance to Eadred. Hence the saga statement about "Eadmund" preferring someone called Olaf to Erik could be true enough, except for the wrong royal name, The real Eadmund would have been unlikely to favour Olaf, since he had been instrumental

in driving him out in 944. (Garmonsway 1972 p110) The fact that Erik too was actually forced to leave for some years is ignored in the saga, but is reflected in the account of him descending on Britain as a Viking. This would occur in conjunction with his supposed eventual expedition as a slave trader to Spain. (Wood 1981 pp167-8) Such abduction of northern Europeans into the Moorish world was rife, and one purpose of Erik's harrying around Britain could well have been the taking of suitable captives. It was a quick way to make the fortune he needed to further his regal ambitions. Yet it would ensure that he became hated as well as feared in the regions thus pillaged.

The way in which Erik replaced Olaf in 950 presents a difficulty. The Anglo-Saxon Chronicles say that in 952 (i.e., 950) the Northumbrians drove out Olaf and accepted Erik. It seems unlikely that they could have done so without a show of military strength by Erik, but the circumstances are described in the vaguest of terms. The 'E' Chronicle simply uses the event as an annal, but it is missing completely from the 'D' Chronicle, the one otherwise most informative about events in the North of England. The event may have been selectively omitted in its entirety because it represented a crushing political defeat for the southern English authority and perhaps a military defeat for its allies.

The reality of Erik having a distinct second spell of two years as king in York is indeed ignored by all sources except for the 'E' version of the Anglo-Saxon Chronicle, where is found:

"952. In this year the Northumbrians drove out king Anlaf and accepted Eric, son of Harald, as their king:" followed by:

"954. In this year the Northumbrians drove out Eric, and Eadred succeeded to the Northumbrian kingdom." (Garmonsway 1972 p113)

According to Sawyer's revised chronology these years should read 1950 and 1952, which is in accordance with the case being presented here. All dates lie within Eadred's reign. Erik's ejection is also recorded in the 'D' Chronicle, (954, for 952) Then there is added that Archbishop Wulfstan was restored to the bishopric of Dorchester.

Perhaps 954 is actually correct for the latter part of the entry, since then we might understand that the archbishop had been imprisoned after

Erik's demise in 952, but, though released in 954, was never allowed to return to Northumbria.

There is an Irish account of a battle in the north between Northmen and a combined force of English, Scots and Cumbrians, with the former named as the victors. (Wood p.170) English sources are silent about this. Without considering the chance of conflation of two battles this can hardly be the occasion of Erik's death.

Although the record appears to be two years too late, is it possible that this refers to an otherwise completely unrecorded battle in which Erik defeated Olaf and thereby could displace him in Northumbria? In this case it is not possible to decide whether this represents the "driving out" of Olaf by the Northumbrians, or that he had been forced to leave because of Erik's approach, but returned to face him unsuccessfully in battle once an army had been assembled from among adjoining lands. The "English" of such alliances probably referred to those north of the Tyne.

It is worth recalling that Erik's earldom of the Orkneys included Scotland north of the Moray Firth and controlled the Hebrides and associated western seaways. Erik's presence in York seriously hemmed in the nations north of the Tyne and Eamont, namely the Scots, the Britons of Strathclyde and the English based on Bamburgh. Erik's most convenient entry points into Northumbria from the west would be the Solway Firth and Morecambe Bay. The latter may seem preferable, since Olaf appears to have had the use of the former and had friends there.

Hakon's Saga may have covered this battle when it states that Erik became very bold and had a large army, and could rely so much on his men that he drove far inland, where he harried and pursued folk. When immediately after this it states that Olaf assembled an invincible army to oppose Erik it is probably showing complete ignorance of his discrete and final two years actually as king in York.

This event can be seen as concerning the army led by Olaf that was defeated by the returning Erik in 950. Olaf survived, but this seems to mark the end of his days as a war leader. Another two years would pass before the Welsh, Scots, Irish-Norse and the English beyond the Tyne under new leadership were finally to get rid of Erik.

After his two further years in power at York, Erik fought the battle in which he was killed. The Anglo-Saxon Chronicles assert that he was "driven out" by the Northumbrians, yet ignore his death in battle. However, in the saga Gunnhild was informed of his death while yet in Northumbria. (Garmonsway 1972 p113, Holtsmark 1959 p84) The Anglo-Saxon Chronicles do not record Erik's death.

Gunnhild was presumably still in residence at York. The "driving out" may be an analogical assumption based on ignorance of the matter being settled in battle and that Erik was slain. It probably simply reflects the wording of the preceding annal stating that Olaf was "driven out".

The one English source to go into any detail about Erik's last stand is Roger of Wendover:

"King Eric, with his son Henricus and his brother Reginaldus, in a certain desolate area which is called Steinmor, were betrayed by Count Oswulf and treacherously killed by Earl Maccus, and afterwards King Eadred ruled in those districts".

This is based on Roger's Latin (Coxe 1841 pp402-3) and the given date of 950 is even two years too early for Sawyer's revised chronology. It may indicate confusion with Erik's earlier victorious battle. *Eirikr* here is rendered Eilricus (Eiricus?). In the saga Snorre does not mention Erik's son and brother, giving Guttorm and his sons Ivar and Harek, while the others mentioned among the slain are Sigurdh and Rögnvald, plus Torv Einar's sons Arnkjel and Erlend, whose father was Earl of the Orkneys. It is not clear how these names can be reconciled with the five kings who are said to have fallen with Erik. (Holtsmark 1959 p84) There is some confusion here, although Henricus may be a corruption of Harek. On this point of personal names here the Norse sources must take precedence over the English ones. Torv Einar was succeeded by his son Thorfinn who was married to Greilad the daughter of Thorstein the Red

Erik's slayer is conventionally referred to as "Maccus", but this cannot be reconciled with Roger's *Macone*. Kershaw quotes Simeon of Durham as recording Eiricus being killed by Maccus, the son of Anlaf, and Matthew Parish, who clearly shared Roger's source, as attributing the slaying to "Consul" Maco. In the latter source the son and brother killed with Eric were Haericus and Reginaldus, apparently confirming the Harek of the saga. (Kershaw 1922 pp33-4) Both Maco and Macone could be in the Latin ablative case. The former would give a nominative *Macus*, the received "Maccus". This is not Norse Magnus, or even a Celtic form of this, for it was first recorded too late, namely with King Magnus of Norway and Denmark, who died in 1047. In any case the Gaelic form became *Manus*. As an ablative *Macone* would be in the Latin 3rd declension, with a possible nominative *Macon*. This might then include the same Irish name as occurs in the surnames O'Mahony and MacMahon (*O/Mac Mathghamhna*). Then as now the name would present problems of presentation in both Latin and the Germanic languages. Otherwise, and more plausibly, it might simply be that *Maco(ne)* was a son of Olaf and consider the Irish form of the latter name—*Amhlaibh. MacAmhlaibh* (MacAuley) may have been recorded as something like "Macolle" and the "-ll-" mistaken for "-n-" in script to give "Macone". In this case indicating him as the son of Olaf would be an unwitting tautology.

It would seem that the son of Olaf did away with Erik in vain, for Eadred took over the running of Erik's former kingdom in person and "Maccus" played no further role worthy of appearance in the pages of Northumbrian history. This battle seems to have finally exhausted those threats to the English kingdom that had lurked so long in the north and west.

Hakon's Saga identifies the English leader as Olaf, but he may not have been at the final battle (952), for only his son is mentioned in the English account of Erik's death. Dealing with the final battle, the saga account suggests that at first losses were greater in the army of "Olaf", but for those that fell there came reinforcements out of the countryside, so that in the end it was the Northmen who were getting the worst of it. Finally they were overwhelmed.

The elderly Olaf eventually took to the cloth and ended his days as a monk on Iona.

Earl Oswulf was leader of the English of Northumberland, north of the Tyne, and he will have been anxious to avenge the earlier defeat. Roger must have copied an annal originally written in Yorkshire and the use of "betrayal" to describe Oswulf's action suggests that thereabouts some of the folk were still loyal to Erik. Stainmore is now thought of as referring to the bleak heights of the eastward dip slope of the Pennines, yet this moorland zone is not stony at all. It is on the steeper scarp slopes to the west that the two hamlets of North and South Stainmore are situated and on this side there are numerous rocky outcrops and strewn boulders. The moor east of the summit is more correctly known as Stainmore Common; this type of name usually denotes where the named village has had rights of pasturage. This all suggests that the "moor" originally called Stainmore was on the rougher western slopes below the western scarp and that the engagement took place there. As a less likely alternative one might consider the name as referring to some remains to do with the Romans or to a prehistoric stone that had been replaced by Rey Cross.

In view of the above discussion one might interpret the battle in this way: Earl "Macone" (or "Macolle", son of Olaf) had established a base camp for his campaign somewhere near the Solway Firth and made his way up the Eden valley, heading for the Pennine crossing at the Pass of Stainmore. Erik decided that he could challenge him successfully and marched out of York to cross the Pennines from the east by that same old Roman route. They met at Stainmore. The two armies seem to have fought where they met, but Erik may have marched into a trap. If Olaf was waiting for Erik in the difficult country near the Stainmore villages it would be hard for Erik to get past him without having defeated him conclusively. Erik was indeed getting the upper hand until he was attacked at his rear from the east by another army, one led by Earl Oswulf. This caught Erik by surprise: he had expected to have to fight only one army, the mainly Irish-Norse one led by Olaf's son, "Macolle". The trap snapped shut on that rough terrain, furrowed by deep gills, west of the summit. Even Erik's hardened troops could not cope when attacked from two directions and with no easy escape route. It was a situation where you won where you stood, or you died. It was Erik's last stand.

Oswulf's army, unbeknown to Erik, had made its way along the Roman road from the east to fall upon the rear of the unsuspecting Erik who until then thought he was winning. Thus can one see a likelihood of a preconceived, devious, but ultimately successful battle plan by his enemies. Hence the reported treachery of Oswulf.

Erik's death is commemorated in the poem *Eiríksmál*, which features in the Icelandic compilation called *Fagrskinna*. It is introduced into this by stating that its composition was at the behest of Queen Gunnhild, who went to the Orkneys with her remaining sons after her loss of Erik. The poem is thoroughly heathen, but contains little historical material, although the saga account of Erik's last battle must have come by this same route. The longest extant version ends with Erik promising to name the five kings who died with him; since he does not the poem is incomplete, thus robbing us of more authentic information as to their names. In the surviving part there is no mention of a "bloodaxe"; this is only neared by the phrase included in the description of his worthiness for entry into Valhalla—*oc blodhoct svardh (ok blódhugt sverð) borit*—"and (has) bloodstained sword borne". (Kershaw 1922 p96, Gordon 1956 p149) This suggests that "Bloodaxe" was not deemed a suitable by-name where the intention was panegyric.

On the summit of Stainmore Pass until recently there stood a small pillar known as Rey Cross on the border between Yorkshire North Riding and Westmorland. In the later Middle Ages it was known as "Rerecros on Stanmore" or similar. During road widening in 1992 this monument was in the way and removed: excavation revealed that the small mound upon which it stood was natural, dispelling all hope that the tradition of it being the grave of Erik Bloodaxe would be realised.

The cross itself may of course have been moved in the meantime. However, across the road there exists a flat rectangular mound: perhaps this might serve to keep the tradition alive. Yet its low flat-topped shape on an ancient boundary may indicate its use as a crude "thing" platform, for meetings of men from both sides of the Pennines. The modern boundary between Yorkshire and Westmorland lies some distance to the west, but the monuments may have been deliberately placed within the bounds of the large Roman marching camp there, whose ramparts survive even today. "Rere-" may be derived from Old Norse *hreyrr*—

"cairn, man-made mound"—and the oblong structure could then even be the *hreyrr* in question.

For the positioning of a cairn on a watershed one can compare Dunmail Raise—"Dunmail's *hreysi*"—using a term related linguistically to *hreyrr*. Dunmail was the last king of the Strathclyde Britons and his demise coincided closely with the time of arrival of Erik in Northumbria. There is a suspected rectangular thing mound elsewhere in Cumbria, but in that case a stepped shape is used. Another monolith at a watershed political boundary occurs at the Three Shires Stone on Wrynose Pass.

Another Nordic word for "boundary marker" is *rá*, but this is more likely to refer to a post or single stone. While this cannot be the direct phonetic basis for "Rey-", the pronunciation could have been influenced by that of "Rere-". The latter would seem to indicate initial use of the Norse dative case, hence *hreyri-rá*—"marker at the mound". Possibly soon after the monument was converted into a cross. "Rey-" could mainly have resulted from "Re'e-", due to dissimilation of the second "-r-" in the compound "Rere-cros". In Sweden *rör* is still used for "boundary marker". For a cross beside a thing platform one can compare the situation at Eivindsvik, Norway, the site of the great Gulathing. However, on the matter of Rey Cross marking the site of Erik's grave one might note the Norse noun *hræ*—"corpse of one slain in battle". It actually features in the poem composed in York by Egil Skallagrimsson in praise of Erik, and by which his life was spared—*Hofuðlausn*—"head ransome". (Gordon 1956 p113) Could the sense of this have contributed to the tradition, right from the time of the slaying of Erik, with the original memorial being also thought of in Norse as *hræ-rá*? A final solution is of course not possible; one might choose between *hreyri*, *hreyr-rá* or *hræ-rá* as the original of "Rere".

It was believed that to qualify for Valhalla one had to fall in battle and this must have given comfort to Erik's kin. Yet it seems strangely apt that, apparently having been hag-ridden most his life, he would be borne off by a horse-riding female Valkyrie to the hall of the fallen. It is then ironic that Egil Skallagrimsson, despite the fearsome risks he took with his life, would not qualify for entry, since, although he was going to die "with his boots on", it was of old age at his home in Iceland.

Chapter 10

Erik's Sons

At the time of Erik's death Egil Skallagrimsson was still in Iceland, but news of the event was to entice him abroad again. He had also heard that Gunnhild and her sons had made their way to Denmark, while Arinbjörn had returned to Norway: he had regained his old estate, for it appears that he had been well thought of by King Hakon. Accompanied by Önund Sjoni, Egil made landfall in The Firths and had a joyful reunion with Arinbjörn. That winter he moved southwards into his own estates in Sogn, collecting his dues from the various properties, then returned north again, for Arinbjörn was to hold a great Yule feast.

> How long had Arinbjörn stayed with Erik in England after the visit of Egil? It is quite possible that he stayed long enough to be ejected from Northumbria with his lord, but he either survived the Battle of Stainmore, or he was not there. It is conceivable that the affair with Egil, together with Gunnhild's attitude then, had seriously weakened his relationship with Erik. Well stocked with goods, loot and other wealth he could have returned to Norway in good time to work his way back into favour with Hakon (claimed above to have been his foster son) and thus to recover his estates. Would not his chances of doing this have been much better as a volunteer still with a strong following, rather than as a suppliant fleeing from a terrible defeat overseas?

Later Egil turned glum, for he did not have possession of the estates he had won from Ljot. Reluctantly Arinbjörn agreed to intercede with King Hakon for him, but without success. Indeed, the king chided him for bringing this up on behalf of someone advised to stay out of Norway; if he persisted he might as well go into exile too. The king warned Arinbjörn that he was aware of his friendship with

Harald Grafell, son of Erik and his foster son. Hakon then found it necessary to express his doubt about Arinbjörn's loyalty to himself and suggested that he went to seek his fortune among those with whom his heart lay.

> While it is possible that Egil was able to go and exploit the ownership of his estates in Sogn because of the goodwill of Thordh Hersi and the friendship of Arinbjörn Hersi, the estates seized from Ljot were clearly beyond their influence and his reach. King Hakon was probably loath to offend powerful men on matters within their own jurisdiction, but the question of Ljot's lands could only be settled by approach to the king. In the event, forcing the issue by making him come to a decision proved to be a bad move for both Egil and Arinbjörn. All past displeasures with both of them were resurrected and brought into focus. Even so, Arinbjörn appears already to have been wavering, but the king may have been rash not to cultivate and get on side a man of his prowess and experience. There again, the affair with Egil may have provided the motivation or excuse Arinbjörn was looking for to place his arms at the disposal of the side with which his destiny was ultimately linked. The saga appears to have been wrong about Harald being Arinbjörn's foster son; he is elsewhere said to have been fostered with King Harald Bluetooth in Denmark. The fosterling in question was Hakon.

Egil was highly disgruntled at having been denied such wealth, so Arinbjörn recompensed him with a chest full of silver. It was thought a just reward, since Egil had taken the part of his kinsman against Ljot, saving his life, if not ultimately his lands. This was the kind of token of friendship that Egil appreciated and he immediately regained his good humour. The next year Arinbjörn went a-Viking with three longships and Egil went with him. After raiding Saxony they sailed back to moor at Hals, at the mouth of the Limfjord in Jutland. It proved the parting of the ways, for Arinbjörn had decided to throw in his lot with Harald Grafell Eriksson, while Egil still believed he had a future in Norway. They were never to meet again. Egil rejoined Arinbjörn's kinsman in The Vik and from there made an expedition into the province of Värmland to the east, in order to enforce taxes due to King Hakon: this was done on Thorstein's behalf. If it was intended to be a means of Egil ingratiating himself with Hakon it appears to have failed. In any case, about this time Hakon was preparing to fare against Harald Eriksson in his refuge in Denmark.

Even Egil must have been able to acknowledge to himself that the gift of silver was really a more realistic reward for him than lands in Norway. These would be difficult for him to administer, let alone hang onto, in combination with the estate he already had in Iceland, a place then regarded as a haven for disgruntled outcasts from Norway. Hakon was clearly right in not putting his trust in Arinbjörn; the rebuff over Egil's land-claim was just enough to tip the balance and send the hersi abroad to seek service with Hakon's enemies. It is evident that, for whatever reason, in giving Arinbjörn the opportunity to leave Hakon was reluctant to take him and his kin on.

To strengthen his status as an exile, Arinbjörn needed to increase his wealth; hence the Viking expedition to get hold of some booty. Harald Grafell was gathering his strength in Jutland, the old homeland of three of his grandparents and his mother.

Egil was quite happy to join with Arinbjörn on raids, but when decision time came he preferred risking Hakon's wrath than to have anything to do with Gunnhild and her sons. Thorstein had been ordered by Hakon to prove his loyalty by entering Värmland to enforce the Norwegian king's suzerainty and collect his taxes. Suspicion had fallen on him because of his kinship with Arinbjörn. Egil carried out these duties in his stead, which entailed a very hazardous undertaking, and Thorstein became thereby reconciled with Hakon; trust was clearly required since Hakon was preparing his offensive against the lands on both sides of the Kattegat. Yet it would seem that neither Thorstein nor Egil could join Hakon in his war, since neither would wish to enter into hostilities against Arinbjörn. Egil must have been rewarded handsomely for his efforts on Thorstein's behalf, but with the war looming things looked distinctly unpromising in Norway, no matter what the outcome.

So Egil set out for Iceland, after sending messages to Thordh in Aurland to look after his estates in Sogn and Hordaland for him, and to sell them if possible. He returned to Borg and never left Iceland again.

When a certain Koll Hersi died in Iceland his estate had fallen to his son Hoskuld. His mother Thorgerdh, daughter of Thorstein the Red, did not want to stay in Iceland, so she sailed to Norway and eventually married Herjolf with whom she had a son Hrut, after which Herjolf died. Thorgerdh returned to Iceland to visit her son Hoskuld and died there. Hoskuld himself had spent time in Norway in the bodyguard of King Hakon the Good. Back in Iceland he married Jorunn, the daughter of a wealthy man called Björn.

He later felt the need to better himself, so he bought a ship from a man from Shetland and set sail for Norway again and made landfall at Hordaland. He initially stayed with friends there, but later made acquaintance with King Hakon again, who assisted him to return to Iceland with a shipload of timber.

After the death of Erik, Gunnhild and her sons had made their way to the Orkneys. Eventually news reached them of the hostilities that had broken out between Norway and Denmark, so they made their way to the latter country. This is how Arinbjörn was able to join Harald Grafell Eriksson there.

Hrut had been born to Herjolf and Thorgerdh in Norway and was hence Hoskuld's half brother. While still in Norway he had become a prominant member of the bodyguard of King Harald Grafell, the son of the late Erik Bloodaxe and Gunnhild and became a particular favourite of the latter. Hrut eventually wanted to go to Iceland, so King Harald gave him a ship for that purpose. He sailed off with Gunnhild's blessing ringing in his ears and bearing her gift of a gold ring. On reaching Iceland Hrut was soon in dispute with Hoskuld regarding the estate of Thorgerdh.

The sons of Erik took the forefront in the incursions against Hakon's realm. Eventually, together with massive Danish backing, they made a landfall at *Fitjar* andcaught Hakon at a great disadvantage. Fighting with the sons of Erik were Gunnhild's two brothers, Eyvind Skreya and Alf Askmann, who so long ago had been forced to leave Norway because of wrongs done to the sons of Skallagrim. Alongside Hakon fought a man called Thorolf Skolmsson. Gunnhild's brothers sought out the king, who shouted: "Keep straight ahead!" So they came at him and, as Eyvind took a swing at Hakon, Thorolf rammed him with his shield and the king was then able to bisect him with a two-handed stroke of his sword Kvernbit. Thorolf then killed Alf.

But after that Hakon was struck by an arrow. Some even say it was Gunnhild's servant Kisping who did it. Well, it proved to be his bane, but before he died, even though his side had won the battle, Hakon bequeathed the realm to the vanquished sons of Erik, because of the lack of male offspring.

The king had wanted to make his way abroad to receive a Christian burial, but agreed, that if he died before this could be arranged, then he might be buried using whatever ritual was the normal local practice. Sailing hopefully towards his seat at Aarstad, he only got as far as "Hakonshelle", which was named after the mode and place of his arrival on this Earth. Thus was it said that Hakon died in the same rock shelter as he had been born in. His funeral rights show how he had really failed in his efforts to convert the Norwegians. One might reflect that this feat was soon after to be claimed by Gunnhild's brother Harald, king of Denmark, on his great runestone at Jelling in Jutland. But this too was a rather idle boast, for it was really left to later converted royal Vikings, like Olaf Trygvason and Olaf the Holy, to coerce the bulk of their reluctant countrymen away from their heathen customs.

The deaths of Erik's brothers in law, Alf and Eyvind, would have given greater satisfaction to Egil Skallagrimsson if they had been accomplished in a manner to satisfy the requirements of the blood feud. As it is, they are not recorded in Egil's Saga, while the death of Hakon only receives brief mention in that it allowed Arinbjörn once more to return to his estates in Norway. (Ref. photos 34-37, App. 5)

Gunnhild still had her ambitions. Though Harald Grafell Eriksson was now nominally king of Norway, her sons only really held sway in the Westland, Erik's old stronghold. In The Tröndelag and The Vik powerful earls ruled like kings. By a stratagem Earl Sigurdh of Lade was killed, but his son took over The Tröndelag and proved a match for the sons of Erik. In the end this Earl Hakon and Gunnhild became somewhat attached to each other; but mistrust was rife. Erik's sons continued to try to master the whole realm, but Earl Hakon was hard to overcome and, when hard pressed, would slip away to the outside world. Eventually he turned up in Denmark, to be welcomed there by Harald Bluetooth Gormsson, and there he met Harald Knutsson, Bluetooth's nephew. He had got rich by being a Viking, whereby he earned the nickname Gold Harald: he thought of himself as future king of Denmark.

Norway did not thrive under the rule of the sons of Erik; famine was rife. Folk blamed them for it, for they had become Christians in England and since coming to Norway had destroyed temples and spoilt sacrificial sites. Attempts had been made against popular resistance to remove the earls of Trondheim and the Vik. Trygvi Olafsson, earl of The Vik, was killed and his wife Astrid must flee with their son, the future king of Norway, Olaf Trygvason.

Earl Hakon made his way to Norway again and egged on Gold-Harald to demand half of the Danish kingdom from Harald Bluetooth Gormsson. The latter angrily replied that no-one had ever demanded of his father King Gorm that he should divide the Danish realm; nor of his father Hardaknut, nor of Sigurdh Worm-in-Eye, nor of Ragnar Lodhbrok. Then Bluetooth had talks with Earl Hakon of Lade, who was of the opinion that, having once raised the matter, Gold-Harald was not going to let it lie. Hakon advised Bluetooth to hang onto his kingdom and to acquire for his kinsman another one; the one he had in mind was Norway. But it later came to pass that King Harald Bluetooth sent word to Harald Grafell to come to Denmark to receive properties that he and his brothers had earlier had in that land. Despite the fact that he was Bluetooth's foster son and had received help from him in the past to gain Norway, the ruse now was to lure him away and cheat him of it, so that it could be given to Gold Harald, his brother's son. Grafell discussed it with his mother Gunnhild and their kin and in the end it was decided that it was safe for him to make the journey. He arrived in the Limfjord, Jutland, with three ships and lay at anchor near Hals. One of these ships had Arinbjörn Hersi as steersman.

The "love" that developed between Gunnhild and Earl Hakon is hard to understand, for she must have been well past her prime. Was it further evidence of her "sorcery"? If so it appears to have misfired. It seems more likely that Hakon's attentions drove a wedge between her and her sons. The resistance to the conversion of Norway to Christianity by its Eriksson rulers was considerable and it eventually must be forcibly imposed by later kings, i.e. Olaf Trygvason and Olaf the Holy.

There was treachery afoot. Earl Hakon was plotting with King Harald Bluetooth against both Grafell and Gold-Harald. The latter of these two attacked the former at Hals and killed both him and Arinbjörn Hersi there. Then Hakon made war against Gold-Harald, capturing him and having him hanged. In this way did King Harald Bluetooth win for himself all Norway, as claimed on his runestone, and gave the government of much of the Westland over to Earl Hakon.

When Hakon sailed northwards to claim his Norwegian domain, Gunnhild and the rest of her sons decided that resistance was impossible and sailed westwards to seek sanctuary on the Orkneys. She had only two sons left, Ragnfröd and Gudhrödh. The former tried to regain Norway, but eventually was overwhelmed in battle against Earl Hakon and must flee the land. The second son took to raiding in The Vik. This was after Olaf Trygvason had become king of Norway. Gudhrödh was killed there, together with most of his men. Thus died the last son of Gunnhild and with it her ambition to provide the chief claimants to continue a royal dynasty on the Scandinavian mainland.

News of the death of Arinbjörn Hersi eventually reached Iceland. Egil Skallagrimsson responded by composing an elegiac poem in memory of his friend.

The link between the kings of Denmark and the earls of Lade persisted. Knut Sveinsson, Harald Bluetooth's grandson, invaded England with his father and later managed to subdue the whole kingdom to become King Canute the Great. A staunch henchman was Earl Eirik of Lade. Knut got rid of Uhtred, Earl of Northumbria, and rewarded Eirik by installing him in his stead. The arrangement did not last long and the earldom was soon ruled by the more durable Siward.

At the battle of Hals the trap snapped shut on Harald Grafell. It had been baited by the (feigned?) fondness of Earl Hakon for his mother Gunnhild. This then gave Hakon the chance to avenge Harald on Gunnhild's behalf by making war on Gold-Harald and killing him. Thus by his scheming did Earl Hakon open the way for the temporary annexation of Norway by King Harald Bluetooth of Denmark, a situation that was to need reassertion by his son Svein and his grandson Knut.

The fact that she had been deceived (apparently by flattery) must have been a bitter pill for Gunnhild to swallow, coupled with the realisation that she had no power base whatsoever left to her in Norway. The efforts of her remaining two sons can be perceived as acts of desperation.

In Iceland the news of the death of Arinbjörn must have struck home with Egil as symbolic of the removal of the last vestiges of any hopes he may have harboured of ever returning to Norway.

Chapter 11

Aftermath

The ill-feeling between the descendants of Egil Skallagrimsson and the Norwegian royal house was apparently not healed until the reign of Olaf Trygvason. One autumn a ship arrived from Iceland at Nidaros (Trondheim) in Norway, bearing a heathen crew. Among them was Kjartan Olafsson, said by some to have been the best young man ever to have come out of Iceland. His father Olaf was the son of Hoskuld, the son of Egil Skallagrimsson's daughter. King Olaf took to those who were Christian, but heathens would have departed in their ships, except that the weather prevented them from sailing. The king, on hearing about this, ordered them to his presence and forbad them to set sail. They all attended the king's mass, but the non-Christians were still not impressed, except for Kjartan, whose enthusiasm earned him an audience with the king, along with a few others. Kjartan was then baptized and thus earned the king's friendship.

The name Kjartan is of Irish derivation and appears to have been introduced into Iceland because Olaf's mother Melkorka was the daughter of king Myrkjartan (i.e. *Muirchaertach* in Gaelic) of Ireland. There are no Irish names elsewhere in the kin of Kveldulf, (although, as discussed above, the form "Olaf" itself seems to be due to Irish influence). In his old age Egil appears to have parted from his own children. Thordis Asgerdhardottir was Egil's stepdaughter, as well as his niece, and he spent his final years living with her and her husband Grim. She may have been the only one prepared to put up with him. If she had any children, none are named.

That same autumn another ship arrived from Iceland and on it was Thangbrand, a priest. He reported a great lack of success in his efforts to convert the Icelanders. This infuriated King Olaf so much that he ordered that all Icelanders in the town should be killed. But Kjartan, and others who had been converted, went to the king and reminded him that he was going back on his word. They assured the king that all the Icelanders in Nidaros would now let themselves be baptized and, because of this, there would be a number of ambassadors with good family connections going back to their homeland, which was bound to further the cause of Christianity there. The king then relented and all the rest were baptized and spared.

The background of Kjartan is gone into in far greater detail in the Laxdale Saga. Thorstein, son of Unn Ketilsdottir, had a daughter called Thorgerdh, who married Koll Hersi. Their son Hoskuld went to Norway and spent some time in the bodyguard of King Hakon the Good. After returning to Iceland and marrying Jorunn, he felt the need to better himself, so returned to Norway and renewed his acquaintance with Hakon by joining him at an important meeting. The king assisted him to acquire a shipload of timber. Here he also acquired a slave woman called Melkorka and took her back to Iceland. The suspicions of his wife Jorunn about the arrangement were confirmed when Melkorka gave birth to a son who was named Olaf after his uncle Olaf Feilan. According to his mother Hoskuld's son *Olafr Pá* was the grandson of an Irish king *Muirchaertach* (in Norse Myr Kjartan).

Koll's widow Thorgerdh Thorsteinsdottir went to Norway where she married. Their son Hrut became a member of the bodyguard of King Hakon's successor, Harald Grafell Eiriksson, and became a favourite of his mother Gunnhild. He eventually went to Iceland where he was soon in dispute with his half-brother Hoskuld over the estate of their mother Thorgerdh. A cattle raid by Hrut led to a defeat of Hoskuld's men, but Jorunn managed to calm her husband down. However these were the first rumblings of the terrible feuds that were going to rack the Laxdale area.

As Hoskuld grew old his son was again in dispute with Hrut, while Melkorka felt neglected and relied more on the support of her son Olaf Pa, who grew somewhat at odds with his father. In order to finance her son on a journey to Norway she reluctantly married Thorbjörn Skrjup. Olaf sailed to Norway on the ship of Orn, a member of King Harald Grafell's bodyguard. At court Olaf pleased Gunnhild. As a result of their friendship Olaf broached to Gunnhild his desire to travel abroad. Harald was agreeable and thought that no better man had come out of Iceland. A ship and crew were provided and together with Orn the 18 year old set out for Ireland, which they somehow reached despite the foggy weather. By some chance they were on a coast near to where King Myrkjartan was staying. Local men abandoned an attempt to take the ship once they realised the mettle of the crew. Olaf convinced the ruler of his identity by speaking Irish and showing his mother's ring. He was offered the succession by his grandfather, but declined because of his need to return to Norway and Iceland. Gunnhild and Harald would have him stay in their service but he persuaded them to help him return to Iceland, where he was greeted by his father and mother, Hoskuld and Melkorka.

That Olaf managed to blunder through the fog to a spot on the Irish coast near to where Myrkjartan resided, depends on how one interprets "near". It seems far more likely that Olaf sought his grandfather out. While his acceptance story seems feasible, the resultant offer of the succession looks like another piece of Icelandic hyperbole.

Hoskuld wished that his son marry and had in mind Thorgerdh, the daughter of Egil Skallagrimsson of Borg. She was dubious, since his mother had been a slave, but her father convinced her by pointing out that Melkorka's father was a king in Ireland. Olaf was displeased by her doubts but a meeting resulted in agreement. The wedding took place at Hoskuld's place. Her brother Thorstein Egilsson was there and Hoskuld presented Egil with a sword he had received from Myrkjartan. This pleased Egil very much. The pair went to live with Hoskuld. She turned out to be a woman who liked to be obeyed. Around the year 960 Olaf built a new house and called it Herdholt.

When Hoskuld died c985 he arranged for his estate to be divided between his grandsons Bolli and Bardh and their uncle, his son Olaf Pa. To cement the arrangement Bolli was fostered with Olaf and Thorgerdh and became a firm friend of their son Kjartan. Olaf needed timber and again sailed to Norway. This was against the wishes of his wife. He stayed there with Geirmund Roar, a member of the bodyguard of Hakon of Lade and who suggested he approach this earl. He was received well and allowed to fell trees. In addition he received the gift of a gold-inlaid axe to take back to Iceland. Geirmund then paid for a passage to Herdholt and soon wished to marry Olaf's daughter Thured. Olaf was not agreeable but was overruled by Thorgerdh once she had seen the colour of Geirmund's money. She soon came to regret this. Their son-in-law wanted to leave for Norway and Olaf even provided him with a merchant ship for the purpose. He intended to abandon his wife and their daughter Groa. In the event he was becalmed off Iceland. Thured sneaked aboard and left Groa with Geirmund, while stealing his sword Footbiter, which she then gave to Bolli. The ship reached Norway, but was wrecked with the loss of the whole crew.

It did not take long for the lack of resources in Iceland to be felt by its inhabitants. This was particularly true in the case of timber, especially for house building. (This tradition was due to be abandoned and other available materials put into service.) For the same reasons shipbuilding became impossible and reliance rested on transport from Norway. For reasons like these the Icelanders lost direct contact with Britain and soon began to slip back into the power of the rulers of Norway. Men found it expedient to visit Norway in order to do service, acquire wealth and bring back home that which was lacking. There was a price to be paid and this was loss of independence. They were reluctantly converted to Christianity and eventually absorbed back into the Norwegian realm.

A man called Thorvald married the daughter of Osvif. The relationship was stormy and later Thordh became her husband. She regularly visited a spring. Here she just happened to keep meeting Kjartan Olafsson and an attraction developed. Then, accompanied by Bolli, he would go to see her at Laugar. However, c996 the pair travelled south to *Borgarfjörðr* to see Thorstein Egilsson, Kjartan's mother's brother. They stayed at Borg and eventually Kjartan told his uncle of his desire to buy a half share of a ship belonging to Kalf Asgeirsson that lay nearby. Kalf was also staying with Thorstein. On returning home Olaf expressed doubts about his desire to travel but would not stand in his way. It was a similar tale at Laugar where Gudrun also lacked enthusiasm for his venture. But it transpired that it was because she disliked Iceland and wished to accompany him. But Kjartan turned her down, so she refused to await his return. The foster brothers eventually boarded the ship together with eight other Icelanders. Together with Kalf they reached Trondheim in Norway and learned that Earl Hakon had fallen and that the kingdom was ruled by Olaf Trygvason who had ordered the conversion of all of its folk. Many Icelanders had already come to Norway and at Nidaros they found three other Icelandic ships moored at the landing stage. It appears that they had all wanted to go home that summer, but King Olaf had refused permission while they remained heathens. Kjartan joined them in refusing to convert.

During a swimming session in the river Kjartan met King Olaf who was impressed by him and gave him a cloak. That winter the heathen Icelanders, already suspicious of Kjartan's closeness to the king, blamed Olaf's Christianity for the persistent bad weather. Some spies sent by the ruler overheard Kjartan say to Bolli that he would not bend to the king's will and proposed to go to his hall and burn him in. This was reported back to Olaf and resulted in the Icelanders being summoned to the royal presence where he gave them a choice. He also wanted to know whose idea it had been to burn him in. Kjartan replied that the king believed that the instigator would not reveal himself. But the king already knew it was him and wondered if he really meant it. Because of his virtual confession his life was spared. The king believed that if Kjartan took baptism several other crews would follow likewise. He urged Kjartan to become a better man by freely allowing himself to be converted. Thus would his visit to Norway have improved him. Kjartan cannily replied that he would accept Christianity in Norway, but reserved for himself the right to indulge in a little Thor worship once back in Iceland. Some of King Olaf's men grumbled about the continuing heathen presence about the king, but he maintained that in Kjartan he saw a better behaved man than some of them.

The king had a church built in the growing town and preached in it himself. Kjartan decided to attend to see what went on and as a result many more Icelanders were also present. The upshot was that Kjartan, Bolli and others were baptised. Kjartan was then so respected that it was said that never before had his like come out of Iceland. However, when he announced to Olaf that he wanted to go to England, the king insisted that he either went to Iceland to convert his compatriots or stayed in Norway. Olaf was understanding when he chose the latter option. The man chosen to go to Iceland was a priest called Thangbrand, but once there he found that only some accepted conversion and this provoked widespread strife. Thangbrand decided it was best to return to Norway. King Olaf was furious and threatened that the Icelanders would regret their behaviour. Some converts did come to Norway and were allowed to stay. However, when others wanted to leave they found that the king had forbidden any sailings to Iceland that summer. In the next season the king sent some converts back, but kept four men as hostages, including Kjartan Olafsson. Among those allowed to return was his foster brother Bolli.

In his refusal to allow sailing to Iceland the king's motives were political as well as religious. He was punishing the island into submission by starving it of resources. Such constraints added to the difficulties being experienced by Icelanders and led to the break up of society that is so evident in the feuding and quarrelling described in sagas such as the Laxdale one.

Once back in Iceland Bolli told how Kjartan was involved with the king's bodyguard and very friendly with his royal sister Princess Ingebjorg. On the strength of this Bolli proposed marriage to Gudrun and Olaf said he would not stand in his way. She at first refused until persuaded by her father to accept. Then Olaf Pa became quite displeased. Came the next summer King Olaf relented, having heard that Iceland had been converted. He even allowed Kjartan to leave, to the chagrin of Ingebjorg. Yet nonetheless she sent a bridal gift for Gudrun. King Olaf presented Kjartan with a sword, and he boarded ship with Kalf and reached Borg. Olaf Pa rode to meet them, but then Hrefna, Kalf's sister, found the coif that was a bridal gift and put it on. Kjartan said it suited her and suggested marriage, even though it was clear that Gudrun really still pined for him. When Olaf persuaded Kjartan to ride with him to Laugar, the latter refused a gift of horses from Bolli, despite his father asking that they stay friends. They parted with some rancour. Kjartan's sister Thured urged him to marry Hrefna. She received the coif and they were well matched. This presaged dark deeds.

At a feast Gudrun asked Hrefna to show her the coif. Later, after the guests had departed, Kjartan found that his sword was missing. It was eventually found in a bog and brought back to him, but the scabbard was never recovered. Then another gathering took place at Laugar. Hrefna had taken her coif with her, but when she was ready to don it the item could not be found. At this Gudrun suggested that she had either left it at home or lost it on the way. Olaf tried to keep things calm, but Kjartan just had to mention the matter of the missing items to Bolli, who denied any involvement. Gudrun by now was prepared to admit that the losses could be due to the acts of folk unknown. This did not prevent the majority from believing that she was behind the theft of the coif and that she had ordered Thorkell to burn it.

When later on Hrefna mentioned to Kjartan that she thought that Gudrun had been wearing the coif, Kjartan raided Laugar. Then he complained that he had had no time to talk to either Gudrun or Bolli. This angered the Laugar men, but Bolli calmed them down. However, open enmity had now developed between them and the men of Herdholt. When Bolli bought some land in Tongue, Kjartan objected and made a counter-offer. But when Thorarin said he still preferred to sell to Bolli, Kjartan offered to let him live on the land. Thus did he secure the land, this to the displeasure of Gudrun, who then proceded to chide her husband Bolli.

Kjartan's travel plans came to the knowledge of Gudrun and she instigated an ambush, and if Bolli would not join in he could consider their marriage to be over. After Kjartan sent some of his men back Bolli was shamed by both sides into taking part and in the event killed his foster brother, who by then was in a battle-weary state. Gudrun was exultant and reminded Bolli of how Kjartan had trodden him underfoot after he belatedly came back to Iceland. She also made the point that when Hrefna now went to bed, she would not be laughing.

Olaf's other sons were bent on revenge and killed some of those who had taken part in the ambush, but Olaf restrained them from including Bolli. Then he sent men to Borg to inform Thorstein Egilsson of what had happened. He gathered together a large force so that the feud could be pursued further. But Olaf still wished no harm to come to Bolli, so a settlement was reached. Kjartan's son Asgeir was fostered out and his father's body taken to Borg for burial at the church there. Those brothers who were considered to be at the heart of the dispute were sent into exile. Even so, the sons of Olaf were still very disgruntled that Bolli had got off so lightly.

Olaf Pa died three years after Kjartan and his son Halldor took over as family head at Herdholt. His mother, Egil's daughter Thorgerdh, was still living there and bearing much ill will in her thoughts. She took revenge on Thorkell, who had held back and watched while Kjartan was being ambushed. Halldor went with some men and slew him. She was well pleased with this, but still nagged Halldor about the fact that

Bolli was still alive and thriving. She emphasised that his grandfather Egil would not have tolerated this. So a plot was hatched. Halldor led a band against Bolli's place and Thorgerdh insisted that she go along. They came to Tongue. Bolli sent Gudrun away so that he could face the attackers alone After being wounded by Lambi with a sword and by Helgi with a spear, Bolli was killed with an axe by Steinthor.

A point that emerges from the above is that Norse women were hardly shrinking violets. They had a good deal to say about the running of affairs and, though they did not wield heavy weapons themselves, they did their best to ensure that their menfolk did so when this was considered necessary. Gudrun is a good example of this and Thorgerdh Egilsdottir seems to have inherited well enough the character of her father. Eirik Bloodaxe's wife Gunnhild has already shown above what she was capable of and her daughter Ragnhild was cast in a similar mould.

Meanwhile with Erik's kin, it must have been a sad and bitter Gunnhild who lived out the rest of her life on the Orkneys. Although her numerous sons were all dead, her daughter Ragnhild survived. She proceeded to acquire a reputation to rival that of her mother. Her first husband was Arnfinn, son of Earl Thorfinn of the Orkneys. He is reported to have died on his sick bed, but other reports state that Ragnhild killed him in Caithness, afterwards marrying his brother Havard. At a feast a guest was Einar, Havard's nephew, who was persuaded reluctantly by Ragnhild that he was more fitting to be earl than his uncle, so he eventually engaged him in battle and killed him. He was considered a coward for this and Ragnhild abandoncd him, while talking another nephew called Einar into taking vengeance. Even this did not win Ragnhild for him, because she married Ljot, another of the earl's brothers. While Einar still had ambitions, the Orkneymen preferred Ljot and eventually he had Einar killed. He then fought for supremacy with his surviving brother Skuli, the latter in the end losing both the struggle and his life.

Thus did this branch of the Yngling dynasty descend into comparative obscurity by way of Nordic notoriety. How Erik's namesake maternal grandfather had fitted into the Danish royal house is not evident, but the father of his spouse Gunnhild, Gorm, and her brother Harald, certainly achieved fame, not least by means of the imposing runestones erected at Jelling. Gorm's kin appears to have had roots in Norway and, apart from driving out rival kings, he cemented his position by marrying Thyra, daughter of Klakk Harald, himself once a royal claimant in Jutland. That the Danish power base at this time was centred on southern Jutland means that it included Angel, the traditional Continental homeland of the Angles. Perhaps some genealogy now lost was considered to link them with the early Anglian kings. Well, both Erik Bloodaxe and Gunnhild were of the royal blood of Jutland and this could have been adduced to try to legitimise their claim to York, which they probably considered to be genealogically superior to the likes of Eadmund and Eadred, who could rightly be considered 'Saxons'.

King Sweyn "Forkbeard" was Gunnhild's nephew. His brother in law was Olaf Trygvason. They fared together in England, but eventually left after setbacks. The converted Olaf promised never to make war there again; Sveyn, obstinately heathen, did not. Afterwards they fell out and Olaf lost his life in a sea battle in Danish waters. Another to fall there was Skuli, son of Thorstein Egilsson, who was serving under Earl Eirik. Svein then returned to promote forcibly his claim to an England in which Northumbria had been reduced to an earldom. Respite for England came with Sveyn's death, but his son Knut soon returned to continue the struggle. Edmund Ironside, unlike his father Ethelred, was able to resist stoutly, but nonetheless was in a mind to settle for Wessex except that he too died unexpectedly. Knut was proclaimed undisputed king and not long after Earl Uhtred of Northumbria was assassinated. Knut installed Earl Eirik of Lade in his place, the son of that Earl Hakon who had supposedly reciprocated a passion for him by Gunnhild.

The earldom of Northumbria continued with earls bearing Nordic names. Siward soon followed Eirik and is noted for his assistance in restoring Malcolm to the throne of Scotland, which, according to William Shakespeare, had been usurped in murderous fashion by Macbeth and his Gunnhild-like queen. The next earl was Tosti(g); he eventually fell out with his subjects, as well as with his brother King Harold Godwinson. The bonds of kin snapped completely. Tosti allied himself with King Harald Hardrada (*Harðraði*) of Norway, the latest Nordic king with ambitions to rule England. It is hardly surprising that he landed in Yorkshire and headed for York. Both he and Tosti lost their lives when attacked by Harold at Stamford Bridge on the Derwent. Yet Harold himself was due to fall soon at Hastings and the victorious Duke William of Normandy assumed the crown of England. He found support for his somewhat tenuous claim to it by asserting that King Edward the Confessor had promised it to him.

Thus did the prize so many had struggled to seize or retain eventually fall into the hands of a man descended from Rolf, that son of Rögnvald, earl of Möre, banished from Norway by Harald Fairhair so many years ago. Despite the great victory, the throne was not yet a secure seat. Some stiff resistance was still encountered, not least from the Northumbrians and especially in 1069; but William was able to quell it. In doing so he needed to snuff out the chances of a supportive Danish expeditionary force by employing a policy of burning, death and destruction, which reached its climax in the infamous "Harrying of the North".

The Danish North Sea empire of Canute the Great (*Knut den Store*) had not survived long after his death. Norway again broke free under its own kings and could claim sovereignty over lands in the west. But this control was crumbling in the British Isles, apart from the Orkneys and Shetland. While the Scottish mainland and Hebridean colonies became nominal parts of Scotland, the Northern Isles remained Norwegian until lost to Scotland in the 15th century and three centuries later the residual insular Norn language was dying out.

The Icelanders were still keen to remain independent and late Viking Age expeditions to America had led to settlements in places like west Greenland, Labrador and Newfoundland. These however struggled to survive due to isolation, worsening climate and conflict with natives. The Greenland venture lasted for a number of centuries, but the settlers became dependent on the Eskimos and finally succumbed.

Conditions in Iceland also became fraught due to few natural resources and difficulties of contact with the outside world. The need to fetch timber from Norway is expressed above. They even suffered from the attentions of Barbary pirates. Norway had absorbed the Faroes in 1035 and formed a union with Iceland in 1262. Norway itself lost its independence and fell into foreign hands. In 1380 it was united with Denmark but in the ratification of the Kalmar Union of 1397 the

King of Sweden became the common head of a Scandinavian block. However, during this period commercial power rested largely with the Hansa League based on the port of Lübeck in north Germany.

After Kalmar there ensued a long period of dynastic and territorial disputes between Denmark and Sweden. In 1521 the Swedes left the Kalmar Union. As a result of a crushing defeat in the war of 1657-1658 the Danes permanently ceded to the Swedes all of their extensive territories east of the Kattegat and the Sound, and constituting the southern part of the Scandinavian peninsula.

In the wake of the Napoleonic wars Denmark was granted control of the Faroes, Iceland and Greenland, but lost the island of Heligoland to Britain, while the Slesvig-Holsten question was soon to be seriously debated. A desire to keep control over the two duchies, effectively taking the Danish border down to the River Elbe, fell foul of the movement for German unification. This was compounded by the High German language which, under the influence of the Lutheran church, was spreading up the Jutland peninsula. After victory over a force from Slesvig-Holsten the Danes were heavily defeated in 1864 by a Prussian led army. The disputed duchies at the base of the Jutland peninsula were then annexed as German Schleswig-Holstein.

In 1874 Iceland was granted home rule. Heligoland was given up to Germany by Britain in 1890. In 1905 Norway achieved independence. After World War 1 Iceland also gained independence but the head of state was still the king of Denmark. The ugly head of the Slesvig-Holstein problem was again raised. A plebiscite decided that the northern half of Slesvig should revert to Denmark, a situation that still exists. World War 2 brought about no changes to the borders of mainland Scandinavia, but Iceland became a republic in 1944 and the Faroes became a self-governing dependency of Denmark in 1948.

After the Viking Age Scandinavia and Britain had largely lost contact. They both became more involved with adjacent continental powers. Some commercial contact had been maintained by the Hanseatic League, but the growth of sea power in the 19th century was among the factors that re-established sustained British interest across the North Sea, headed by the importation of timber from the Baltic area and later that of iron ore from Sweden. Denmark developed a nice little earner by shipping off huge quantities of bacon and butter to Britain.

The Hanseatic League caused the Scandinavian languages to borrow heavily from Low German, while the later influence of the Lutheran church resulted in the borrowing of many words from High German. The Viking legacy has left little visible influence in Britain and what there is mainly relates to language. Standard English contains a number of loan words, such as 'window' and 'law'. The effect was much greater on northern dialects. However the Nordic languages have left very clear footprints over relevant areas in the form of place-names, as with settlement elements such as '-by' and '-thorpe' in the Danelaw and nature names containing words like 'gill' and 'fell' in areas subjected to Norwegian influence. In this respect the names of the two main characters of this work appear in island names, in the Hebrides as Eriskay - *Eiriks-ey* - and in the Orkneys as Egilsay - *Egils-ey* - although without any direct reference to those very men.

While forms of Old Norse must have persisted in Britain around the end of the first millennium, its decline was rather rapid in face of competition from English, Norman French and Gaelic. Since World War 2 English has been the invader and has become a *lingua franca* in Scandinavia as in many other places.

In modern times Scandinavia presents itself as the reverse of its Viking past, with culture replacing brutality. There have emerged a number of productive men, some of whom have remained relatively obscure in the outside world. In the 18th century the Swedish botanist Carl von Linné presented his binomial classification method (Linnaean system) without which taxonomy the groundbreaking work of Charles Darwin would have been nigh impossible. His countryman, the writer Johan August Strindberg, obtained a certain notoriety at home but failed to find the worldwide fame and literary influence acquired by his contemporary the Norwegian playwright Henrik Ibsen, who also greatly eclipsed his own countryman the poet Björnstjerne Björnson in the realm of international acclaim. Norway also was the homeland of Edvard Grieg, a composer of delightful music that has left its mark of popularity in the outside world in a way that the acclaimed foremost Danish composer Carl Nielsen never will.

The seafaring nature of the Viking spirit remerged towards the end of the 19th century with the Arctic explorations of Fridtjof Nansen in 1888 and 1893-6. Then in his expedition of 1910-12 Roald Amundsen became the first man to reach the south pole. Both men used the same wooden ship, which was called *Fram*, i.e "Forward". Oceanic adventures continued when Thor Heyerdahl sailed over the ocean in unlikely craft in order to prove his migration theories. The raft used to cross the Pacific was made of balsa wood, while the boats in which he sailed on the Atlantic and Indian Oceans were constructed using reeds. One way in which they still reflected Viking traditions was that they were propelled by single large square sails.

However a man had been produced by Denmark whose work was to become very well known abroad, something of an achievement for someone who wrote in Danish. Hans Christian Andersen was born in Odense in 1805 and has grown to fame mainly because of the "fairy tales" he wrote. Oddly the English speaking world seems to have failed to notice that, like the Emperor's New Clothes, fairies are totally lacking. This collection of Andersen's works are known as Adventures and Stories (*Eventyr og Historier*), which, apart from the odd mermaid, elf or troll, are full of charming folk who are quite quaint and usually find themselves in odd situations while doing extraordinary things, as do also the toys and animals that feature.

Erik Bloodaxe was certainly no fairy either, but rather like the Emperor he is thought to have acquired an attribute that to the present day observer seems to be quite absent from his weaponry.

Appendix 1

The Times of Erik Bloodaxe Haraldsson

Scandinavia and the North

Anno 863
Birth of (Skalla)Grim
Kveldulfsson.
Anno 865
Birth of Harald Halfdansson
(Hairfair)

Anno 885
Harald Hairfair won the Battle
of Hafrsfjord. This united
Norway under him, so he had
his shaggy hair cut off.
The coast of Norway was being
raided by Vikings based on the
Scottish islands.
Anno 890
Ketill Flatnose left Norway for
Scotland.

Britain and the South

Anno 793
The Viking raid on Lindisfarne.

Anno 871
In this year Alfred defeated the
Danes at the Battle of Ashdown.
Anno 875
Halfdan shared out agricultural
land to his men in Northumbria.
Hrolf (Rollo), son of Earl
Rögnvald of Möre was in
Normandy.
Anno 877
Halfdan killed in Ireland.
Anno 878
Alfred defeated Guthrum's
Danes at Edington. Treaty of
Wedmore (Somerset). The area
to be under the "Law of the
Danes" was established.
Guthred became king of
Northumbria.
Anno 885+
To quell hostile Vikings and to
bring them under his suzerainty,
Harald Hairfair made a foray
to the northern and western
seaboards of Scotland and as far
as the Isle of Man .
Anno 894
King Guthred of Northumbria
died

Scandinavia and the North

Anno 895
Unn Ketilsdottir left Faroes
for Iceland. Thorgerdh, Unn's
granddaughter, married Koll
Hersi.

Anno 900
Birth of Thorolf
Skallagrimsson.

Anno 905
Halfdan Halegg and Einar in
dispute over the Orkneys.
Anno 910
Birth of Egil Skallagrimsson.
Anno 911
Björn Brynjolfsson sailed from
Shetland to Borg in Iceland.
Anno 912
Birth of Asgerdh Bjarnardottir.
Anno 914
Thorolf Skallagrimsson sailed
from Iceland to Norway
together with Björn. He made
friends there with Prince Erik
Haraldsson, foster son of Thori
Hersi.
Anno 916
Erik and Thorolf made a foray
into the Arctic. There Erik met
a certain "Gunnhild", who was
learning sorcery among the
Lapps.

Britain and the South

Anno 896
Danish army in England broke
up. The parts dispersed to
Northumbria, East Anglia and
the future Normandy.
Anno 899
In this year King Alfred of
Wessex and England died. His
son Edward became king.
Anno 902
The Irish took Dublin back
from the Norwegians.
Ingimund left Ireland and settled
on the Wirral.

Anno 911
The Scandinavians acquired
Normandy.

Anno 912
Ealdorman Ethelred of Mercia
died.
Anno 914
The Norwegians returned in
force to Ireland.

Scandinavia and the North

Britain and the South

Anno 919
Lady Ethelfled of Mercia died
at Tamworth. Her brother, King
Edward, took Mercia under his
direct rule.
Rögnvald fought at Corbridge
(Northumberland) and subdued
Northumbria. He took York and
became king there.

Anno 920
Death of Unn.

Anno 920
King Edward accepted as
overlord by the Strathclyde
Welsh, the Scots and the
Northumbrians (King
Rögnvald). Sigtryg Gali (his
brother) came to England from
Ireland and sacked Davenport
(Cheshire).

Anno 923
King Edward built a fort on the
Mersey at Thelwall (Cheshire)
and restored the one at
Manchester.

Anno 924
Rögnvald died in York. Sigtryg
took York and became king of
Northumbria. King Edward died
at Farndon-on-Dee (Cheshire).

Anno 925
Björn's wife Thora died.

Anno 925
Athelstan, Edward's son,
crowned king. He met with
King Sigtryg of Northumbria
at Tamworth and gave him his
sister in marriage.

Scandinavia and the North

Anno 926
Thorolf Skallagrimsson returned
to Iceland bearing the gift of an
axe to his father from Erik
Haraldsson. Skallagrim spoiled
the axe
Anno 927
Thorolf and Egil sailed from
Iceland to Norway, taking
Asgerdh with them. the axe was
dumped at sea. Egil made friends
with Arinbjörn Thorisson

Anno 928
Thorolf married Asgerdh
Bjarnardottir. Egil killed
Atley-Bardh and others of Erik's
men at the island called Atley

Anno 929
Thorolf and Egil made a Viking
expedition into the Baltic.
Captured by Courlanders they
escaped, while also freeing a
Dane called Aki. Homeward
bound, they raided Lund,
then in east Denmark. They
reached the seat of Thori, who
reluctantly allowed Egil to stay
after Arinbjörn threatened also to
leave. Birth of Hakon Haraldsson

Anno 930
Egil was kept away from a festival
at Gaular, a cult site. There
Gunnhild's brother, Eyvind
Skreya, stabbed Thorvald Ofsi to
death, a

Britain and the South

Anno 926
King Sigtryg died. King
Athelstan drove his sons out
of York, the "would-be" King
Gudhfridh and his brother
Olaf. Athelstan then took
Northumbria under his direct
rule. While at York he apparently
received the gift of a ship from
Harald Hairfair.
At a meeting at Dacre
(Cumberland) by the River
Eamont, Athelstan was accepted
as overlord by the kings of the
Strathclyde Welsh and the Scots

Scandinavia and the North

Britain and the South

henchman of Thorolf
Anno 931
Thorolf and Egil returned to
being Vikings. Egil attacked and
looted Eyvind's ship off the
west coast of Jutland.

Anno 932
Arinbjörn was in England and
joined Athelstan's forces as a
mercenary. A sword was
presented to him at the time of
his oath of loyalty. He founded
Londesborough between the
Humber and York and Thorolf and
Egil were obliged to join him there
Anno 933
King Athelstan harried Scotland.
His navy
reached Caithness. Hauk Habrok
supposedly forced Arinbjörn to
accept Hakon Haraldsson as a
fosterling
Anno 934

Anno 935
In Iceland Hoskuld Kolsson
married Jorunn (Björn's daughter)

Gudhfridh died, father of Olaf
Anno 937
During a skirmish at
Bromborough before the
Battle of Vinheidh Gudhfridh
Sigtrygsson was killed. During
the main battle Athelstan.
and Eadmund defeated the
Irish-Norse(under Olaf
Gudhfridhsson), the Scots
and the Cumbrians. Thorolf
Skallagrimsson was killed

Anno 938
**Egil reached Norway and
stayed**
with Arinbjörn Hersi, at whose
home was living Asgerdh, his

Anno 938
Thori having died, Arinbjörn
needed to leave England to claim
his estates. Egil Skallagrimsson
followed him.

Scandinavia and the North

brother Thorolf's widow. She
and Egil were soon to marry.
Anno 939
King Harald, 80 years old and
infirm, handed over the realm
to Erik. A civil war ensued,
with Erik fighting others of his
kin. He eventually succeeded,
although leaving much residual
unrest.
Egil sailed from Norway to
Iceland to stay with
Skallagrim at Borg. Thorfinn
Strangi married Egil's sister
Sæunn

Anno 943
Deaths of Bjorn Brynjolfsson
and Harald Hairfair.
Erik assumed the kingship in
Norway. Egil sailed
from Iceland and confronted
Erik and Gunnhild at the
Gulathing. Erik and Arinbjörn
went on an expedition.
Egil

Britain and the South

Anno 939
King Athelstan died.
His half-brother Eadmund
became king

Anno 940 or 941
The Northumbrians accepted
Olaf Sigtrygsson as king. St.
Catroe visited him in York. Olaf
stormed Tamworth. King
Eadmund besieged him
and Archbishop Wulfstan in
Leicester. By treaty
Olaf retained some "Danelaw"
territory south
of the Humber, bounded by
and north of Watling Street.
Olaf Gudhfridhsson died after
attackingTyningham in
Lothian
Anno 942
King Eadmund asserted his
control over north
Mercia and established a
northern border for it
Anno 943
Eadmund stood for Olaf
Sigtrygsson and
Rögnvald Gudhfridhsson at
baptism

Scandinavia and the North

killed Bergönund and kinsmen
of Erik while he was away and
then sailed back to Borg in
Iceland.
Anno 944
Erik left Norway after
giving way to his 15 year old
half-brother Hakon (the Good)
for the throne. Arinbjörn went
with him.
Death of Skallagrim at Borg.

Anno 946
Egil Skallagrimsson sailed from
Iceland

Britain and the South

Anno 944
Erik Bloodaxe reached the
Orkney Islands.
King Eadmund drove Olaf
Sigtrygsson and Rögnvald
Gudhfridhsson out of
Northumbria and brought
it back under direct English
rule. This was with the help
of Erik Bloodaxe, who was
then installed in York as a
replacement sub-king by
Eadmund (although regarding
himself as a full king).
Anno 945
With Erik's help Eadmund
subdued Strathclyde and ceded it
to Malcolm, King of Scots, but
with conditions. This excluded
the likes of Olaf and Rögnvald
from the Solway area
Anno 946
Egil shipwrecked in the
Humber and over wintered with
Arinbjörn at Londesborough.
King Eadmund killed at
Pucklechurch. His brother
Eadred became king

Scandinavia and the North

Britain and the South

Anno 947
King Eadred met with
Archbishop Wulfstan and other
Northumbrians at Tanshelf
to receive their pledges of
allegiance. But soon after they
proclaimed Erik as their "king".
Eadred responded with an
expedition. Ripon Cathedral
was burnt down. Erik's army
sortied from York and destroyed
Eadred's garrison at Castleford.

Anno 948
Egil and Thorstein arrive in
south Norway

Egil Skallagrimsson, together
with Arinbjörn, met with Erik
and Gunnhild in York. Together
with Arinbjörn and his men,

Anno 949
Egil and Thorstein journeyed to
Trondheim to meet King Hakon
the Good. Despite claiming
support from Arinbjörn, Egil
was frustrated by Hakon and
left. Parting from Thorstein, he
came to Blindheim. He rescued
Arinbjörn's sister Gydha from
the depredations of Ljot.
Egil summoned Atli to the
Gulathing, after which he killed
him in a holmgang duel. After
visiting Thorstein in The Vik
he sailed from Norway and
returned to Iceland

he left the city. Being favoured
by Eadred, Olaf Sigtrygsson
returned to Northumbria, intent
on regaining the throne

Anno 948
Under pressure from Eadred,
the Northumbrians abandoned
Erik. He was replaced as
sub-king by Olaf Sigtrygsson.
Egil and Thorstein Thoruson
acquired a ship from Arinbjörn
and sailed from England

Anno 950
Harald Bluetooth succeeded his
father Gorm as king in Denmark

Anno 949
Erik Bloodaxe went on an
expedition to Spain and the
Mediterranean

Scandinavia and the North

Britain and the South

Anno 950

Erik returned and defeated a combined force of English, Scots and Cumbrians. Thus did Olaf Sigtrygsson lose Northumbria and Erik was again accepted as king there.

Anno 952

Arinbjörn returned to his home in Norway.

Anno 952

Erik Bloodaxe betrayed at Stainmore by Earl Oswulf and killed by Earl "Maccus", i.e. Olafsson. Arinbjörn left England. Gunnhild and her sons fled from York and reached the Orkneys. Archbishop Wulfstan imprisoned

Anno 954

King Hakon attacked the Denmark of Harald Bluetooth

Anno 953

Archbishop Wulfstan released, but given the bishopric of Dorchester in the south

Anno 955

Egil left Iceland for the fourth time and visited his estates in Norway. He spent Yule with Arinbjörn at his seat. Gunnhild and her sons arrived in Denmark

Anno 955

King Eadred died. Eadmund's son Eadwig became king. Gunnhild and her sons left the Orkneys

Anno 956

Arinbjörn was distrusted by King Hakon because of his friendship with Harald Grafell Eriksson. The hersi thus decided to leave Norway. He and Egil went on a Viking

Scandinavia and the North   Britain and the South

expedition together. They
parted at Hals, Denmark, with
Arinbjörn joining Harald, while
Egil returned to Norway, where
he made a journey eastwards into
Värmland on behalf of Thorstein
Thoruson.

Anno 957

Egil's final return to Iceland from
Norway. Harald Grafell invaded
Norway. Gunnhild's brothers
killed in battle. King Hakon also
mortally wounded. The realm fell
tentatively to the sons of Erik.
Thus could Arinbjörn settle again
in Norway as a wealthy man.

Anno 959

Earl Sigurdh of Trondheim
killed by the sons of Erik.
Olaf Pa married Thorgerdh
Egilsdottir.

Anno 962

Truce declared between Sigurdh's
son Hakon and the sons of Erik.
Earl Hakon and Gunnhild became
fond of each other.

Anno 972

The Battle of Hals won by
Gold-Harald. King Harald
Grafell and Arinbjörn Hersi
killed there. Thorstein Egilsson
married Jofrid.

Anno 981

Olaf Cuaran (Sigtrygsson) died a
monk on Iona

Anno 990

Egil Skallagrimsson died a natural
death in old age

Scandinavia and the North	Britain and the South
	Anno 994 Olaf Trygvason converted to Christianity in England and left while promising future peace.
Anno 995 Kjartan Olafsson met King Olaf Trygvason at Trondheim	
Anno 1000 Olaf Trygvason killed at the sea-battle of Svold against Svein Forkbeard. Skuli Thorsteinsson also fell there. Svein and his son Knut (Canute) set sail for England	**Anno 1000** Svein and Canute invaded England. Svein died Canute left and returned. He was proclaimed king of England after the natural death of Edmund Ironside.

Notes:

The above sequences of events are based on the presentations in the main text. However, these results are not to be considered as cut in stone; some statements may indeed be marginally wrong, even though they seem to represent the most probable of any alternatives, while some dates may be out by a year or two, but are meant to facilitate understanding of the relative chronology of events, rather than to be absolutely accurate. Given the state of the records, the last is indeed impossible to achieve with certainty. Events are usually dated in English records, even though the sources may quote years that are slightly at variance to one another; interpretation is hence required in these cases. Scandinavian events are normally undated and timing needs to be worked out in comparison with dates from elsewhere.

The time-lines incorporate a re-assessment of the historical value of Icelandic records, especially Egil's Saga. While the latter in the past has been widely claimed to be severely wanting, with certain provisos one can regard the recording of events to be as true as the reports reaching Iceland could make them. Even so one must take account of varying amounts of hyperbole, omission, misunderstanding and obfuscation. In post-Viking times Iceland became a very isolated community and the oral histories became trapped there, with little possibility of checking details. This was less applicable to contact with Norway than with the British Isles. With regard to England, confusion arose about the names of the kings concerned, while "Arinbjörn" was often replaced by "Athelstan". A main instrument of obfuscation was a desire to promulgate a supposed special relationship between Egil Skallagrimsson and King Athelstan and thereby enhance the Icelander's reputation.

Another attitude leading to inaccuracy was the desire to brand Erik's wife Gunnhild as an evil sorceress. This was presumably due to contribution from Thorfinn Strangi, who accompanied Egil on earlier adventures and apparently had to endure an unavenged death; her brother had killed his. He became Egil's brother-in-law. Even so, apart from the biased contributions of Egil himself, others of his companions must have provided personal and eye-witness experiences. Such a one was Önund Sjoni. There are however discrepancies in degree of accuracy in which events were recorded. While much is sketchy, there is considerable detail in the accounts of the Battle of Vinheidh and the confrontation with Erik at York. The former presents Egil as a formidable warrior and a figure of exaggerated political importance. One might suspect that a main contributor here was Thorfinn Strangi. There is a quite different tone with the York encounter. Here Egil wrecks his ship, must shelter behind Arinbjörn and grovels before Erik. This is not the way that Egil liked to be presented. One must suspect the influence of Önund Sjoni on the account of these events. This would be the reason why Egil came to dislike him and harm his prospects when the opportunity arose. The "Athelstan" myth is perhaps no mistake, but rather a deliberate attempt to improve Egil's reputation, which had been badly sullied by this episode.

Appendix 2

Genealogies

List of Tables

TABLE 1

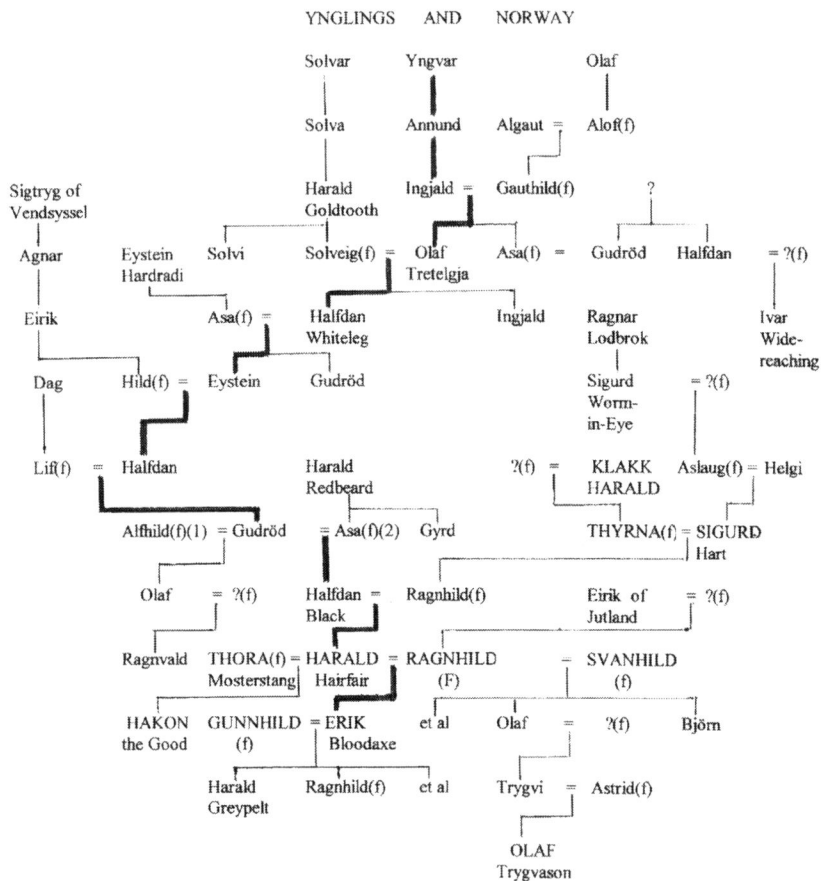

YNGLINGS AND NORWAY

TABLE 2

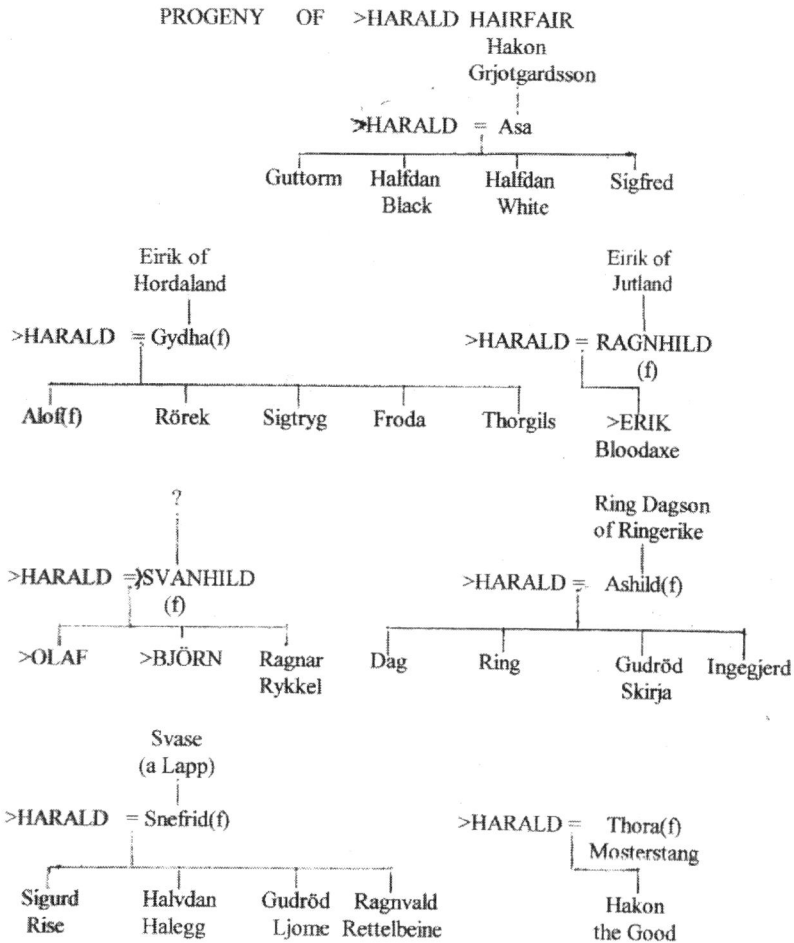

PROGENY OF >HARALD HAIRFAIR

TABLES 3 & 4

Table 3

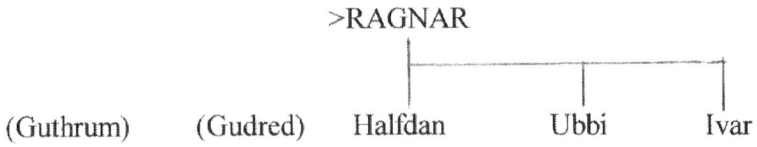

KIN   OF   >RAGNAR

>RAGNAR

(Guthrum)   (Gudred)   Halfdan   Ubbi   Ivar

Table 4

IRISH-NORSE

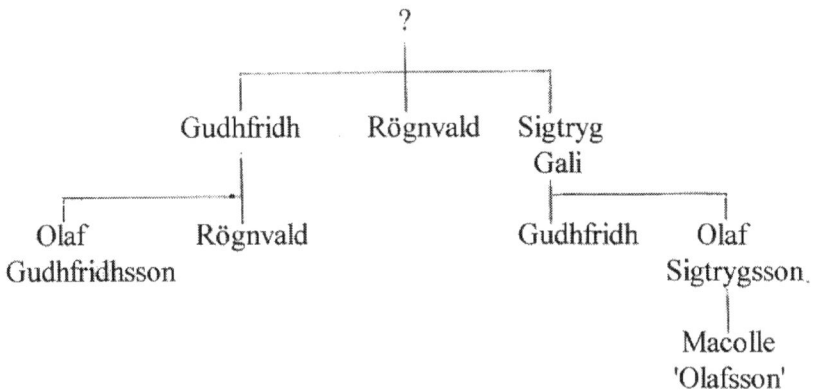

?

Gudhfridh   Rögnvald   Sigtryg
Gali

Olaf   Rögnvald   Gudhfridh   Olaf
Gudhfridhsson   Sigtrygsson

Macolle
'Olafsson'

TABLES 5 & 6

Table 5

DENMARK

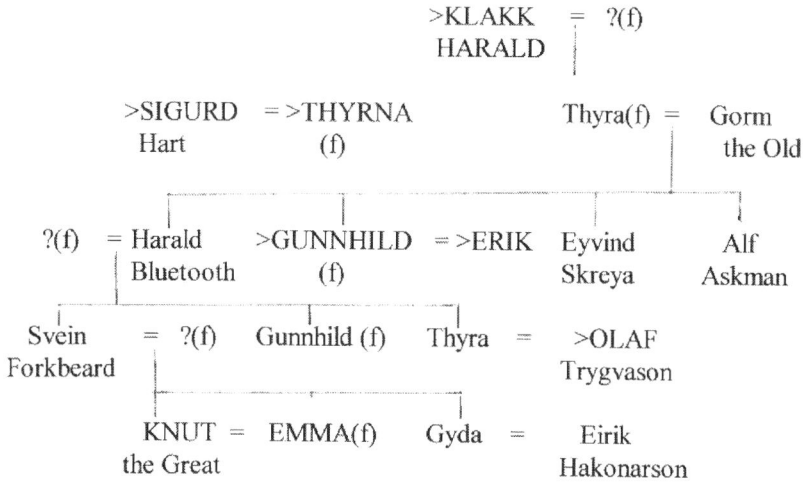

```
                        >KLAKK    =   ?(f)
                        HARALD    |
                                  |
  >SIGURD   = >THYRNA              Thyra(f) =   Gorm
   Hart        (f)                              the Old
              |                              |
  ?(f)  = Harald   >GUNNHILD  = >ERIK  Eyvind      Alf
         Bluetooth   (f)               Skreya      Askman
    |     |
  Svein    =  ?(f)   Gunnhild (f)   Thyra   =   >OLAF
  Forkbeard  |                                  Trygvason
             |
      KNUT = EMMA(f)      Gyda   =   Eirik
      the Great                     Hakonarson
```

Table 6

ENGLAND

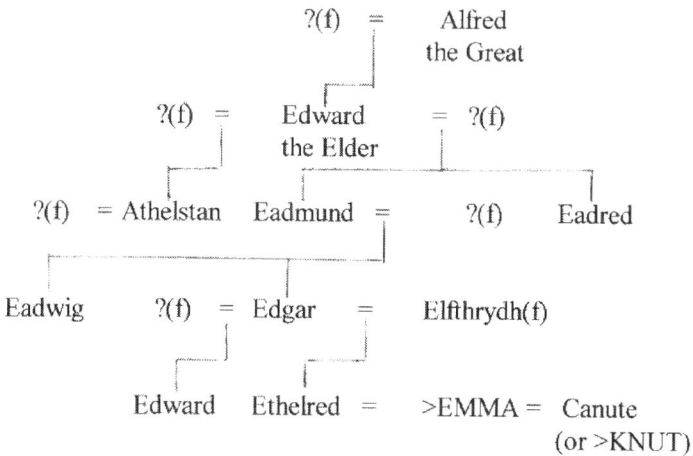

```
               ?(f)    =    Alfred
                            the Great
                            |
       ?(f)  =   Edward        =  ?(f)
               the Elder
               |                  |
  ?(f)  = Athelstan  Eadmund  =   ?(f)       Eadred
    |
  Eadwig      ?(f)  =  Edgar  =  Elfthrydh(f)
                      |          |
            Edward   Ethelred  =  >EMMA = Canute
                                          (or >KNUT)
```

TABLES 7 & 8

Table 7

SOGN   AND   THE   FIRTHS

?(f) = Brynjolf   Hroald = ?(f)

Thordh   Alof(f)   = Björn = Thora(f)   Thori = ?(f)

Gydha(f)   Arinbjörn   Thora = Eirik
                                                                    Alspak

Bergönund = Gunnhild(f)   THOROLF = ASGERDH(f) = EGIL   Thorstein
                           Skallagrimsson   Skallagrimsson

Table 8

TORGAR,   SANDNES   AND   BORG

Helga = Björgolf = Hildiridh(f)

Brynjolf = ?(f) Sigurd   = ?(f) Harek   Hraerek   Kveldulf = ?(f) Yngvar = ?(f)

Bardh   = Sigridh = Thorolf   Skallagrim = Bera(f)
          (f)

>THOROLF = >ASGERDH   = >EGIL   Sæunn(f) = Thorfin
            (f)   Strangi

Grim = Thordis(f)   Thorstein   Thorgerdh(f) = Olaf Pa   Bodhvar Gunnar

TABLE 9

This assesses the dating of deaths and the lengths of reigns in the Anglo-Saxon Chronicles and "Simeon". The figures in brackets are calculated insertions by your author based on the dates quoted in the texts. The reigns of 14+ and 6½ in "A" and "D" and 23+ in "Simeon" are from the sources, but do not agree with the quoted dates (Stephenson p, 88). In the cases of "A" and "D'" the 6½ year reign of Eadmund will be correct because Athelstan's death should be October 939, while Eadmund did die in May 946

Reigns and Death Dates (from the death of Alfred in 901 to that of Eadred in 955)

The rationalised dates can be set against the careers of Erik Bloodaxe and Egil Skallagrimsson.

	Alfred	Reign- Eadward		Reign- Athelstan		Reign Eadmund		Reign- Eadred	
'A'	901	(24)	925	14+	941	6½	946	9½	955
'D'	901	(23)	924	14+	940	6½	948	(7½)	955
'E'	901	(23)	924	(16)	940	(7½)	948	(7½)	955
'Simeon'	899	23+	924	15+	940	5½	946	9+	955
Rationalised	899	24½	924	15½	939	6½	946	9½	955

.

Appendix 3

Maps

Map 1. A Viking's View of North-Western Europe in the 10th Century. Place-names are in Old Norse (except for Bö).

Map 2. Southern Norway.
Place-names are in modern Norwegian form.
There are two places called Naustdal, but it must have been at the one on Nordfjord that King Vemund and his men were burnt in by Rögnvald. It is specifically stated that he came over the *eið* - 'isthmus'. The place-names Eid and Eidsfjord exist there to this day. Earl Hroald and his descendants Thori Hersi and Arinbjörn Hersi took over The Firths. It is possible however that they abandoned the seat on Nordfjord as being too vulnerable and moved to Sunnfjord, where they were nearer to their friends in Sogn, yet taking the place-name with them.

Map 3. The Westland (The Firths, Sogn and Hordaland), Norway.
The inset shows the position of Borg in Iceland relative to its fjord, for comparison with Bö in Sogn. However one must be aware that the inset is only at half the scale of the main map. The main point to be brought out is the lie of the places in relationship with the orientation of the fjords.

Map 4. York.
The street plan and street-names are shown insofar as they are relevant to the text. While the later medieval city walls are indicated, other features are generally omitted as being irrelevant, e.g. post-medieval streets and other bridges over the Ouse and Foss. This does not imply that every feature relative to the period of Erik Bloodaxe has been shown.

Map 5. Middle Britain
This shows Britain between the Forth and the Severn. The inset indicates the position of Map 6.

Map 6. The Humber Basin.
The inset shows the position of Map 7.

Map 7. Bramham Moor
This and the surrounding area are significant for the Battles of Brunanburh and Vinheidh.

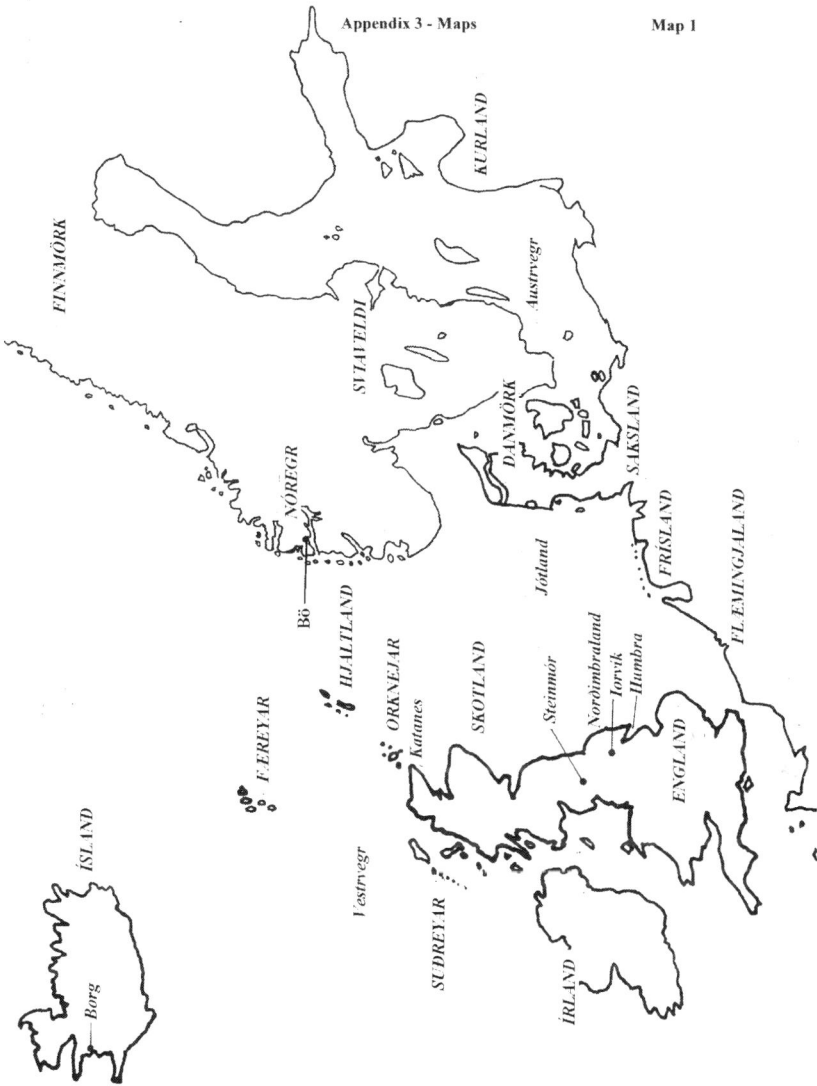

Appendix 3 - Maps   Map 1

Appendix 3 - Maps   Map 2

Sandnessjöen
Alsten
Vefsenfjord
HELGELAND
Torget
NAMDALEN
Leka
Beitstadfjord
Elda
Skarnsund
TRØNDELAG
JÄMTLAND
Solskjel
Lade
NORDMÖRE
Vigra
ROMSDAL
Stad
Blindheim
SUNNMÖRE
Nordfjord
Eid
Dovrefjell
Naustdal
FJORDANE
SOGN
Sognsjö
VALDRES   OPLAND
Aurland
Asköy
HÖRDALAND
Årstad
ROMERIKE
Stord
RINGERIKE
Haugesund
Tönsberg VIKEN   VÄRMLAND
VEST
Avaldsnes
ROGALAND   FOLD
Utstein
FOLD
Hafrsfjord
AGDER   Trömöy
Lindesnes

184

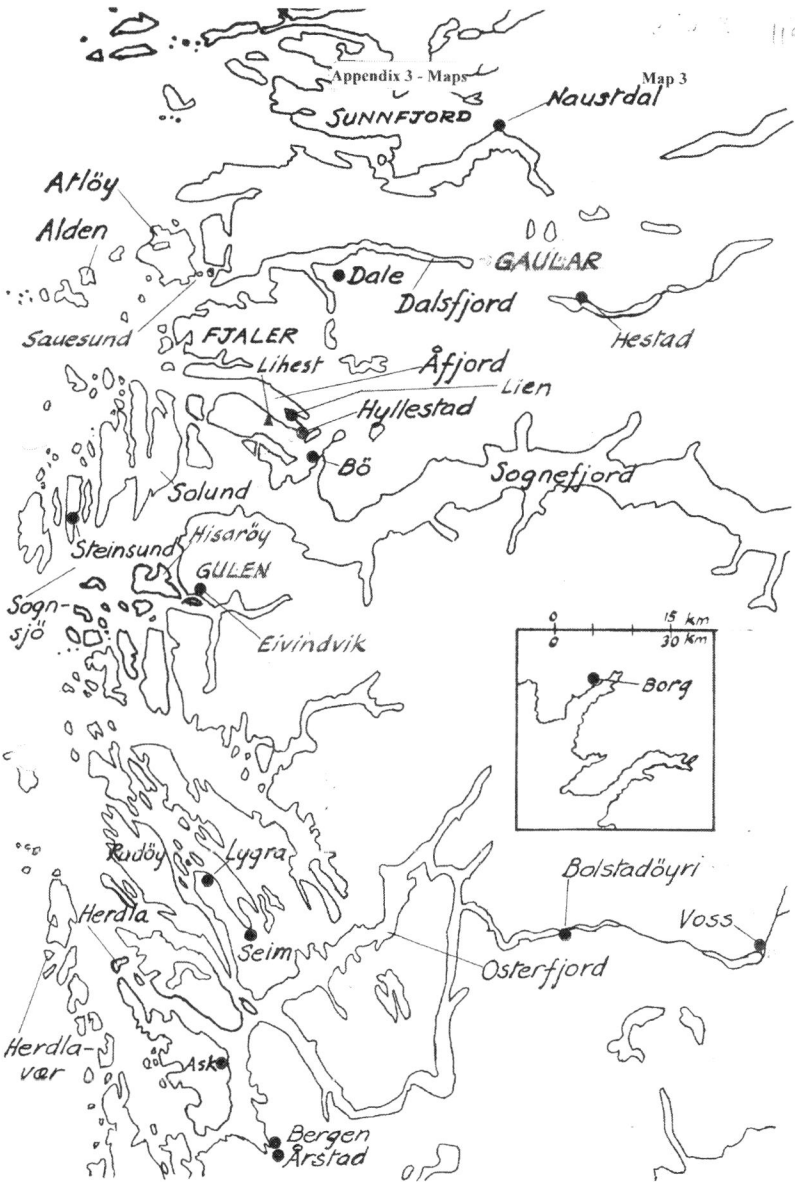

LEGEND FOR MAP 4

Full lines: City walls and streets

Dashed lines: Roman walls and streets

Dotted lines: Lost streets

AW Aldwark

BB Bootham Bar

B Bootham

BG Bartle Garth

BS Blake Street

CHS Chapter House Street

CLG Colliergate

COS Coney Street

CPG Coppergate

CS Church Street

FG Feasegate

FL Fetter Lane

FS Finkle Street

FOG Fossgate

GIG Gilligate

GL Groves (or Shoter) Lane

GOG Goodramgate

HEG Hertergate

HL Haver Lane

HUG Hungate

JG Jubbergate

KM King's Manor

KS King Street

KSQ King's Square

KST King's Staith

L Lendal

M Minster

MIG Micklegate

MOB Monk Bar

MOG Monkgate

MS Market Street

NOS North Street

NSG Nessgate

NWG Newgate

O Ogleforth

OG Ousegate

P Pavement

PG Petergate

PP Patrick Pool

S Shambles

SB Stonebow

SAG St. Andrewgate

SHS St. Helen's Square

SKG Skeldergate

SSG St. Saviourgate

SSS St. Sampson's Square

STG Stonegate

SWG Swinegate

TG Thursgail

WAG Walmgate

WG Whip-Ma-Whop-Ma-Gate

MAP 4

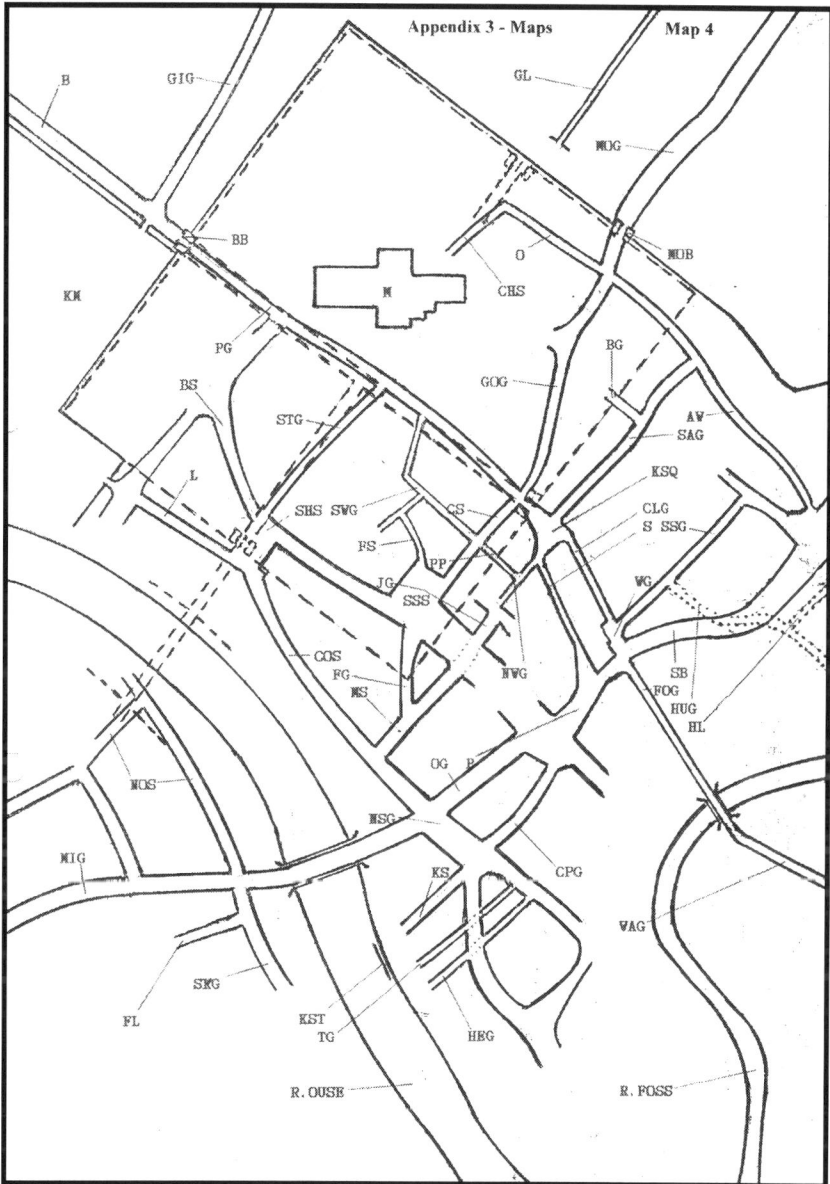

Appendix 3 - Maps   Map 4

MAPS 5 & 6

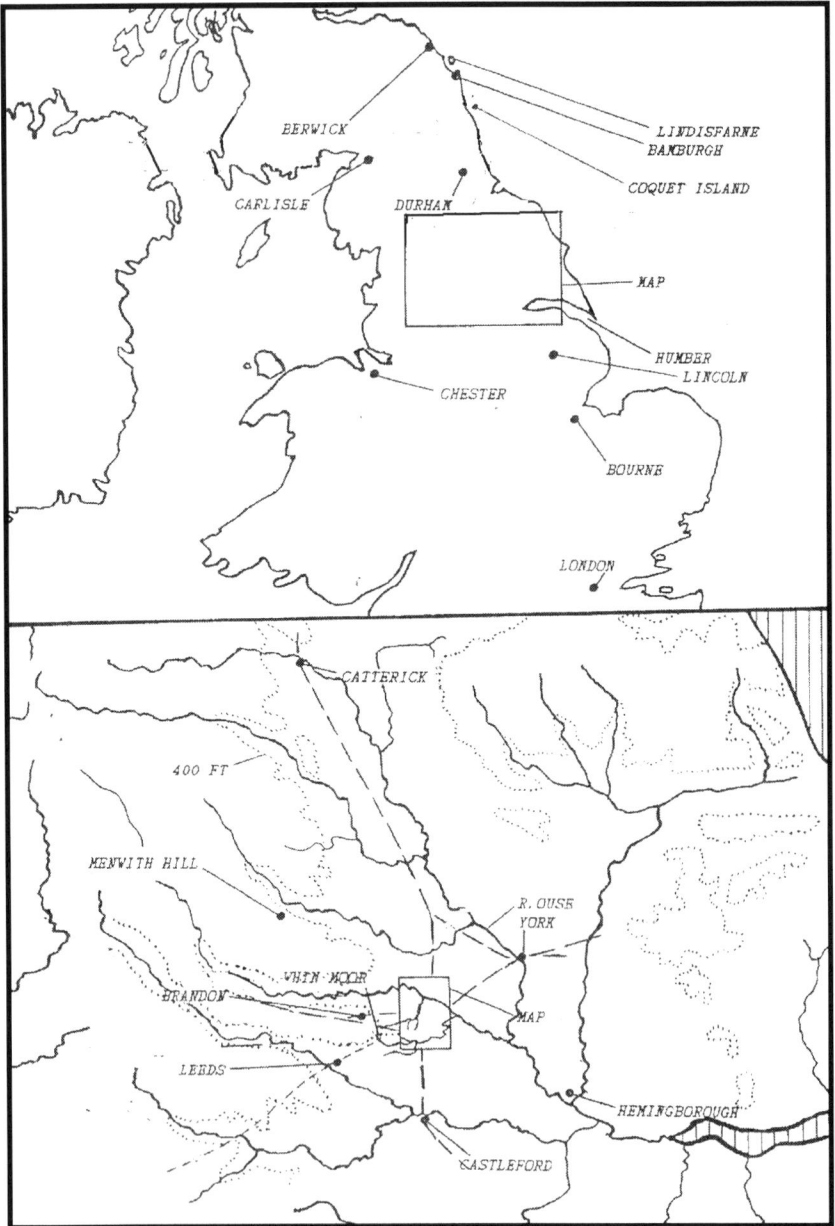

MAP 7

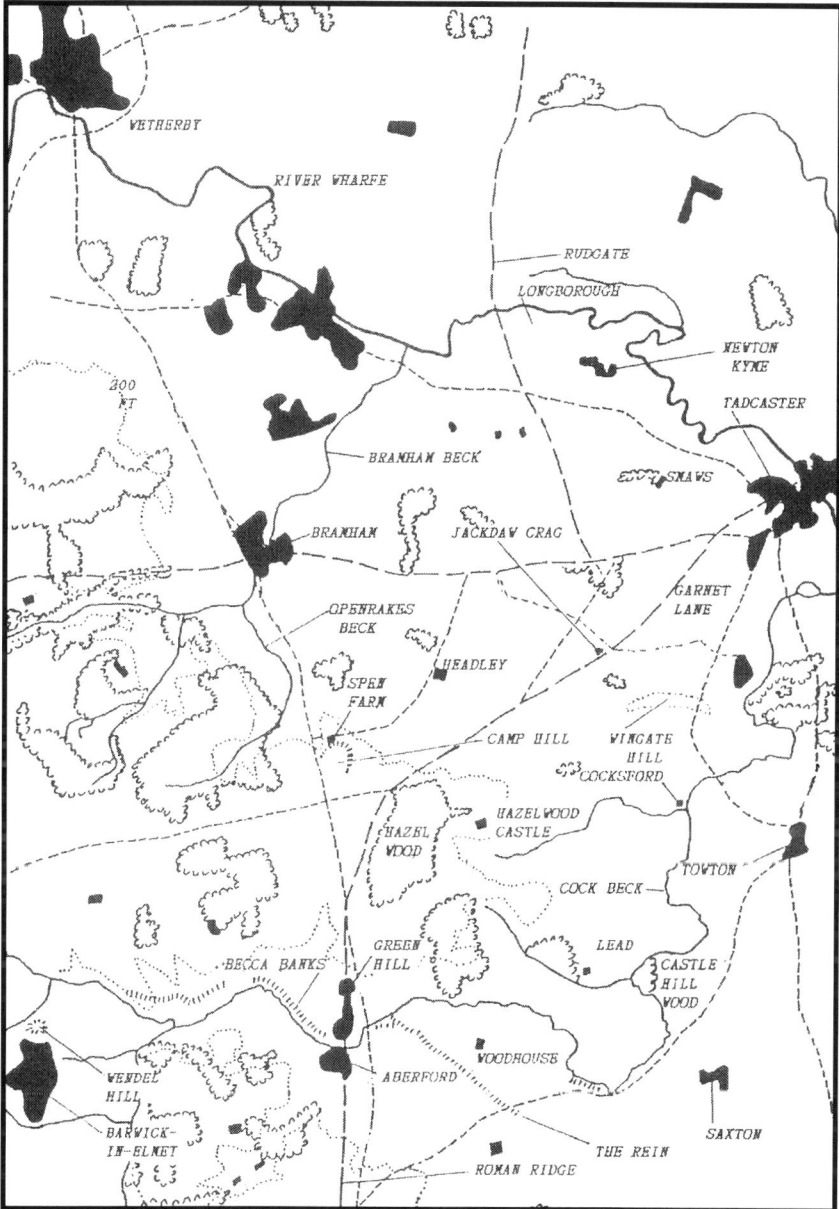

WETHERBY

RIVER WHARFE

RUDGATE

LONGBOROUGH

NEWTON
KYME

TADCASTER

300
FT

BRAMHAM BECK

SNAWS

BRAMHAM

JACKDAW CRAG

GARNET
LANE

OPENRAKES
BECK

HEADLEY

SPEN
FARM

CAMP HILL

WINGATE
HILL
COCKSFORD

HAZELWOOD
CASTLE

HAZEL
WOOD

TOWTON

COCK BECK

LEAD

CASTLE
HILL
WOOD

BECCA BANKS

GREEN
HILL

WOODHOUSE

WENDEL
HILL

ABERFORD

BARWICK-
IN-ELMET

SAXTON

THE REIN

ROMAN RIDGE

Appendix 4

The Structure of York
in Viking Times

Appendix 4

The Structure of York in Viking Times

(App. 3, Map 4)

York was founded by the Romans as the legionary fortress of *Eboracum*. This took place towards the end of the first century AD at the confluence of the rivers Ouse and Foss. It had the usual rectangular plan with four gateways and using a standard internal layout of major features. The *Via Praetoria* leading straight to the headquarters building was approached directly by a bridge over the Ouse. Because of its importance, civilian settlement was attracted so that Eboracum became a town which extended onto the western bank of the Ouse. In the 3rd century it was elevated to the status of a *colonia*, being the largest urban community in the north. Decline set in during the 4th century and by the beginning of the 5th organised civil life was ebbing away.

The state of (Caer) Ebrauc in the post-Roman British period is unclear, while the encroaching heathen Angles apparently had no use for it, except perhaps that it featured as a decaying centre for British resistance that must be overcome and denied to them. With the coming of Christianity activity was renewed. This was not by the Northumbrian Columban church centred on Lindisfarne, but through the coming of the Roman mission of Augustine and, in the north, Bishop Paulinus. With the conversion and baptism of King Edwin in 627 the first minster was built, though small and of timber. In the united kingdom of Northumbria, Bernicia had nothing to compare with *Eoforwic (Ceaster)*, the urban centre of Deira, despite the ruling house of the northern realm achieving dominance. Towards the end of the 7th century the bounds of Northumbria shrank, while throughout the 8th century dynastic squabbles and the threat of schism were ever present. The Roman defences at Eoforwic remained fairly intact, although repairs consisting of a tower and a length of wall have been attributed to this ensuing period.

A civil war between the two persistent factions was under way in the 9th century when the Danish "great heathen army" advanced on Eoforwic and defeated the two English contenders, who had been forced into a pact against a common foe. Thus did *Eorwik* become the capital of Danish Northumbria, which a victorious King Alfred later limited to the Tees in the north. The Southumbrian Danes were eventually to lose their struggle with English Mercia and Wessex, and their growing weakness was spreading north of the Humber, until the Northman Rögnvald seized Eorwik. For three decades it came intermittently under the control of Northmen from the Celtic west, mainly Ireland, who the English kings of the royal house of Wessex were ever trying to overcome, if not dislodge. In 924 King Athelstan came to Eorwik and slighted defences built there by the Danes. The final Norse king in *Iorvik* was Erik Bloodaxe who himself fell foul of the Irish dynasty and other foes.

After Erik *Iork* became the centre of an English earldom, which reverted to being a Norse one after King Canute's accession. The last earl, Tostig, fell out with his brother Harold, king of Wessex, and allied himself with Harald, king of Norway, who had regal ambitions in England. They tried to seize York, but both were killed at Stamford Bridge north-east of the city. After William the Norman won at Hastings in 1066 the north became a centre of resistance to the conquerors. The result was a "scorched earth" policy which devastated much of north-east England and left York in ruins. The Normans secured the city and the Ouse approach by building two castles, one on each side of the river. Although due to suffer further vicissitudes of fortune, medieval York regained its status as a centre of strength and culture, not least by the construction of the city walls and the huge Minster

A feature to note in Yorkshire place-names generally is the suppression of genitive "s" in many, particularly from the Nordic period. This did not occur either with the earlier "Danish" settlers, nor with the later incomers fresh from Norway; it was largely due to contact with the Celtic folk of Britain. This feature is not to be confused with Norse weak or feminine genitives. In York the effect of it can be seen in names like St. Andrewgate, Petergate and maybe Goodramgate; it must be taken into account when considering names. Of course no genitive "s" will feature anyway where the first element is a plural.

There are two surviving references to "king" near the lines of the Roman ramparts. King's Square is mainly just outside of—but includes—the position of the south-east gate of the Roman fort. This open space is oriented towards the ancient commercial area by the Foss, and is actually a "triangle". Any original direct line of the Roman road here is hypothetical, but may have been realigned southwards to become the streets called Colliergate, Whip-Ma-Whop-Ma-Gate and Fossgate. There is also a divergence from the "base" of the triangle presumably developed from a way created outside of and parallel to the Roman wall, eventually to become Newgate, from which The Shambles forked to run roughly parallel to Colliergate. Newgate now continues to a small offset, where it becomes the wider Jubbergate and then Market Street, the latter reaching Coney Street at a right angle beyond the southern corner of the fort. Coney Street runs close to the line of a Roman road from the south-west gateway towards the ness formed by the confluence of the Ouse and Foss, and presumably led directly to a bridge over the latter. The name may mean "King's Street" (rather than "Kings' Street"

In an "Official Guide To York" it is stated about Coney Street (in the other direction) that: "It led by way of Ald Conynge Strete to Earlsborough, the palace of the famous Danish jarl (earl) Siward". "Old Coney Street" was the former name for Lendal (Booth 1990 p156). On the whole the word "street" in York is of later usage than "gate". However, where "street" is preserved in the sense "Roman Road", the reverse will apply and it is suggested that this is the case with Coney Street. This would then represent Old English *Cyninges Strat*, but with later Nordic influence. Thus might one consider that the river frontage under the Roman wall was long regarded as a royal preserve, with wharfage under direct control of the Anglian kings of Deira. There could be a tendency for this to move further downstream with the development of the city into the "Ness" between Ouse and Foss. Eventually the upstream section would tend toward disuse for wharfage, having been supplanted, with its fate finally being sealed by the construction of the Ouse Bridge in stone. Henceforth, sea-going ships would not be able to reach the upper berths without the facility to step masts. "Earlsborough" would appear to have been in the general location of the present. "King's Manor". There was possibly an annexe to the Roman fort on this north-western side near the river, which ultimately formed the basis for the precinct of the high medieval St. Mary's Abbey. The existing King's Manor received its name when this home of the abbots was assigned to Henry VIII at the dissolution of monasteries, but earlier appears to have been *Jarls-borg* (or *Eorles-burh*), which presumably relates to earls such as Eirik of Lade and Siward. The evidence for this name is that Marygate was anciently called "Earlesburgh".

Names like King's Square and King Street are of modern English type, but the former at least should have developed from earlier Norse, or even Anglian usage; the latter appears to have been suggested lately by King's Staith. One side of King's Square is marked as King's Court. The latter version of this name suggests strongly the presence here of the Norse *kunungsgarðr*—"King's garth". The Nordic "kings" of Northumbria needed to be prepared for attack; their realm was surrounded by hostile entities. Of any surviving habitable Roman remains, the internal buildings were probably dominated by the ecclesiastical establishment, and the safest place for a military royal court would be that gateway which was most remote from the outside world, namely the King's Square one, and other gateways were perhaps used as quarters by the main henchmen, such as Arinbjörn Hersi. Leaders ensconced in such defensive structures would also be protected from any enemy within. What "King's" and "Coney" do suggest is that the kings of York did live around the military fringes of the fort and that the access openings associated with them were the south-east and south-west gateways, facing Foss and Ouse respectively.

Rather than "gate" some York streets have used "gail". This is from Norse *geil*, a natural groove or gully, but often implying "hollow way". In York street-names it probably referred to unplanned ways and they sometimes have appeared in use before the Nordic period. Later all were replaced by other names. The use of "lane" in the street-names can be considered as too late to be relevant here, but often replaced "gail". [The data used here for street-names is extracted basically from Booth (1990) pp149-162, Smith (1970) pp275-300 and Ordnance Survey (1988)].

No street in York has survived as a "gail". Several of them that are now "gates" or "lanes" were earlier "gails", although most were never so. One should not take the differentiation as haphazard, but understand that a "gail" was originally simply a worn track not significantly lined with houses or other urban structures. Those that stayed thus into the later middle ages became "lanes", but if they attracted formal buildings at an early date they usually became "gates". It follows that some could have been "gails" without ever being recorded as such. Right from the start a "gate" was something more formal than a "gail". As well as becoming fixed as the typical term for "street" in northern borough developments, "gate" also encompassed meanings such as "open place, pasture, road".

Feasegate was more usually "Fesegail". This appears to be from Old Norse *Fe-husa geil* - "Lane of cow-houses". It has been cut right through the southern corner tower of the Roman fort. The reason for its existence can be seen in later terms as direct access from the old crossing upstream of Ousebridge, by way of Market Street to the Thursday Market (now St. Sampson's Square). Feasegate would provide direct and specific access for cattle drovers.

A lost street on a similar subject was Nowtgail, from Old Norse *naut-geil* - "cattle lane". It was beyond the Foss, the present George Street, and presumably a way for driving cattle into York from this direction using Foss Bridge and Fossgate.

Just to the north of St. Sampson's Square is Swinegate. Unlike cattle, pigs can be kept on a permanent basis in urban surroundings. This would be the case here, with the way through them being called "Swinegail" according to earlier spellings. Against this one can compare Hungate which ran from St. Saviourgate to the Foss. It has never been recorded as a "gail". It can be likened to the Danish street-name Hundegade, as well as Hungate in Lincoln and Houndgate in Darlington. *Hunda-gata* would seem to be a convention brought over from Denmark. Whatever its sense elsewhere, Hungate in York seems to have led to a tip at a marsh by the Foss; it was particularly the refuse from the butchery area to the north-west that was attractive for the keeping of dogs there. A side street is Haver Lane, which suggests the keeping of goats, because the tip provided food which these beasts of catholic taste could devour. Although not recorded one might suspect that this name originated as Old Norse *hafra-geil* - "lane of goats".

The produce of slaughter was later marketed just outside the old fort near King's Square, namely at The

Shambles—"Fleshamelles"—trestles from which meat was sold. This seems to have been included in the ward called Marketshire and referred to in the Domesday Survey Latin (1086) as *in marcello*. Yet the area of The Shambles was earlier the haymarket (i.e. Haymongergate). The parallel lines of The Shambles and Colliergate outside of the south-east Roman gateway suggest that the whole was an open space leading from King's Square and whose centre was built over to leave two narrow streets, thus becoming unsuitable for a haymarket. From an early date "Ketmongergate" appeared; it is Old Norse *kjötmangara-gata*—"meatmonger street"—and is identical to Købmagergade in Copenhagen, earlier "Kødmangergade". This name again looks like a convention imported from Denmark. Yet it originally seems to have been applied as a description, rather than a name, because it was used for both the streets running eastwards from the haymarket, now St. Andrewgate and St. Saviourgate.

The main slaughtering cannot have taken place far from King's Square. This would explain further the position of Swinegate, namely to receive offal as pig-food. One can see further evidence of the industrial use of the by-products of butchery in the street-names Hornpot Lane and Girdlergate (now Church Street), involving the working of horns and hides respectively. The availability of the latter commodity can also be seen as responsible for Glover Lane (earlier Glovergail), an alley joining Low Petergate to Swinegate. Sheep are not separately in evidence, but Hosier Lane (earlier "Hosier Row") was that part of Pavement adjoining The Shambles, while Fetter Lane (earlier Feltergail) was across the Ouse near the Ouse Bridge. The concentration of industries not involving animal products can be observed in other areas, e.g. Spurriergate (spurs) and Coppergate (woodwork).

A "gail" with a bake-house is recorded with "Bacusgail'" It reached Pavement nearly opposite The Shambles and may have been the route for driving cattle from Foss Bridge before Fossgate was created, or to provide means to avoid this.

Finkle Street is of a kind that is associated with many borough developments in the North of England. Elsewhere it appears to have been applied specifically to the way leading to the entrance of such boundered official markets. The York one was written as Finclegayle in 1356, before becoming Finkullstrete by 1370. The change may have been made to suit the convention established elsewhere. Since it connects St. Sampson's Square (i.e. the cattle market) with Swinegate, it is apt to note that in the 19th century it had come to be known as Mucky Pig Lane. The first part is probably from Celtic, i.e. Gaelic *muca* (rather than Welsh *moch*)—"pigs". "Finkle" resists explanation. However the association with market entrances suggests it to be derived from an early practice of controlling such narrow access by means of a "funicule" or rope (from Latin *funiculus*). Such a term would then be due to the Normans, with initially a derived pronunciation "fünkel". That the Thursday Market in St. Sampson's Square is descended from an earlier "borough" entity is indicated by the former presence of a Tollbooth and Guildhall there. (Smith 1970 p289)

Skeldergate lies over the Ouse and probably is a name derived from one of two origins. If it embodies the personal name Skjold to give *Skjaldar-gata*, it would be unusual in York's earlier "-gate" names. More in common with these would be the featuring of *skjaldari*— "shield-maker"—hence *skjaldara-gata*—"shield-makers' street". Early spellings are not decisive, unlike those of Skelderskew, near Castleton, which consistently suggest *Skjaldar-skogr*—"Skjold's wood".

Across the Ouse a street was once called Hertergate (later Far Water Lane and now Friargate. It is ostensibly in the same vein as Skeldergate and suggests a personal name, i.e. *Hjartar-gata*—"Hjort's Street". Old Norse *hjortr* means "stag". But it is one of three ways down to the Ouse at King's Staith, the others being King Street, a continuation of Coppergate, and Cumberland Street between the two. Earlier forms were Cargate (or Kergate) for King Street and Thursgail for Cumberland Street. These suggest the presence of Old Norse *kiarr*—"wetland"—and *thurs*—"giant"—but there are problems with the old names for all these three streets that are two complex for discussion here.

The above suggests that, while the Ouse frontage was at an early date under direct royal control, the Foss frontage was not and became the main wharf zone for the merchant classes who were to be concentrated in the south-eastern quarter of the city. The triangular King's Square (or King's Court), outside the Roman south-east gateway, has a name of recent form, and indeed was largely filled by Christ Church until 1937. This casts some doubt on the royal connections of the open space. Yet there has long been a convenient way from King's

Square via Colliergate (or The Shambles) and Coppergate to King's Staith. Also, as already noted, from King's Square a route parallel to the rampart passes from Newgate to Market Street via Jubbergate, which last may be the original name for all this thoroughfare. The whole route suggests a former way from the "King's Square" gateway to a ferry or wooden bridge in use before the first stone "Ousebridge" was built. It lines up with the main run of Micklegate opposite, which then can be assumed to have been diverted southwards when such permanent bridge was built a little downstream.

Not. all street.-names using "gate" can be assumed to have origins in the Norse period; the word became naturalised in the local dialect and indeed was used to create names in more recent times, e.g. Davygate and Deangate. It also follows that if names using "street" are not relatively recent, then they are very old, preceding the "-gate" names absolutely. Three surviving such names have been identified, i.e. Coney Street, North Street and Blake Street. (Booth 1990 pp149, 151, 157). North Street now lies along the Ouse west bank, but originally included a stretch at right angles away from the river and running from Toft Green. Now called Tanner Row, where this reaches the river it is in line with the Roman bridge. This could explain the origin of Anglo-Saxon North Street and Danish derived Toft Green, these being along the Roman road, the latter name even suggesting occupation in Roman times, a *vicus*. Blake Street. is not likely to include Old Norse *bleikr* (adjective) or *Bleikr* (personal name) directly and meaning "pale", since one would then have expected Blakegate. It probably originated in Anglian times as Old English *blæce-stræt* - "street where bleaching took place". On its present. line it cannot have had a Roman origin; it perhaps became a "street" by being considered an off-set continuation of Coney Street. Its line suggests part of a convenient diagonal track which evolved between Bootham Bar and the gateway at St. Helen's Square. The rest of this route is still well marked by the curving boundary between the Theatre Royal and St. Wilfrid's Catholic Church.

Kunungsgardh is the name given to Erik's quarters in York. After Egil's men and all Arinbjörn's housecarls had armed themselves: *ðá gekk hann í konungsgarð*—"then went he (Arinbjörn) into king's garth". The term persisted in English records of the 13th century as *kuningesgard, conyngesgarth*, etc., which indeed strengthens the claim of identity with the present King's Court. (or Square). The use of *durum* (dative plural) to describe the entrance where Arinbjörn knocked to proclaim his arrival, could be construed to refer to the usual double gates of a Roman fort.(Gordon 1927 pp108, 230)

A feature of the York street-names is that people were segregated into types, usually relating to status, race or occupation. Thus Coney Street (already mentioned), Bretgate—"Britons", Coppergate—"carpenters" (from Old Norse *koppari*) and Colliergate—"charcoal burners or sellers". Colliergate leads to the medieval bridging point of the Foss via Whip-Ma-Whop-Ma-Gate and Fossgate. The first of these is really a small square and suggests a place used for public floggings. But such "silly" names are usually corruptions of forerunners no longer understood and these may often be Celtic. However, in this case it is proposed that the name was Norse and derived from the the verb *vapna*—"to arm". The whole would be a standard cry, something like *vapnaðir með vopnum (i gatu)*—"armed with weapons (in street)". A mustering point for warriors, perhaps before embarking at the King's Staith, is inferable. With repetition, loss of some unstressed elements would give "vapna-me-vopnum-(i-gate)". In England Norse "v-"regularly gave "w-"later and "h" here would be intrusive, suggested by the notion of "whipping". The 16th century spelling "Whipnam Whapnamgate" supports this assertion. One might note a similarity with the language used as Egil was about to confront Erik in York, when Arinbjörn said: *Taki menn ða vapn sin*—"Let men take then (each) his weapon". After this they are immediately described as *vapnaðir*—"armed". (Gordon 1927 p108) *Með vopnum* also occurs specifically in association with York, namely in the account of the Battle of Stamford Bridge in *Fagrskinna*. (Gordon 1927 p160)

It is reasonable to surmise that there was originally a Roman parade ground at this location. If so, the area will have been much larger. It would eventually be the site of a special "holy cross" and the church of St. Crux would later be built there, while the wide street called Pavement, stretching away to the south-west, might relate retrospectively to that same Roman feature.

Of the four Roman gateways, three have remained as openings until the present, namely Bootham Bar and the King's Square and St. Helen's Square ones. The Roman roads from the gates have tended to be lost. The basic reason for this is that once the Roman bridges over the Ouse and Foss were destroyed passage became difficult and the roads fell into disuse. The later arrangements were governed by activities both within and without the fort walls in the Anglian, Viking and later Medieval Periods. Only the road out of Bootham Bar to the north-west maintained its line as a thoroughfare, because no river crossing was involved. The route to the north-east was broken by the loss of the relevant gateway and replaced both by Gillygate, running externally from Bootham Bar and the Medieval Monk Bar, this being a new opening further south-east and reached internally by the thoroughfare called Goodramgate. However, even though the route through the Roman north-east gateway has been interrupted, it apparently still exists externally as Groves Lane, earlier Shoter Lane, and internally as Chapter House Street, the Roman *Via Decumana.* As with all such Roman ways in York there has been a tendency to stray somewhat from the original line.

The internal framework of the fort was rather disrupted by the building of successive minsters (St. Peter's) on their diagonal orientation, while much of the northern angle became an ecclesiastical precinct. The loss of the north-east gateway was probably due to the church authority wishing to deprive mammon of the old access close to the cathedral, and the instigators of this change are suggested by the names Monk Bar and Monkgate. Yet the old *Via Principalis* is still preserved as Petergate, although with a bulge to the north-east, while the *Via Praetoria,* from the south-west gateway to the fort centre, is represented by Stonegate, although now veering somewhat to the right as it approaches Petergate. These deviations cannot represent any form of planning; they suggest haphazard reassertions of thoroughfares after periods of complete ruin, rather than creeping developments resulting from successive rebuilding, There are three periods when such is likely to have taken place: in the sub-Roman period before the Anglian kings of Northumbria revitalised York; in the 8th century (Booth 1990 p9) or in the wake of the Norman conquest (Booth 1990 p20).

The south-west gateway survived the loss of the Roman Ouse bridge. A road to the north-west is now only represented by the short street called Lendal, external to and closely parallel to the line of the rampart. It was earlier known as Lendinge street or Old Coney Street. Coney Street itself, as remarked above, represents the Roman road to the south-east, but appears to be only good for approach to the

"Ness". "Coney" owes its form to a compromise between Old Norse *kunungr* and Old English *cyning*, but in any case it can be argued that it constituted the approach to the royal wharfs along the Ouse. This appears to be confirmed by "King's Staith", which is reached by way of King Street, an extension of Coppergate. The latter itself is approached by way of The Shambles and Pavement. The medieval Ouse Bridge was built upstream of King's Staith and was served by a new route from Pavement, namely Ousegate, which was then connected with a realigned Micklegate on the far bank. The date of the first bridge to replace the lost Roman one cannot be established, but may have been before the Norman Conquest, presumably on the line of Jubbergate, as mentioned above. In Norman times the hindrance to shipping of such a wooden structure may have been avoided by including a drawbridge. King's Staith as a name did not come into general use until Tudor times, but is associated with visits to York in the 13th and 14th centuries by kings Edward I, II and III. This may be considered in conjunction with the first stone bridge probably having been built towards the end of the 12th century (Booth 1990 pl19) and the movement of the royal staith downstream because of this.

The frequency of street-names in "-gate" is a testimony to the Nordic presence in York. Stonegate, rather than "stanegate", would appear to be a later Anglicisation: both "stan-" and "stein-" feature in the 13th century. The name would appear to date from a time when it still lay directly on the line of the metalled Roman way. Goodramgate should contain the Nordic personal name Guthrum *(Guðormr)*, although the feminine name *Guðrun* is also possible; or it may even have a descriptive sense. Like Blake Street it seems to have been a way that evolved obliquely between two Roman gates, but its north end has been captured and redirected to the repositioned medieval gate known as Monk Bar, which replaced the Roman one.

The Norse kings who ruled in Northumbria before Erik had strong links with Dublin and it might be expected that there would be Irish material among York's nomenclature. They were also frequently allied to Britons; so where is reference to the Welsh or the Irish? Erik Bloodaxe had no such firm Celtic connections and neither did the earls later installed as a result of Cnut's conquest, i.e. Eirik and Siward. Such potentates and their followers could be expected to introduce Nordic language into Yorkshire untainted with either Celtic or English. Can one see signs of these points at York?

Jubbergate was earlier recorded as "Brettegate", apparently from Old Norse *Breta-gata*—"Street of Britons (Bretons?)". *Bretir* meant "Welsh" and Jubbergate—"(Jew)Bretgate"—may have been a concentration of such just outside the fort wall. At some later time it was taken over by Jews. (Little) Bretgate over the Foss is inside of and strictly parallel to the city wall there and hence seems like a later medieval development. Are these people who moved from Jubbergate, perhaps even because of the encroachment of Jews? If (Jew)Bretgate is pre-Norman conquest, Bretons cannot be involved.

A name that seems to involve Britons is Penley's Grove Street. The earlier rendering "Paynlathcrofts" indicates an ancient origin. "Payn-" can hardly be Welsh *penn*—"top, hill". The name becomes interesting if one thinks of "Paynlath-"in terms of Welsh *paun-llaet*—"peacock of milk", *paun-llaid*—"peacock of mire", or *paun-llaith*—"peacock of death" or "damp peacock". These appear to make little sense, but one can extract *paun-llaid, paun-llaith* and compare them with Peasholme, a little further down the Foss at the end of the city wall across this river from Layerthorpe. "Holm" is a word of Nordic derivation often meaning "raised land in a mire", while "pea" is a peafowl. But. *Pá*—"peacock"—was used as a by-name by Northmen. Indeed, Egil Skallagrimsson's daughter Thorgerdh was married to Olaf Pa. Peasholme can thus be regarded as an Anglicised version of "Pa's island in the mire", rather than "island in the mire where peas were grown", as suggested by the earliest medieval spellings. In this case the name could have existed in Welsh either as *paun-llaid* - "peacock of the mire" - or *paun-llaith* - "damp peacock". The Norse version would be original and this is a sign that folk were indulging in word-play, a Celtic trait.

What then were the "crofts" of Paynlath? If not the obvious solution, one can associate them with the "groves" of Penley's Grove Street and Groves Lane. To the north-east of the fortress wall there have been found Roman fields with scattered burials. Such use may have continued in the neighbourhood of the road leaving the fortress on this side, but with the "graves" later being known as the "groves". The confusion between Old English *græf* and *graf* is quite common in place-names. If the "crofts" do not relate to anciently visible Roman *vicus* type remains, the reference may have arisen by *græf* once being thought of as meaning "pit, ditch" and represented as Norse *gröft* of that sense. Whether the word-play was ever taken to its logical conclusion in that 'Paynlath' was thought of as Welsh *poen-laith*—"pain of death" in the sense "grief"—is a moot point. Groves Lane had an earlier name Shoter Lane. Both Old English and Old Norse had words like "shoter" meaning "archer". Welsh warriors were more likely to be bowmen than Angles or Scandinavians. But the connections with "archery" may have had to do with Welsh *bwa* meaning "bow" in this sense, as well as "arch" in the sense "gateway".

Ogleforth is a fascinating name. It was recorded from early in the 12th century in forms like "Vgle-", "Huggil-", "Ugel-", "Ogul-", "Huggleford" and, in 1546, "Ogleforth", but there seems no way that it can mean "ford" in the usual sense. It is just inside the rampart from the "Welsh" area described above, so perhaps it involves Welsh *ffordd*—"way, road"; but this does not help with "Ugle-", which one can however better clarify with recourse to Gaelic.

Before proceeding the reader must prepare himself for more word-play. The pervading notion is that of "arch", which is also expressed by the word "bow". With Ogleforth the cosmopolitan nature of York's population in the 10th century is to be borne in mind, even though the various ethnic groups tended to be segregated. The presence of Gaelic speakers from both Ireland and the western isles of Scotland is to be expected. Beginning with Gaelic *bogha*—"bow"—this could be readily compared with *bothar*—"road, lane, street"—if the "-r" be neglected. Indeed, *bothar bogha* means "road of (the) arch (bow)". One might then suspect that the "Shoter Lane" mentioned above has been derived from this; there were no actual "archers"! Hence the road passing through the north-eastern Roman gateway may have been *bothar bogha* in Gaelic and *ffordd bwa* in Welsh—"way of (the) bow".

Returning to "Ogle-", one can choose between two solutions in Gaelic, *Ui Gaedhil*—"descendents of (the) Gaels"—or *Ua Gille*—"descendent (grandson) of (the) servant". Anyhow, either could lead to "Ugel-" or "Ogel-" once understanding was lost. The "U-" may also have been confused with various words for "yew". One can refer to the name York itself being derived from a Celtic name meaning "yew"—*Eburos*. (Smith 1970 pp275-80) Gaelic *bothar ui gille*—"way of (the) descendent of the servant"—could be rendered in Welsh as *ffordd yw gelli*—"way of (the) yew of (the) grove". Here one must recall that yew was the wood used for bows and also the "groves" already mentioned! But Old Norse *yr* is said to have had the meaning "bow of yew" (Houken 1956 p246). It is just possible that the earlier Celtic forms of "Ugel-" came to be recognised by Scandinavians as *y-geil*—"yew (bow) lane". Ogleforth was really the way of the "yew bow", itself being a reference to the north-east gateway of the Roman fort. This has since vanished, being replaced by Monk Bar. Outside of the gate "yew grove" perhaps had an additional significance here in view of its traditional association with burials.

The use of "bow" can be seen in the street-name Stonebow (with comparison to "yew-bow" to be noted. This is a modern resurrection, but was earlier applied to a narrower way in the same area. It apparently refers to a lost stone arch, which must have been of Roman origin. Just. to the north lies Aldwark. This term was used by the Angles to refer to defensive earthworks of earlier folk; in this case surely referring to one by the Romans. The relevant "old work" would be a rampart of similar purpose to the one proposed above at King's Manor to the north-west of the fortress, being required to close the gap between the main rampart and the river, here the Foss. The "old work" was probably an earthwork with an arch set in it, from which the way within took its name. Outside this "stone-bow" the way eventually led via Peasholme Green to Layerthorpe over the Foss, the crossing now being marked by Layerthorpe Bridge. The element *thorp* in England can generally be regarded as Danish and Layerthorpe could well include Danish *ler*, Old Norse *leir*—"clay, loam"—and be identical to the Danish place-name Lerdrup. However, the earliest spelling (11th century) gives "Legerathorp". This can be compared with Old English *legerstow*—"burial place". It is not suggested that this is the original sense of Layerthorpe, but that it shows influence from the general association with cemeteries that is evident to the north-east of the site of the Roman fort.

Many street-names referred to activities taking place in them, some still obvious, some not. Among these one can name Horsefair, The Shambles, Colliergate, Swinegate, Grape Lane, Hosier Lane, Girdlergate, Fishergate, etc. St. Leonard's Hospital was descended from a pre-Norman establishment in the western corner of the Roman fort. Two reminders of activities there are the lost Lop Lane and

Footlessgail. The latter is from Old Norse *fot-lauss*—"footless"—while the former may also refer pithily to amputation and other primitive surgery, while both could be different names for the same way. One can readily surmise that Lop Lane eventually became associated with folk infested with fleas. The names probably both referred to the unfortunate inmates of the former St. Leonard's Hospital. The choice of the name "Leonard" may even have been influenced by the nearby area called Lendal.

Gaelic connections with the north-west zone of the fortress were already established in the 10th century when King Athelstan entrusted the early hospital to the Culdees in 937. They were a sect of obscure origin whose main areas of activity were Scotland and Ireland (Booth 1990 p126). They were the *cuildeach,* from *ceile-de*—"spouse of God". Lendal seems to contain some derivative of the word "land", such as Danish *lænde*—"strip of land"—and one can particularly look at Old Danish *ålænding*—"strip by a river"—and Swedish *länning*—"landing place" (Houken 1956 p124). Without early forms the exact nature of the name Lendal cannot be confidently determined, with the "-a" creating a difficulty. However, owing to the links with Gaels this just might be derived from Gaelic, i.e. as in Modern Irish *leana-dala* (Scots Gaelic *lon-dalach)*—"meadow of assembly"—in other words equivalent to a Norse *thing-völlr* and presumably with early reference to the eventual King's Manor precinct. To the English "leana-d-" could easily be understood as referring to some compound in Old English leading with something like "Leonard", i.e. *Leonard-hall* or *Leonard-halh.*

Bootham, outside the fortress's north-west gateway, is Old Norse *(á) buðum*—"(at) booths". These were usually structures for temporary accommodation, but may here have referred to poor housing. Running off to the north is Gillygate. It is natural to assume that the street-name refers to a church dedicated to St. Giles. If so one must wonder why the name was not Gilesgate, as indeed is the case in Durham. Otherwise why is the "St" missing in this case, in contrast to other York place-names of this type, e.g. St. Andrewgate? One might surmise that the association with St. Giles was suggested by an existing way-name. If there were Irish retainers in the area they would be "gillies", from Gaelic *gille*—"servant"—borrowed into Norse as *gilli*, so that the way they lived along would become *gilla-gata*. If this were right it would add weight to any proposition regarding an earlier precinct at the eventual King's Manor, and one might have caught a glimpse from there of Irish gillies dwelling in booths "beyond the pale".

The association with St. Giles occurred early enough, with a reference to St. Egidius in a 12th century Yorkshire charter. (Smith 1970 p288) Giles is another name for Egidius, the latter name being based on Greek for "kid", and both owe their introduction to the Normans. The "booths" of the "gillies" would be there earlier than this and one can recognise the extramural settlement involved in the charter entry *in vico Sancti Egidii*. One can perhaps recognise a reference to Egidius in the lost Kidcotes, a prison belonging to the Archbishop. Yet oddly enough Giles is actually the patron saint of cripples, beggars and lepers, while Leonard was the one for captives! The two saints, appear to have exchanged functions here. One might note that there is still a persistent element of word-play involved in this discussion.

A feature of the Norse heathen religion was hanging, this being done as an aspect of the cult of Odin. Such heathens would be active very early in the story of Nordic York, but one can imagine that they were excluded from the fort itself. Let it then be proposed that they operated near the above-mentioned *thing-völlr* on the site that eventually was occupied by St. Mary's Abbey. Two names point to this proposition being just, Galmanhowe and Galmanlythe. Galmanhowe can be localised in that Earl Siward built a church there dedicated to St. Olaf. The '-lythe' is from Old Norse *hlið*. In York a word like this, but with short vowel, is used for the gateways until replaced by French-derived "bar", hence "Bouthumlith" and "Bouthumbarre", both for Bootham Bar. Old English *geat*—"gate"—is not in evidence, apparently eventually avoided to prevent confusion with "gate" meaning "street". *Hlið* was also used at Micklegate Bar, but not at the later Monk and Walmgate Bars. But *hlið* (with long vowel) had the meaning "slope, bank, hill", and there is evidence to show that it was frequently used in connection with heathen sites (see Chapter 3 above). One can hence propose this sense at Galmanlythe, especially in view of the evident "long" vowel. Galman can be taken to represent *Galge-mann*—"gallows man"—perhaps meaning "hangman". However the name "Odin" was taboo, so he had alternative names, e.g. Grim; Galgemann may have been one of them. Galmanhowe appears to be the same name, except that Norse *hlið* has been replaced by Old English *hōh* of similar sense.

The Galmanhowe site appears to have been first Christianised by the construction of a "minster" (i.e. church) there by Earl Siward early in the 11th century and dedicated to St. Olaf. This is the present St. Olave's. Because of the Gaelic congregation hereabouts it is not surprising to find the form Olave prevailing, since this reflects the Irish version *Amblaibh*.

The oddly named Patrick Pool was a street which earlier included Swinegate, which lay in line to the north-west. The elements are both of Celtic origin, although the word order is Germanic. Old names in "-pool" are scarce in the east (e.g. Hartlepool), but more common in the west (e.g. Liverpool, Blackpool). Pooley Bridge at the foot of Ullswater suggests the general area whence this name came. At the head of Ullswater is Patterdale, with earlier spellings with and without genitive ending, i.e. "Patrichesdale" (1184) and "Patricdale" (1246). This suggests strongly links with Ireland, but there is no cause to associate it with St. Patrick; it is more probably the name of a landholder. The same should apply with the "Patrigpole, Patricpol(e)" recorded in York in the 12th century, but probably dating from earlier times. Celtic order of elements is shown by Aspatria in Cumberland, "Ascpatric' (c1230)—"Patrick's Ash". Patrick Pool was apparently named from a pond, whose presence in later times caused flooding enough to make the way impassable, but possibly associated with the former water supply to the nearby Roman baths on the north side of St. Sampson's Square. The original pond may have been valued as a watering place for the pigs kept in this area and the beasts that were marketed nearby.

While the historical geography of York throughout the first millennium has been rather unevenly explored above, the state of the city around the time of Erik Bloodaxe still needs to be clarified. This was specifically in the late 940s. One firm date is the entrusting of that hospital to the Culdees in 937 by King Athelstan. This followed his victory at Brunanburh, where he had been helped by Egil Skallagrimsson. Yet why should he show favour to this particular Gaelic sect, since the army opposing him had been largely recruited in Ireland and Scotland? Athelstan was an astute ruler, so one might suspect appeasement of the Irish as a motive.

It is self-evident that the Norse kings from Ireland would have Gaelic speakers in their retinues, some of mixed race and some probably bilingual. Mainly in the North Riding, there are the place-names of the Nordic "-by" type, but embodying Irish personal names, namely Carperby, Melmerby, Bretanby, Melsonby, Gatenby, Lackenby and Duggleby. The last actually involves Dufgal, the Norse form of Gaelic *dubhgall,* meaning "dark stranger" but considered to be used specifically for "Dane". The distribution suggests that the main access route of such incomers was through Wensleydale or over Stainmore by way of Morecambe Bay or the Solway. None of these names exhibit the "-s" genitive and Patrick Pool in York is in the same "Irish name" tradition.

On the whole there are no further signs of Celts within the Roman walls beyond Ogleforth and Patrick Pool. Patrick may have considered himself a Northman, despite his Irish name. Inside the old fortifications the dominant languages would be English and Norse. The same would apply in the external south-western zone, towards the Foss, where the latter tongue probably predominated. The main stronghold of English would be the Minster precinct in the north angle of the fort, with political York being conceived as an alliance between the Anglian archbishopric of the north and the Norse secular domain.

At the time that Egil visited Arinbjörn and the pair confronted Erik, the internal street pattern would include Petergate, Stonegate and Ogleforth. The north-eastern gateway would still be usable and Goodramgate would be a diagonal lane intersecting Ogleforth near it. Such diagonal lanes would be precluded across the north and south angles by the Minster precinct and cattle market respectively. The western diagonal lane had probably recently been curtailed and redirected by the Culdees hospital, the remnant retaining the name Blake Street.

As probably also being the case with his rival Irish-Norse kings, Erik would be using the gatehouses of the old Roman fort as fortlets, but elsewhere there must have been a place of open-air assembly where the "thing" could meet. These gatherings traditionally involved a raised platform from which the law-speaker could address the appointed thingmen and the crowd. There are signs that this could have been near the eventual Lendal. Here there was a river "landing", but the name "Lendal" arose because of a later concentration of Gaelic speakers drawn by the presence of the Culdees. It could well be that the remains of the Roman multangular tower served as the law-speaker's platform. Hereabouts Irish speakers came to be present near the river and a ferry nearby can be suspected. The other side was marked by Devlin Stones. The reference specifically to Dublin is obscure, but the stones perhaps referred to the remains of a pier or abutment of the Roman bridge surviving to serve as the opposite ferry landing. The Culdee site itself occupied the western angle of the fort. Its south-east boundary formed the basis for the later Footless and Lop Lanes, the eventual Museum Street and Duncombe Place. Gaelic retainers were concentrated in "booths" outside the north-west wall and such "gillies" gave their name in the course of time to Gillygate.

The Britons appear to have been concentrated outside of the north-east wall. York must always have had an attraction for them and they still have their own name for it, i.e. Welsh *Caer Efrog*. They had a historical tendency to ally themselves with the Northmen, since both had the common need to overthrow the dominant kingdom of Wessex. Yet if one judges from those Britons who fought against Athelstan at Brunanburh, the Welsh most involved in Northumbria were those from Strathclyde (Cumbrians) rather than from the present Wales.

The Britons implicit in Jubbergate appear to be a detached community, hence their special mentioning. However, this is next to Feasegate and one might deduce that the herding of animals was in the hands of such Celts, so that those associated with the running of the cattle market lived here. This market suggests that the fort as a whole was made to operate as a closed commercial borough. While the gates limited access to all, dealing was confined to the southern quarter. To facilitate access for beasts it was found "feasible" to cut a special way through the southern corner tower to create Feasegate. Butchery would take place somewhere in this general southern zone and the meat taken out through the south-east gate for sale in streets north-east of the haymarket (later Colliergate). Outside the gateway itself was an open space where the haymarket was held, but also used for assembling troops, thus reflecting its origins as a Roman parade ground. Inside the gateway industry flourished that depended on animal by-products, such as horns and hides. Patrick Pool provided a watering place in an area where swine were kept. Celtic elements in this name again point to animals while still on the hoof being the charges of folk of Celtic background. This leads one to believe that manufacturing and trading were the spheres of operation of Germanic folk, particularly the Northmen. They were mainly to be found in the areas to the south-east and south towards the Foss, and also over the Ouse in the Micklegate-Skeldergate area.

By the very nature of the problems involved the above cannot claim to paint the full and final picture with regard to the social and physical structures of York in the 10th century, but one can perhaps observe an expansive ecclesiastical core within the Roman ramparts, with regal authority being vested in a military fringe and using the Roman gate-houses as quarters. In addition to the expected Anglian and Norse material there is indication of British and Irish presence, although direct evidence for this is sparse and it has been greatly obscured from us by the Celtic liking to indulge in esoteric word-play.

Appendix 5

Photographs

All taken by William Pearson or his wife June

Photographs Nos 1 to 4—Naustdal (Nordfjord)

1. Naustdal. The head of the wyke, this being a minor coastal indentation and with its row of wooden "nausts".

2. A farmhouse on its platform. The higher vacant platform is on the right. This could well be where Vemund was burned in by Rögnvald on behalf of King Harald.

3. A view from near the higher platform showing its view down the Nordfjord and over some of the farmland.

4. The higher platform with the monolith near its edge.

Photographs Nos 5 to 8—Voss

5. The church (whose spire can be seen) stands on a low ridge that runs to the right where the river (behind the trees) enters the lake. Behind is the large "vang". In the foreground the sloping beach remains, but can be seen to have been built up in front of the church. The alternative site for the hall would be to the left of the church, on slopes off the picture.

6. St. Olaf's cross on its mound on the south end of the low ridge.

7. Looking north from the infilled quay area towards the railway station. The church spire is on the right. An alternative platform site for the hall where Skallagrim confronted Harald would be where the ridge met the foot of a slope just behind it, rather than near the hotel and railway station (as indicated by the figure). The longer distance to the shore would better serve the description of Skallagrim's escape.

8. Looking eastwards from Vossevangen. Skallagrim's return by rowing boat would have been to the distant dale, along which the sea can be gained at the head of Bolstadfjord.

Photographs Nos 9 to 12—Hestad

9. Hestad church on its knoll, looking north.

10. Hestad church among trees at the end of the spit. The hamlet is at the landward end of the spit to the north. This place is proposed here as the site for Erik Bloodaxe's heathen gathering at Gaular, where he was enraged by Egil Skallagrimsson. The short water link between the two lakes (the Kyrkjelisund) is now bridged.

11. Looking west from Hestad church over Lake Hestadfjord.

12. Looking east from Hestad church along Lake Vikdalsvatn.

Photographs Nos 13 to 16—Eivindsvik

13. The high cross at Eivindsvik.

14. The high cross at Eivindsvik showing the harbour below. The place is screened from the main body of the Gulefjord by the small island seen beyond, on which is Fonna.

15. View westwards across the harbour from the doorway of the church. This stands on a ridge of rock that overlooks the wyke, but which has been cut through by the main road immediately beyond the figure.

16. View across the wyke showing the church on its rocky ridge. There is only one location where "a level place" exists that could be "marked out with hazel wands set in a ring and strung with ropes" and wherein sat the judges of the 10th century Gulathing gathering. This lies to the left of the church and is now mainly filled by the cemetery. The low cross is among the trees to the left of the church and from this position one can overlook the small plain. It is from here that the thingmen and attendant crowd could have been addressed by law speakers. The level area has since been increased in size by infill in front of the white house to the left to provide a deep water quay with space behind it.

Photographs Nos 17 & 18—Hisaröy

17. On this view looking north-westwards, the island of Hisaröy is on the left. The water is the sound along which Arinbjörn would sail to his home further north along the coast. After the Gulathing assembly broke up in disarray, he was pursued by Erik through here and overhauled further to the north.

18. On this view looking south-westwards, the south end of Hisaröy is on the right. The way from Eivindsvik (i.e. the Gulathing) is from the left in the foreground. Beyond is the main Gulefjord and to the right, beyond Hisaröy, is the route proposed for Egil's escape to the outer Solund islands. In this case Egil would have been out of sight behind Hisaröy before Erik reached this junction and was misled into turning right in the wake of Arinbjörn. (See also Photo 30)

Photographs Nos 19 to 24—Bö and Hyllestad

19. View across Böfjord. Bö can be seen on its platform, with its fields spread below it along the shore and with the crag that overlooks it partly overgrown with trees. The white church can be made out at the water's edge to the left.

20. View looking south-west showing Bö on its platform under the crag. The tree-covered low ness on the left encloses a small natural harbour.

21. The small natural harbour as seen from Bö when looking towards Leirvik.

22. Looking down the Böfjord from Bö to the Sognefjord. The approach is now obscured by a small industrial area built out from the shore.

23. View of the platform at Bö, with its modern houses, as seen from the fjord-side church. This platform is proposed as the site for the former home of Kveldulf, later the essential part of Björn's legacy that Egil was determined to possess. It was the ancestral seat of his kin, the property he was so bent on regaining

24. Hyllestad church, with Lihest across the fjord, resembling a horse's head and back. The present position of the church may not be historically relevant here, for the original heathen shrine was more probably on the peninsula partly visible beyond the church tower and now known as Lien.

Photographs Nos 25 to 27—Borgund

25. Borgund hamlet on its rocky platform. The stave church is some distance away to the right.

26. Borgund hamlet from the dale bottom near the church.

27. Borgund stave church with its unchurch-like construction. The hamlet is behind the trees to the left. There is no sheet of water here, but there is a "ness": this is formed by a rugged "hairpin bend" of the river immediately downstream of the church, which stands near the base of the loop.

Photographs Nos 28 and 29—Aurland

28. View of the settlement from across the Aurlandselv river. The white gable of the church can be seen centrally beyond the riverside buildings. The flat land to the left is a spit that has formed between river and fjord. The church stands at the root of this ness and the "hall" of Thordh Brynjolfsson was perhaps at the foot of the slope beyond.

29. The houses beyond the churchyard are on a platform. The situation of the church at the root of a ness between river and fjord or lake is redolent of Voss. The arguments made about Hestad (above) indicate that such nesses in front of halls were originally sites of heathen shrines, maybe on plots later usurped by churches.

Photographs Nos 30 to 33—Atlöy and Naustdal (Sunnfjord)

30. The island of Atlöy seen across the Dalsfjord from Fjaler. Between Atlöy (on left) and Askvoll is the strait of Sauesund. This is where Erik finally caught up with Arinbjörn after they left the Gulathing in turn. Although not clearly visible, in the middle of the picture, in front of Atlöy, lies a small island - a holm: this would be the Saudhey to which Egil Skallagrimsson swam after he slew Atley-Bardh.

31. This is Naustdal, with its prominent church. The wyke in front of the church has been considerably filled in, especially in recent times to construct the new road. The church is on slightly higher ground, while the river runs out at the foot of the fell-side to the right. The situation is again similar to those of Voss and Aurland, except that here there is no surviving pronounced ness between river and fjord. Behind the church there is now a large 'vang' that probably mainly consists of later infill. To assert that there was once a ness here implies this and that the course of the river has been diverted. The hall here would most likely have been on the higher land towards the slopes to the left of the church, that is if the analogy with Voss and Aurland holds; but see below.

32. Naustdal church showing its raised position relative to the houses beyond. It is clear that if the 'hall' was to the right here, as suggested above, the view down the Fördefjord would be sacrificed; but the oldest part of the settlement does seem to be here and an excellent view of the farmland could be obtained.

33. The 'vang' behind the church. It is noticeable how the modern dwellings avoid encroaching on this land, a rare and valuable asset today, just as it presumably once was to Thori and Arinbjörn.

Photographs Nos 34 to 37—Seim

34. This is thought to be the burial mound of Håkon the good at Seim. It is reported in three sagas that he was buried in a mound at 'Sæheim' in Hordaland. The relevant quotations from these are inscribed on rocks near the entrance of the monument. Whether he was indeed buried here may be debatable; the important point in this contest is that folk in the past have claimed or believed he was.

35. The green mound is in an elevated position overlooking the Lurefjord. The church spire protrudes beyond the barrow.

36. This view of Seim church shows how the Lurefjord is overlooked by the site. Since it is stated that Håkon received a heathen burial against his wishes, it follows that no church was present at the time; this does not preclude that a site at or near the church was occupied then by a heathen shrine, which made the site attractive for the burial of a king. Conversely one could argue that the church was eventually built because of the supposed presence of the buried remains of an early Christian king nearby. The elevated position of this church is comparable with those at places like Sogndal and Kaupanger, which contrast with the low-lying sites at Hestad, Naustdal, Aurland, Voss, Nordfjordeid and Bö, which all show a preference for situations right down beside large sheets of water. Old churches elsewhere, e.g. in England, are generally found on available hilltops, so that it may seem that the lowly placing by water is an ancient trait in Norway derived from a heathen past. This is not to assume that such sites were all on a par with the temple proposed at Hestad, but that some were private shrines of the landed men whose 'halls' would stand nearby.

37. View over the Lurefjord from near Håkon's Howe at Seim.

Photographs Nos 38 to 42—York

38. St. Helen's Square, York, looking north-east in 1993. The River Ouse is behind the viewpoint and the Roman fortress wall used to run across the middle of the square as viewed. The actual gateway was to the left of the line of this later arch and the *Via Praetoria* (now Stonegate) was well to the left of the church.

39. King's Square, looking north-west. Beyond is Petergate, running towards the Minster; but the line of the original Via Principalis would be straight and hold further to the left, thus missing the site of this great church. The opening to the left is Church Street, while on the right lies Goodramgate; the actual gateway would be just in front of this junction. The position of the gate tower appears to have stood rather to the right of the present opening; this may indicate a sometime blocking off of one of the twin doorways that were a feature of Roman gates. It is suggested that it was in just such a gatehouse as this that Egil Skallagrimsson composed his "Head Ransom" poem. However, the name of the square may indicate that this gate tower was traditionally used as headquarters by Norse kings in York, such as Erik Bloodaxe.

40. The Roman road now called Bootham leading to Bootham Bar, beyond which gate it continues as Petergate. On the right can be seen part of the stone wall of the St. Mary's Abbey/ King's Manor precinct (earlier Earlesburgh).

41. View from within the King's Manor precinct towards Gillygate. On the right is Bootham Bar, which once had a barbican. The demolition of the fortifications here was due to the creation of the wide thoroughfare in the foreground, called St. Leonards. To the right of the parked van is Queen Margaret's Arch

42. View across Bootham through Queen Margaret's Arch, which is slightly offset from the present street called Gillygate seen beyond. Both features lie well outside of the city wall, preseumably because of the need to accommodate the barbican, which stood to the right.

Photographs Nos 43 to 44—Bowes Moor

43. Stainmore Pass looking westward towards the summit and the large Roman marching camp. This visit by members of the Teesside Archaeological Society was on 13th August 1989 during the archaeological project prior to the conversion of the A66 road to a dual carriageway. The moor can in no way be considered to be stony on these eastward dip slopes.

44. Rey Cross being examined by members of TAS. It stood then beside the A66 and within the Roman marching camp, but was soon to be removed to accommodate the roadworks. The skyline crags mark the summit and it is only from this point that Stainmore can be said to be stony. The name was hence only applicable to the summit and the scarp slopes to the west. This implies that Erik Bloodaxe met his death in battle there in 952, rather than near Rey Cross, a name that has nothing to do with rex(genitive regis) - 'king' or any supposed Norman French version of this.

Appendix 6

Bibliography

Select Bibliography

Anderson J. (edited) 1981 (1873)—*The Orkneyinga Saga* - Edinburgh

Bæksted A. 1968—*Jyske Runestene* - Copenhagen

Booth R.K. 1990 - *York: The History and Heritage of a City*—London

Burne A.H. 1952—*More Battlefields of England*—London

Campbell A. (ed) 1930—*The Battle of Brunanburh*—London

Carruthers F.J.—*People Called Cumbri*

Cavill P., S. Harding & J. Jesch 2004—English Place-Name Society: Journal 36—*Revisiting Dingesmere*

Coxe H.O. 1841 - *Rogeri de Wendover - Flores Historiarum*—Vol 1—London

Ekwall E. 1960—*The Concise Oxford Dictionary of English Place-Names*—Oxford

Elgee F. 1930—*Early Man in North-East Yorkshir*—Gloucester

Garmonsway G.N. (trans. & ed.) 1972—*The Anglo-Saxon Chronicle*—London

Gordon E.V. (Rev. A.R. Taylor) 1927 (1956)—*An Introduction to Old Norse*—Oxford

Hall R. 1990—*Viking Age Archaeology in Britain and Ireland*—Princes Risborough

Holtsmark A & D.A. Seip (trans. into Norwegian) 1959—*Snorres Kongesagaer*—Oslo

Houken A. 1956—*Håndbog i Danske Stednavne*—Copenhagen

Jones G. 1975—*A History of the Vikings*—London

Kershaw N. 1922—*Anglo-Saxon and Norse Poems*—Cambridge

Leadman A.D.H. (1891)—*Battles Fought in Yorkshire*

Loyn H.R. 1977—*The Vikings in Britain* - London

Mawer A 1920—*The Place-Names of Northumberland and Durham*—Cambridge

Olsen M. 1939—In *Nordisk Kultur—Stedsnavn—Norge*—Oslo

Ordnance Survey 1988— *Historical Map and Guide: Roman and Anglian York*

Ordnance Survey 1988—*Historical Map and Guide: Viking and Medieval York*

Pálsson H. and P. Edwards (translated)—1976—*Egil's Saga*—Harmondsworth

Pearson W. 1995—Yorkshire Archaeological Journal: *Bramham Moor and the Red, White and Brown Battles*—Vol 67

Pearson W. 2004—Cleveland History:: *Gaelic Placenames in North-East England: Even Cleveland and Teesside—Part 1*—No 87

Ibid 2005—*Part 2*—No 88

Press M.A.C. (translated) 2011—*Laxdæla Saga*—Oxford

Riley D.N. 1977—Yorkshire Archaeological Journal: *Aerial Reconnaissance in Central and Southern Yorkshire in 1977*—Vol 49

Sawyer P. 1995—Northern History: *The Last Scandinavian Kings in York*—Vol 31

Smith, A.H. 1970—EP-NS: *The Place-Names of the East Riding of Yorkshire and York*—Vol XIV

Stenton F.M. 1971—*Anglo-Saxon England*—Oxford

Stephenson J. (trans) 1858—Facsimile 1987—Simeon of Durham: *A History of the Kings of England*—Llanerch

Stephenson J. (trans)—Facsimile 1989—William of Malmesbury: *The Kings before the Norman Conques*—Llanerch

Surtees Society 1868—*Symeonis Dunhelmensis*—Vol 1—Durham

Thorpe B. (ed) 1848—*Florentii Wigorniensis*—Vol 1—London

Thorpe L. (trans) 1969 (1966)—Geoffrey of Monmouth: *The History of the Kings of Britain*—London.

Vaughan R. (ed.) 1958—*The Chronicle Attributed to John of Wallingford*—Camden Miscellany—London

Willams ab Ithel J. 1860—*Annales Cambriae* - London

Woolf A. 1998—Northern History: *Erik Bloodaxe Revisited*—Vol 34

Wood M. 1981—*In Search of the Dark Ages*—London

Appendix 7

Index of People

Index of People

Appendix 8

Index of Places

Index of Places

Printed in Great Britain
by Amazon

36446283R00163